MEDITERRANEAN SUMMERS

HOW A MAN, A WOMAN AND A DOG SPENT EIGHT SUMMERS EXPLORING THE ANCIENT SEA IN A SMALL BOAT

Karen Heath Clark

Published by BookLocker.com, Inc., Bradenton, Florida, U.S.A.

Printed on acid-free paper.

BookLocker.com, Inc.
2015

First Edition

Front cover: *Avanti* at anchor near Croatian island of Rab
Rear cover: Roka is ready to start our journey in Palma, Mallorca;
      Colorful harbor in Mali Lošinj, Croatia

For my sweet dog Roka and my helpmate in life
and on this book, Bruce,
both lovable and fun travel companions

"The sea can do craziness, it can do smooth, it can lie down like silk
breathing or toss havoc shoreward;
it can give gifts or withhold all; it can rise, ebb, froth like
an incoming frenzy of fountains, or it can sweet-talk entirely."

— Mary Oliver, *A Thousand Mornings*

TABLE OF CONTENTS

For more stories and photos about our *Avanti* journey,
visit our blog at www.karenandbruce.com.

Avanti anchored at the Tremiti Islands, Italy

PREFACE

HOW AND WHY DID THIS HAPPEN?

Our easyJet plane, full of noisy, cheering British tourists, touched down in Palma on the Spanish island of Mallorca. My husband, Bruce, gathered our luggage while I let our small black dog out of her under-seat travel bag. We hailed a taxi. "Marina Real Club Nautico," Bruce said proudly, feeling superior to those mere tourists surrounding us. We belonged here. We owned a boat in the marina. Several minutes later, the taxi pulled up to the marina and the guards waved us through. The taxi rolled slowly down the long dock past hundreds of expensive yachts waiting in the water for their owners to reappear.

"Stop here. That's it," Bruce commanded. A bit stunned, we unloaded the taxi and stood in front of a decidedly unimpressive "yacht" bearing the name *Avanti*. I looked down at our piles of luggage, then over at the waiting boat, and finally started to laugh. Bruce glanced at me, confused, then finally smiled. "This is ridiculous," I sputtered, "This can't really be happening"

We boarded *Avanti*, opening her door with the key we had never used before. After dumping our belongings in a pile in the "main saloon," we headed straight for the marina bar to attempt to gather our wits. We sipped gin and tonics and reminisced about the past five years, pondering what had brought us to this surprising place and time.

Bruce and I are both Type A workaholics with a thirst for oddball travel. Tours horrify us, and even extensive planning is anathema. We study possible destinations, buy airplane tickets, then improvise. Our now-grown children, Adam and Andrea, hated our travels when they were young. Like most children, they wanted routine, certainty and comfortable hotels with swimming pools. We rarely had reservations and often didn't find a place to stay until late in the day.

Sometimes it was well after dark – often after hours of driving, looking and squabbling – and there was rarely a swimming pool.

The dawn of the plan that resulted in our standing here on the dock in Palma had occurred in Turkey five years earlier. We had spent three weeks driving through the country on one of our typical vacations, just offbeat enough to raise eyebrows among our friends about our safety. After spending a few days browsing Istanbul in miserable cold and rain, we rented a car and headed for Ankara. We quickly realized that we actually should worry about our safety: the Turkish highways are absurdly dangerous. Picture three giant buses racing to pass each other on a two-lane road, all speeding directly toward your underpowered subcompact car.

In Cappadocia, we stayed in a hotel carved into the cliffs a thousand years ago, and then visited the ascetic, fundamentalist home of the whirling dervishes in Konya, where alcohol was not available anywhere, even in our Western-style hotel. From there we headed on a small winding road over the snow-covered Taurus Mountains to the sublime southern Turkish coast on the Mediterranean Sea. At Antalya we turned west and followed the coast past ruins from at least a half-dozen ancient civilizations. At Marmaris in the southwest corner of Turkey, we turned north, leaving the Mediterranean for the Aegean Sea. Our next stop was the popular tourist town of Bodrum.

From first appearances, Bodrum was not going to be a highlight of the trip. A series of monstrous white condo developments greeted us as we drove into town. Although the town boasts a stunning crusader castle, it was otherwise uninspiring. Cruise ships stop here, resulting in an abundance of tacky tourist shops. The available hotels were unattractive.

We stopped for a late morning coffee at the harbor's edge contemplating driving on to the next town. As we discussed our options, we noticed the rounded sterns of dozens of Turkish gulets lining the town's main wharf. Turkish gulets are gorgeous boats –

quaint, beamy, wooden, with small sails, looking like misplaced Chinese junks. Their sails are rarely used; gulets usually run under power.

Several of the larger gulets posted signs advertising their availability for charter for the day, the week, or the month. It was only May, too early for the swarms of tourists that appear in July and August. The boats were still being varnished and polished for the season. Here and there a shill stood on the wharf beside a gulet, hoping to scout up tourists to take out to sea, but without much luck so early in the season. The weather was chilly and the water too cold for swimming.

Eying the charter signs, I suggested idly that perhaps we should try to spend the night on one of these boats. Bruce unexpectedly agreed with me. He's not one who normally takes well to something new. We started looking more carefully at the gulets. Could we charter one of these gulets for just one night and avoid the dreary hotels?

We paced the harbor's edge, inspecting the boats. Some were way too big – they could hold at least a dozen people. Some of the smaller ones looked shabby, even unseaworthy. Then we saw her – the *Adorga* – her perfectly-sized, varnished hull glowing in the late morning sun. There was no sign advertising that she was available, only two young people sitting on board watching us.

What should we do? "Okay," I whispered to Bruce, "Let's go for it. What do we have to lose? You ask." Bruce is used to being asked to do awkward or embarrassing tasks and usually complies. He paused, then called out, "We like your boat – is it available for charter?"

Three hours later we were aboard while the young couple, Adil and Lynn, maneuvered *Adorga* out of the Bodrum harbor. Our lives would never be the same.

That morning in Bodrum was the beginning of our new journey. Had it been earlier in the day, had the town been more appealing, had

Bruce not worked up the nerve to ask, what would we be doing in retirement? Traveling in a Winnebago? Bored at home snapping at each other? Driving a golf cart in Leisure World? We'll never know.

Adil was a Turk, but spoke good English as do most coastal Turks. He was the owner and skipper of the *Adorga* and appeared to be serious and hard-working. His girlfriend, Lynn, was the cook, and Adil's total opposite. Lynn was British, demanding, critical, funny, chatty and irreverent. Adil claimed to be a devout Muslim; however, it was obvious even to us that his religious views were unorthodox.

Adil and Lynn took our pre-paid trip money to town to shop for dinner and breakfast for the four of us, telling us to return in two hours. And then we were off, *Adorga's* tiny two-cylinder motor churning up a miniature wake behind us. As *Adorga* sputtered slowly out of the harbor, Adil brought out a round of beers.

An hour or so of cruising brought us to an isolated bay. Adil dropped the anchor and turned off the engine. *Adorga* was enveloped in total silence except for Lynn's outbursts from the galley where she was cooking dinner. She complained loudly in her cockney accent, mostly about Adil and other Turkish men. "Those Turks!" she declared. "They are so pig-headed and opinionated!"

Eventually Lynn brought out a glorious fish dinner and the four of us ate together. We watched the sun set and talked, and then the fiery, licorice-flavored Turkish liqueur, raki, appeared on the table. Adil and Lynn told us about their lives – how she had met him in Turkey many years ago, then bounced back and forth to and from England until four years earlier when she returned to Turkey and Adil for good. Her family was not pleased. She and Adil had a stormy relationship. At first they tried to conceal their fighting from us, limiting their battles to surly bickering and sniping. By morning, they had stopped trying to hide the fighting and openly screamed at each other. We decided fighting was part of how they kept their relationship exciting.

Adil had recently found God and had become a committed, though eclectic, Muslim. Muslims are not permitted alcohol, but Adil seemed to have no issues with downing both beer and raki. Lynn was not impressed by his new-found faith.

"Would you like to hear some Sufi music?" Adil asked us.

Lynn roared at him in exasperation, "They don't want to hear it! Stop bothering them! They're not interested."

But Lynn was wrong. "Actually, we're fascinated by your religion" I told Adil. "We'd love to listen to some Sufi music." We talked for hours with Adil, about his beliefs and the Koran and about his theories of how the world will end.

We were deeper into the heart of Turkey than at any other time on our trip. We spent the evening with the atonal chants of the Sufis, drinking raki, watching the stars, rocking gently with the boat, and listening to Adil talk about the glories of Islam while Lynn angrily banged pots in the galley.

When the sun came up the next morning, Lynn appeared with a breakfast of cheese and salami to go with the pot of strong Turkish coffee. We explored some of the nearby islands and I swam in the icy water. Early in the afternoon, chugging back into Bodrum, we sighed with regret, wishing we didn't have to leave *Adorga*.

Bruce had talked vaguely about going somewhere on a sailboat when we retired. I wasn't convinced. Our only multi-day sailing adventure had been a disaster, resulting in a tangled genoa, a fire on board and a close encounter with a giant cargo ship. I had vowed that I would never spend more than half a day on any boat. Overnight trips were banned.

But *Adorga* was different. She was comfortable. A thick Turkish carpet covered the floor of our cozy bedroom. The galley was not large, but workable. We could stretch out in the sun on the large aft deck. The small bay where we rocked through the night was isolated and serene.

Bruce has always hated searching for hotels in our travels, along with the requisite unpacking and packing of suitcases. The idea of taking our home with us from port to port sounded unusually civilized to him. We both hated searching for meals. With our own boat, we could cook on board as much or as little as we wanted.

Driving out of Bodrum that day, our enthusiasm was hard to contain. The more we talked, the more excited we became. Perhaps leasing a boat would work, or maybe even buying one and spending a year, maybe two years, cruising in the Mediterranean.

We were nearing retirement after many years of two heavy-duty, long-hour careers. I was a partner in a large international law firm, putting in 10-hour days. Bruce was a geologist, formerly a university professor, now running a large geotechnical consulting company. Both us of were burning out on work. Our children were on their own. It was time for something new. We loved travel. Our travel history was checkered with strange adventures and the occasional mishap. We had hitchhiked with backpacks in our childless years through Greece and Yugoslavia. Later we spent a year in Australia with one-year-old Adam, meandering home through Africa and South America. When Adam and his younger sister, Andrea, were a bit older, we took them on trips through Europe and Australia, driving them crazy with our lack of planning. Then it was on to family camping in Wyoming, Idaho, Washington and Oregon. After our children left for college, we ventured through Chile, visited the Galapagos, biked with another couple through the Czech Republic, and trekked in Nepal. And then there was the visit to Turkey.

Thoughts of retirement had started to edge into our brains, but we had no idea how retirement could possibly work for us. Suddenly, there in Bodrum, everything changed. We now had a plan.

The idea snowballed. We started telling friends that we would retire to cruise the Mediterranean even though we barely believed it ourselves. When we heard that sailboats could be a problem in the Mediterranean since the winds were not reliable and that a powerboat might be better (the kind we'd always called "stinkpots"), we decided to try one out. We chartered diesel trawlers for a few days in San Diego, then the San Juan Islands, and even Alaska. It was fun, never a disaster. The closer we came to retirement, the more committed we became to our crazy idea.

We started researching, expecting to be hammered with the many reasons why our harebrained scheme could never work. We took tiny steps forward, always ready to jettison the whole idea if we hit a brick wall. The wall never appeared.

We searched for resources to help us – the library, the Internet, Amazon, bookstores – but there was nothing. Most travel guides were not helpful. Land-based travel books miss what a boating visitor needs and wants to know. Traveling by boat is a vastly different experience from traveling by car or train. Many villages and towns on the water, where boaters spend most of their time, don't rate even a mention in most travel books. And some towns that are tourist favorites provide a terrible boating experience – often they have miserable or no marinas and do not cater to boaters. The best sources for the Mediterranean are a group of boating handbooks written by Rod Heikell and a number of his friends, and published in the UK. They provide all the little details necessary to find a good marina or town wharf and settle in, including the amenities available. They also provide information on the history and ambience of the harbors and port towns themselves. His descriptions are often the only information easily available in English about these places. But even Heikell couldn't answer the big questions we would face. Instead, we learned by picking up snippets of information available locally and from other cruisers, and from a long list of hit-or-miss experiences along the way. It wasn't pretty, but it did produce its own type of excitement. We hope this book will make it easier for others who are game to try an adventure like ours by providing the type of information that was not available to us.

We started and ended on the island of Mallorca in the Balearics. We traveled along most of the east coast of Spain, the entire Mediterranean coast of France, the west coast and islands of Italy plus the sole of the Italian boot and its spur (the Gargano peninsula) and Venice, the entire sea coasts of Croatia and Slovenia, approximately 40 Greek Islands plus parts of the Greek mainland, both the Aegean and Mediterranean coasts of Turkey and, finally, Northern Cyprus. Although we originally expected to travel the Mediterranean for only a year or two, we ended up spending eight years cruising there, between three and five months each year.

This book is divided into two parts. Part I is a description of our actual travels, with a full chapter devoted to each country. Included are descriptions of our favorite ports, bays, and cities, and some of the unique boating joys and troubles we found along the way. Part II discusses the nuts and bolts of traveling by boat in the Mediterranean. This section includes how to decide which boat to buy, where to buy it and how to handle the purchase, things to consider when leaving home for a long period, how to manage and maneuver in the marinas, harbors, and bays in the Mediterranean, how to estimate the costs of the whole adventure and, finally, for animal lovers, what you need to know if you want to take your dog or cat along for companionship.

PART I: THE STORY OF A MEDITERRANEAN ADVENTURE

"The journey is the thing."
— Homer

CHAPTER 1
WE TAKE THE PLUNGE

The initial idea was straightforward: retire, then lease or buy a boat to live on for a year or two in the Mediterranean. That was it – no details. But soon we learned about the many decisions we needed to make. The first big decision: when to start? That question led to discussions about retirement.

The whole retirement issue is tough and depends on a myriad of economic and psychological factors. We always talked about retiring early and getting out of the rat race. But we found reasons to delay, to hang on to our working lives a bit longer. We, like most, find that avoiding change is the easiest path. Financial considerations limit retirement for many, but others who can afford to retire often continue to hang on because they don't know what else to do, and retirement is a scary unknown. Often people who talk big about retiring end up working until they are forced to retire, either by their employers or because they suffer a health setback. It's not easy to quit working. The main source of self-identity is often one's career; it provides a sense of competence and self-worth as well as income. People often work far longer than their financial conditions demand.

Bruce and I each had successful careers that provided psychological rewards and financial comfort. Bruce ran a large geotechnical firm. A Yale graduate with a Stanford Ph.D., he left his tenured geology professorship at the University of Michigan to join a consulting firm in California, driven to this change for various reasons related to both his work satisfaction and my discontent with living in Michigan. He became CEO of his company. His industry was prone to extreme economic cycles and he had guided his firm through a terrible downturn in the early 1990s when over half of the company's employees were laid off; it was a painful and depressing time. The expectation of another downturn drove Bruce to want to retire while business was good.

My path was more circuitous. I met Bruce at Stanford as an undergraduate and we moved to Ann Arbor after we married and Bruce accepted the university job. Ann Arbor is a fun college town, but I could never adjust to the bugs and humidity in the summer, the lack of an ocean, and the cold, bleak winter weather..

I earned a master's degree in history at the University of Washington to further my career goal of teaching history at a community college. But the only position I could find was teaching part-time at a college an hour's drive from Ann Arbor. Good teaching jobs at any college were hard to find, particularly near a university town. When I realized that my hopes for a college teaching career were unrealistic. I switched gears. A few months after the birth of Adam, my first child, I enrolled at Michigan Law School. I didn't take it particularly seriously and had no specific career goal. Perhaps I could write wills for my neighbors or help them buy houses. I reconsidered when I realized that law firms in California were eager to hire me when I graduated. Returning to California was my fondest dream. I missed the beach, the sun, and especially my mother and my old friends.

I managed to convince Bruce that it was time to return to California, a shocking feat since he gave up a tenured professorship at a world-class university. Likely he was driven partly by the realization that life with a cranky wife for the next few decades might not be fun. Also, his field of expertise was earthquakes and earthquake-triggered landslides, a field more interesting to pursue in California than in Michigan. So when I graduated from law school, now with two babies in tow, we packed up and moved to Corona del Mar, a village in Newport Beach, where I began my job with a large, international law firm and Bruce joined a geotechnical consulting firm. Twenty years later, I was a partner with the same firm and Bruce was the CEO of his firm. I was tired of the long hours and high pressure.

Still, the thought of retirement made us nervous. We viewed ourselves as important professionals in our respective fields. What would we become of us once we no longer had that identity?

That's when we took our momentous trip to Turkey. After that trip, the idea of cruising on a boat in the Mediterranean became a positive goal and the central theme in our retirement plans.

I took the advice of another attorney in my firm who left her career to become a stay-at-home mom. She saw a psychologist to deal with her fears about moving from a high-prestige, high-income career to becoming "just a wife and mom." She advised me that the professional therapy helped. I took her advice. It was a smart move and I was lucky to get the right therapist. She made me see retirement in a different light, as a new and exciting adventure that would let me, for the first time in many years, shape my life in any way I wanted. She allowed me to laugh at my worries and myself and let go of my fears.

For Bruce, it was equally difficult, but being a macho guy, he had no interest in seeking help. It was the fear of a new economic downturn that was his driving force. He sold his interest in his company and retired in mid-2002. While I continued to work for another year and a half, it was Bruce's retirement that led us to start serious retirement planning.

The decisions came fast and furious. Buy or lease a boat? Where to go? What sort of boat? Did we have the funds? What about our house and our sweet dog, Roka? Would we like living on a boat? Would we soon grow to hate each other in such a small space? How could we keep ties with our family, friends and activities at home? How would we handle mail and communications? We were hit with so many pesky details that we wanted to throw up our hands in despair.

Finding the best answers became a challenge. We'd already decided two of the biggest questions: we'd go to the Mediterranean and we'd buy a powerboat. Those were easy. It was the personal decisions about our lives that were hard. In hindsight, we muddled through the decision process pretty well. We may have stumbled a few times, but nothing was fatal and no decision was disastrous.

Our house. Would we sell it? Rent it? Just leave it empty? If we left it empty, who would watch it? Could we afford our adventure if we continued to have all our house expenses with no rent to offset them? It was easy to decide to keep the house and live there for part of the year. This decision was reinforced when we learned that there is a distinct boating season in the Mediterranean – from mid-May to mid-October. The rest of the year the weather is too stormy and the seas too rough to be on the water. There are year-round boaters who live on their boats, but in the winter they stay in one marina, only venturing out from time to time when the weather is calm.

We decided that wasn't for us. We wanted to be home in the winter. But should we rent out our house? Bruce was against it. I was in favor. Bruce finally agreed to offer the house for rent if the perfect renter appeared. We listed it as a short-term lease with a realtor friend and, sure enough, the perfect renter showed up.

The dog. That was easy. Our sweet little Roka was small, so we decided to take her along. That of course led to many future complications, but also some joyful and entertaining adventures.

We hated leaving our children for such a long time until we came to accept the cold realization that they would do just fine without us. They were both living far away anyway – our daughter was moving to San Francisco and our son lived in Seattle. Because of the distance, most of our contact with them was by phone or email anyway. We thought that would stay pretty much the same whether we were in Europe or Corona del Mar.

How would we get our mail? We decided to have our mail forwarded to my office to be opened by my assistant, who could email me about anything important. Later we had our mail forwarded to our daughter, Andrea.

And what about paying bills? We found we could set up most bills for automatic payment. Others we could pay from an Internet cafe through our bank's "bill-pay" feature. That system worked fine.

We both sat on various non-profit boards. Would we have to resign? No, we decided. We would simply miss meetings while we were gone. Bruce and I each sat on one public board whose meetings we hated to miss, so we tried to time our departures to Europe and arrivals back home to miss as few of those meetings as possible. We vowed not to miss any other meetings during the year, and as a result we attended more of the meetings than many others who sat on the same public boards.

How would we adapt to the boating life? We'd had sailboats for 40 years and loved sailing, but in reality we were day sailors. Our one overnight trip from Newport Beach to Catalina was filled with disasters, including setting the galley oven on fire. We had also bareboat chartered a sailboat for a week in the Caribbean with friends and had a blissful time, although we didn't care much for the cramped sleeping quarters.

Living on a boat sounded nice, especially if we could find one with a little more space below decks than we had on our previous trips at sea. Neither of us was prone to being seasick. We knew we didn't want, and couldn't afford, a skipper and crew, meaning we would need a fairly small boat that we could operate and maintain ourselves.

Being careful people, we decided we should try out life on a boat before making a commitment. We had already decided on a powerboat but we'd never owned one and never spent any time on one, so we needed to figure out if we even liked them. We chartered a small Grand Banks trawler in San Diego for a weekend. We had no idea what we were doing and were shocked that anyone would let us near such a nice vessel. A surprisingly brief lesson was all it took and suddenly we were cruising nervously around the harbor with brave friends, sipping wine and crunching crackers. We pulled into a dock by the Hotel Coronado for the night, impressed that we hadn't destroyed the boat. After dinner at a local restaurant, we returned to sit on the quiet bay in the evening, enjoying the gentle roll of the boat and good conversation. This seemed easy. The boat was returned intact.

Giddy with success, we chartered a slightly larger Grand Banks out of Anacortes, Washington, to cruise the San Juan Islands for an entire week. Various family members visited, apparently fooled into thinking we were competent to handle such a boat. It was a remarkable week that included anchoring in total seclusion at night in quiet bays, watching a pod of killer whales pass by, hiking uninhabited islands, cooking most of our meals on board, and reconnecting with family. We started making lists of what we liked and didn't like about the boat, of "must haves" and "don't wants." This was starting to work out just fine.

The following year we chartered a small 32' powerboat in Juneau, Alaska for a trip out to Glacier Bay with another couple. The boat was far too small, but everything worked out, even after Bruce accidently disabled one of the two engines. We glided through fields of icebergs, watched glaciers calve into the fjords and whales breaching, and visited pristine bays on the kayaks we took along with us. Only a handful of private boats are permitted into Glacier Bay at one time, so there was rarely another boat in view. Our self-confidence was growing.

Could we spend months at a time on board together? We've always done most things together, but this would be far more intense. We love a good fight, but at home we can go to our separate corners to recover after any all-out battle. That wouldn't be possible on a boat.

Surprisingly, we found that we get along better on a boat than we do at home. Perhaps it's because it's us against the world on the boat instead of us against each other, as it is at home. It's hard to figure.

Were we flexible enough to embark on a path for which we had no experience and no guidance? All our off-the-cuff travel without itineraries or fixed plans proved to be good training, although the flexibility actually required was sometimes almost beyond our reach. We learned to shed a tear and move on when forced to abandon a much-anticipated adventure. Weather can spoil any perfect itinerary, as can a broken fuel pump, or a rough sea. The truth is that any boating plan must be flexible. Even the best plan, when it goes bad, must be quickly killed and a Plan B, or even Plan C and D, created. We learned to make a general schedule at the start of a year, but not worry when we strayed. Guests had to adjust to us – they could request when or where to visit us, but usually not both. Anyone with problems being flexible will have trouble with this sort of life. While we were forced to give up long-planned adventures several times and had to accept the disappointment, we learned that Plan B, Plan C, or Plan D, often turns out to be an even greater adventure than Plan A.

We decided to buy a boat – chartering would be too expensive for the length of time we wanted to stay in the Mediterranean. For a cruise of only a couple of months, chartering would make sense. But we thought we'd be on the water for at least two summers. And Bruce had the skill and interest in fixing engines, boat parts and other mechanical problems that seem to crop up more often on a boat you own than on a professionally maintained charter.

Picking the Mediterranean as the destination location was easy. We love that part of the world; plus the practical benefits seem obvious.

Many people speak English, yet the culture of each country is unique and fascinating, especially to me; European history was my field of interest throughout college and graduate school. Most harbors were built in ancient times and are still surrounded by ancient city centers. The historic harbors are generally located about 50 miles apart, the maximum travel distance by oar or sail in ancient times, and a perfect distance for us to cover in a day.

To locate a boat to buy, we headed for the Internet. There are thousands of boats for sale on the Internet in every part of the world. We found boats of interest in Mallorca and Barcelona, places where Brits and Germans congregate. We started emailing brokers who were advertising these boats. Several brokers responded to our emails. Many did not. We told them we planned to visit to inspect the boats in the near future.

The first time our plan seemed truly real, and we felt genuinely committed, was the day we bought our airplane tickets to Barcelona to go look at boats, along with tickets on easyJet.com from Barcelona to Mallorca to see a few more. It was November 2002. Off-season fares were low, hotels were cheap and brokers were eager to see some action.

We saw three Grand Banks trawlers near Barcelona, but none were right. So it was on to Mallorca where we met with five different brokers to see eight different boats. Mallorca is a cosmopolitan spot and the brokers we consulted were of British, French, American, Dutch and German origins. Our list had been narrowed to eight boats based on their descriptions on the Internet. Most looked pretty worn or had other big flaws. Some were difficult for us to actually see. One required a long drive to an inland boat yard where it was stored on land; another was shown to us by the French broker who, upon arrival at the boat, realized he had no key, resulting in our standing out in a cold rain storm while he desperately crawled around the boat trying to find a way in. He failed.

The one standout was *Avanti*, a ten-year-old 39-foot Ocean Alexander that had almost all the qualities we were seeking. And the price was far below what we had thought we would have to spend. We were prepared to spend around $350,000 – still far less than the cost of a similar vintage Grand Banks – but far above the $180,000 being asked for *Avanti*. Ocean Alexanders are popular cruising boats in the U.S. as well as Europe. They are built in Taiwan and are known for their dependability and good workmanship. We returned home optimistic.

Avanti had been for sale for over a year, so we felt no pressure to move quickly. Our broker was Colin, a helpful and generous Brit. He worked with the seller, Dieter, a retired executive from Germany. After some back-and-forth offers and counter-offers, an agreement on price and terms was reached, subject to a satisfactory "marine survey and sea trial" – an inspection by a specialist to determine that there are no hidden problems and a spin on the water to make sure all the boat systems work properly. The contract was signed.

In January we were back on a plane, bound again for Mallorca, to be on hand for the marine survey and sea trial. That trip was not strictly necessary; many buyers are not present for the survey and sea trial. But we thought that watching the survey would be informative and would make us comfortable that the inspection was thorough and honest. And we wanted to see how *Avanti* handled on the sea. The sea trial was fun, out of the harbor at Palma past the Spanish king's palace and back.

We gulped, wired our funds and we were soon the proud owners of *Avanti*, still sitting at the dock in the Real Club Nautico marina in downtown Palma, Mallorca.

It turned out that our surveyor didn't find everything. The surveyor saw black smoke billowing from *Avanti*'s engines but didn't think it was a problem. We don't know why. It's easy as an "outsider" to be suspicious of the close relationships between brokers and surveyors in the cozy world of boating. But we trusted our broker and had confirmed with others that our surveyor had an excellent reputation. The problem continued to worsen for us until, by the end of our first summer, the engine was diagnosed as having a cracked cylinder head, requiring an extremely expensive engine repair. It was painful. A new cylinder head was installed (along with new diesel fuel injectors) and we never again had any black engine smoke.

That engine repair made us unhappy. But we learned that it's important to let go. One piece of useful advice we received was that we should assume that we would often be over-charged, and perhaps even totally ripped off, but that we should simply accept this as the price a visitor pays in almost any foreign land. There's not much you can do about it unless you speak the local language fluently and have some powerful friends in the area. Most service providers are honest and try to do a good job for you, but there are always a few who are incompetent or a bit shady. We learned to assume that we would overpay and people would take advantage of us, but that it just wasn't worth stressing over.

Now we were almost ready to start. We packed up our house, throwing piles of junk away and giving box after box of clothes and household goods to charity, unburdening ourselves of many years of accumulated stuff. We packed our remaining clothing and personal items in boxes and stored them in the one locked room in our house that remained ours, out of bounds to the tenant. We had our airplane tickets in hand and our house rented out to a stranger. Together with our mutt, we officially became vagabonds.

In the middle of May, our daughter, Andrea, took us to the airport and waited until we were checked in. We'd never traveled on a plane with our dog in the cabin and worried that something would go terribly wrong. Roka was slightly over the airline's maximum weight and she could not stand up in her bag as required by the airline regulations. She had papers, but it was never perfectly clear what we needed. Andrea was our fallback. If something went wrong, Andrea would take Roka home with her. We had reserved business class seats through our frequent flyer mileage, gobbling up a huge number of miles, with the idea that things might go more smoothly in business class and that our looming dog crisis would be easier to resolve if we were seen as "big hitter" customers.

The United Airlines official who checked us in was stymied by Roka. She fretted. She had no clue what to do. She made calls, studied her computer screen, thumbed over manuals. We worried, working ourselves into a frenzy, chattering mindlessly. After 15 minutes of indecision, our official finally concluded we owed a $125 dog fee – exactly what we told her when we arrived at her counter. She barely glanced at Roka's papers, worrying only about her own paperwork and the restless people in the line behind us. "Traveler's check or credit card?" she asked. Mistakenly thinking traveler's checks would be quicker, we handed over several signed checks. Wrong choice. It took another 15 minutes for her to figure out how to cash our checks. The masses in line behind us started to grumble. Feet shuffled. Roka was tightly zipped into her doggy suitcase to hide her over-the-limit size. Despite our worry, she was completely quiet. We thought she might bark or whine, leading some bureaucrat to want to look her over, perhaps weigh her. But the airline official was so flustered by the time she finally got our traveler's checks cashed, she just wanted us to leave. Relief! We sighed deeply as we left the counter, boarding passes for three in hand. Roka now had her own boarding pass under the name "The Dog." We tearfully hugged Andrea who was starting to feel abandoned. We all cried. With a bit of angst, we were off on our new life.

Our flights were scheduled to allow plenty of time between legs for Roka to visit friendly lawns and dirt along the way. We overdid it. After eight hours in JFK, followed by nine hours in Frankfurt – enough to visit the medieval old town and take a boat ride on the River Main – we finally arrived at the marina in Palma and dragged ourselves onto *Avanti*, only one suitcase short and exhausted to the bone. Fortunately, the missing suitcase arrived at the marina the following day.

We knew we were poised for a grand adventure, and we had no idea how it would turn out. The plan had become reality. Stepping into this new life had been surprisingly easy, each step an obvious result of the prior one. Before realizing that we could not possibly be competent enough to carry this off, here we were, Mediterranean boat owners. It all felt serendipitous and accidental, even though we had imagined it for years. We felt like careless children who had waded into a puddle for the fun of splashing, then suddenly found themselves trapped in quicksand, sinking fast. Everything in our lives had changed so quickly. This was surely the first day of the rest of our lives.

CHAPTER 2
SPAIN: OUR ADVENTURE BEGINS

Mallorcan boy at Festival
of the Patrona de Pollença on
Mallorca

Granddaughter Sienna admires
Miró sculpture in Barcelona

Avanti satisfies her diesel greed
at pricey Ibiza marina

Roka in front of the Knights
Templar Castle, Peniscola

Polar bear at entrance
to Salvador Dali's
home

The beach at Formentera is crowded
even in May when the water is
still too cold for a decent swim

Yes, this male sunbather in
Barcelona is in fact nude

Famous Bullfighter Bruce
takes on Roka the Bull in
bullring in Vinaros

Spain is a colorful, friendly place. It helps to speak a little Spanish, but many locals speak English. Our fluency in Spanish was far better than our fluency (or lack thereof) in any other Mediterranean language. But even if you can't speak a word of Spanish, it usually doesn't matter. The Spaniards are open and helpful. The food is good, but dinners start shockingly late. It took a long time to adjust to finishing dinner at midnight. The culture is delightful and comprehensible. The wines in Spain are inconsistent, but many are world class. And the prices are reasonable. In short, Spain was an easy place to start.

Yet, at the end of our eight years, when considering our favorite countries, Spain didn't fare all that well. The food is good, but it's not French. The harbors and marinas are better than those in Greece, but don't stack up well against those in Croatia, Turkey, France or even Italy. The people are friendly, but not so outgoing as the Croatians or Turks. The countryside is pretty, but not so dramatic as Italy, Croatia, Greece or Turkey. It's an ok place for dogs, but much less dog-friendly than either France or Italy. We had no serious problems with Spain, but other than the amazing world-class cities of Barcelona and Palma, it doesn't rank at the top of our list.

Our Spanish cruising route began in the marina at Palma where we acquired *Avanti*. From early May to mid July we ventured from the island of Mallorca to the Spanish mainland, then up the east coast of Spain to the southern tip of France.

The Balearic Islands

Mallorca

We'll always have a soft spot in our hearts for Mallorca. The island was desolate when we first arrived to look for boats during that stormy, cold November week in 2002. There were no tourists. We stayed at the elegant but almost empty Nixe Palace Hotel west of town, where we watched surfers take advantage of some rare big waves caused by a recent storm. The tavernas in the ancient town center were empty. In one restaurant in the town center, we were totally alone for two hours, not counting the hired entertainment, a guitar player.

After actually acquiring *Avanti*, we returned to Mallorca in April to get her ready for her journey. The weather was warming and life had returned to Palma. It was Easter Week, Semana Santa, and we were joined by our daughter, Andrea, a fluent Spanish speaker. Her language skills were helpful, but Mallorcans, like natives of the other Balearic Islands, have a Catalonian heritage similar to Barcelona and prefer to speak in Mallorquin, similar to Catalan. There are heated arguments on Mallorca over whether Mallorquin or Spanish should be the main language of instruction in the public school. Still the locals are willing to converse in Spanish and display none of the hostility toward Spanish speakers found in Barcelona.

Palma celebrated Semana Santa with parades each day in which hundreds of marchers donned what appeared to be Ku Klux Klan robes, even down to the pointy hats. Rather than bed-sheet white, however, the robes were colorful, each color representing a different church from around the island. The ancient town was brimming with visitors and the cozy tavernas hosted boisterous crowds of diners.

Our marina, Real Club Nautico, was mere steps from the narrow streets of the medieval town with its soaring cathedral and dozens of tiny restaurants. We visited the cathedral often. Its dazzling stained glass windows washed soft, colored light onto the few elderly parishioners attending morning mass. Throughout Europe, churches and cathedrals stand mostly empty, and only a handful of those who attend are young. Europeans are far less religious than Americans.

On a hill on the other side of town, visible from our deck on *Avanti*, stands the Castillo de Bellver, a 14th century castle, offering a sweeping view of the entire coast of Mallorca from its ramparts. Nearby is the final home and sunlit studio of artist Joan Miró, now open to visitors. A modern museum devoted to Miró's art has been constructed beside his home and studio and contains dozens of his iconic paintings.

We loved Real Club Nautico. Its proximity to the ancient heart of Palma made it easy for us to explore the city center on foot. The other major marina in town, Club de Mar, seemed less convenient and snootier, but it is extremely popular. It was home to the largest private boat on the island, a sleek four-story 250-footer owned by a Saudi sheik, alleged to have a permanent crew of eighteen and a cruising crew of more than fifty during the three weeks of the year when the sheik is aboard.

The island is easy to visit by rental car. The interior is covered with wooded hills, broad fields of grain and pastures, and views of the jagged mountain range that makes up the backbone of the island. We drove north and east to visit a few of the ancient villages, including Valldemossa, where Chopin and his lover George Sand lived in the local monastery for a brief and reportedly unhappy period in the 1830s. We enjoyed lunch at the elegant and extremely expensive Grand Hotel Son Net, then owned by a friend from Orange County.

At the end of our eight years of travel, we returned to Mallorca. On that visit, we cruised to Puerto Pollença, a quiet seaside town at the opposite end of the island, where the Fiesta de la Patrona de Pollença was being celebrated in the village of Pollença, a few miles inland from the port. All of the residents, even tiny babies, dressed as either Christians or Islamic Moors and participated all week in reliving a traditional historical battle between the ancient Christians and Muslims.

We ate well on Mallorca. The Spanish noon meal is often the largest of the day, while the evening meal might consist of a selection of small dishes, or *tapas*, along with a couple of glasses of wine, at one of the universally delicious restaurants filling the tiny cobbled streets of old Palma. My favorite meal was *gambas al ajillo*, a hot shrimp and garlic appetizer, and I ate it often. Because of the small plates of food in the evening and the late starting time – usually after 10 p.m. – early evening snacks on board *Avanti* were a necessity.

I hung out for hours in Internet cafés to work on my legal matters. We eventually obtained an expensive Internet hook-up for the boat and I loved it, but it soon broke.

The Iraq war began that spring and the Spaniards, like most Europeans, were opposed to our invasion. We put anti-war signs on our boat, partly so the Spaniards wouldn't confront us as hated American aggressors. We joined an anti-war march through the town. The war in Iraq was an issue of constant discussion with locals during our first few years in the Mediterranean. When George W. Bush was re-elected, the Europeans were stunned. Several told us that they had not met a single American who favored the war or supported Bush so they could not understand how he could have been re-elected. We suggested two possibilities. First, most of the Europeans we met were involved in boating, as were most Americans they met. Since American boaters tend to come from the coastal areas of the U.S. which are more blue politically than America's heartland, the cruisers with boats small enough to use local marinas (not the giant yachts that are completely self-sufficient), tend to be more blue than Americans as a whole. And second, the more conservative Bush supporters were more likely to travel more conservatively, perhaps on a cruise ship or guided tour, making it less likely that our European friends would come in contact with them.

Our boat broker told us that local law required that we obtain captain's licenses. Since no one actually ever asked to see our licenses in our eight years of cruising, we're now skeptical of his advice. But we were insecure about our skills and lack of experience with powerboats, and with *Avanti* in particular, so we dutifully signed up for a class with a British couple to satisfy the requirements for the Royal Yachting Association Captain's license. The couple spent two full days with us on *Avanti* teaching us tricks about running our boat and anchoring, as well as navigating with paper charts and compasses. Much of what we learned would be important only if all our boat navigation systems failed. On the other hand, Bruce learned a lot about *Avanti's* engines and navigation systems and their occasional quirks. We weren't feeling invincible yet, but certainly more cocky after officially becoming licensed captains.

Suddenly it was June 1, the time we had set for our departure from Mallorca. Panic set in. The idea of continuing to loiter in the streets of Palma for a few more weeks seemed excellent. We grew nostalgic for the narrow streets and late-night tapas dinners. But the days were bright, the seas were calm and the town that had once belonged solely to us was becoming packed with summer tourists. It was hard to find a table at those restaurants that were empty in January. The "season" was upon us; we knew it was time.

Ibiza

Our first stop after Mallorca was the famous Balearic party island of Ibiza, home in the '60s to many hippies and counterculture wannabes, including some dear friends who lived an impoverished hippie life there for a year before returning to the U.S. When they got back, they founded one of the largest bookstore chains in the world. We concluded that they weren't sufficiently committed to the counterculture.

It was a huge relief when Ibiza popped into view from the upper helm. This was our first foray out of sight of land for a few hours, and no matter how you prepare for it, those "blue-water" trips are tense. Seeing our destination meant that we had survived the first leg of our journey – no one overboard, no engine failures, no killer waves. Once inside the harbor, we pulled into the nearest marina for the night. This was our first bad decision; the price was appalling.

The scary price we were quoted for two nights at the Marina Botafoch was the highest we paid anywhere in the Mediterranean during our eight years of travel, at least until we returned in 2010 to the same marina and found that the price was even higher. The services were non-existent unless we were willing to pay even more. The marina seemed intended for a jet-set crowd visiting the Ibiza casino and nightclubs, not for us. But it was our first marina stop and we were giddy that we had completed the first leg and were still alive.

The old Phoenician-walled Ibiza Town, a UNESCO world heritage site known as Dalt Vila, towers over the harbor, providing both a dramatic sight from the sea and a fun place to walk. During the summer season, Ibiza hosts crowds of partying, wealthy young people to enjoy its beaches and its famous, trendy and expensive nightclubs. Since the clubs are open only during the summer, the town was still quiet. We biked to the local beach, rented beach chairs and froze in the early June sea breeze. We still got sunburned.

The cost of the marina definitely influenced our opinion of Ibiza. We were also still on edge about our cruising skills. Although we'd survived one day, there was no guarantee of surviving a second or third. Returning to Ibiza seven years later, we still didn't care much for the Ibiza scene. It still looked to us like a shallow jet-setter experience. We did manage to make friends with some genuine jet-setters in a water taxi coming back to the marina after dinner in Dalt Vila. They were happily tipsy Brits who owned an ocean-liner-sized boat in the marina. When the water taxi arrived at our marina, they insisted that we join them for a few more drinks in the marina bar; we were there for hours.

Formentera

Only four miles from Ibiza lies the island of Formentera, the anti-Ibiza.

We stopped at Marina de Formentera, just three miles from the tiny capital of San Francesc. While eating at the marina restaurant, we watched the sun set, then promptly fell into bed, exhausted even though our trip from Ibiza had taken less than an hour. The adrenaline rush of beginning a new and mysterious journey had worn us out.

The next morning we rented a small motor scooter and all three of us piled on. I carried Roka on my back in her doggy backpack. This turned out to be unstable and dangerous – the scooter's center of gravity was too high with Roka on my back. We abandoned the backpack on later motor scooter trips and just stuck Roka on the seat between us. We traversed the 11-mile string-bean shaped island, wending our way up the island's mountains, past vineyards enclosed in rock walls into a sweet-smelling pine forest overlooking a calm turquoise sea. A local jewelry shop at the top on the mountain offered silver gecko necklaces that I couldn't resist. Geckos are everywhere on Formentera – we had to scramble over hundreds of geckos to get to a local beach.

The island of Formentera is sleepy, shrouded in pines; the beaches are quiet and the sand is soft and white, with many nude bathers even in early June when the water is far too cold for comfortable swimming. We could find no trace of the trendy Ibiza-style nightlife. Most of the locals are farmers. Villages are tiny. Formentera feels like a small Caribbean island misplaced in Spain.

We decided to be courageous by spending our last night in Formentera at anchor, another new experience. The water was calm and shallow and the marina was close by in case of a problem. We edged *Avanti* out of the marina and traveled only about 100 meters before anchoring. We were nervous and watchful, sitting for several hours on *Avanti* checking the landmarks we had noted when we anchored to make certain they were not changing position relative to the boat – a necessary test to confirm that the anchor is holding. We seemed secure. In an exaggerated fit of caution, I later learned to dive in my snorkeling gear after we dropped anchor to see for myself whether the anchor was firmly embedded in the sea floor, but I hadn't yet learned that trick in Formentera.

By mid-afternoon, we were convinced the anchor was not dragging, so we hopped in our dinghy and headed for shore where we sat, watching *Avanti* and sipping sangrias, still fearful that her anchor would drag and she'd either disappear over the horizon or crash into one of the other boats anchored nearby. We returned after an hour or two of watching and sipping to cook dinner on board and finally relax.

That night, our first night ever at anchor, the sea was bouncy. We were distraught. The anchor chain rattled and clanged in the dark, frightening us. Was our great adventure over, having lasted all of three days before *Avanti* was dashed on the rocks? Of course there were no rocks visible, but it was easy to imagine in the middle of the night that they were lurking just below the surface. How would we ever explain the inevitable sinking to our family and friends, who had wished us a hearty *bon voyage* only a few weeks earlier? But when the sun rose the next morning, we hadn't moved at all. Another milestone reached!

Then we faced a new bone-chilling challenge: crossing the sea to the Spanish mainland, a genuine blue-water cruise out of sight of any land for many hours. The day was bright and the sea calm, so it was time to be brave. We took off. The seas suddenly became rougher and a menacing storm appeared – okay, it was actually just a local 10-minute squall – but it put us on edge. We breathed a sigh of relief when we caught sight of land and realized that a genuine blue-water crossing was possible in our little boat.

When we returned seven years later, we encountered the same bouncy seas. It was August and the marina in Formentera was packed so our only option was to anchor. We decided to stop for lunch to check out the situation. The rough seas wouldn't let us finish eating our food; we were rocking and reeling and miserable. Even though we had hoped to visit Formentera again, we had to pull up anchor and head off to our nemesis: that same expensive marina in Ibiza.

Denia

When we pulled into the ancient Phoenician port of Denia on the Spanish Costa Blanca, we radioed to the harbormaster in our best nautical English. The response crackled back through the radio speaker – in Spanish. Oh no! We had been told that English would be spoken in all European ports throughout the Mediterranean. It is the official language of the sea. Spanish was tumbling out of the radio much too quickly for us to understand. Bruce kept repeating "berth" while I struggled with our Spanish dictionary to try to find the correct Spanish word. As it turns out, most pocket dictionaries don't contain the word for "berth" or any other boating terms for that matter. Even worse, the Spanish word for "berth" found in the big dictionaries isn't the one the Spanish actually use for a boat berth. Finally we understood from frantic exchanges in Spanish that the actual port officials were not there and would not return for another hour. That's how we learned another lesson: often there is nobody "official" at the port office in the middle of the afternoon. They come to work later in the day, about the time most of the sailboats are arriving for the evening. We did manage enough communication to find a berth, but we needed an hour and a good stiff drink to recover from the ordeal.

The highlight of Denia is the crumbling 11th-century castle on a small hill in the middle of town. It took us a while to figure out how to reach it since many of the streets that head toward the castle are dead-ends, but it is worth the effort. The castle is well preserved and the view is worth the climb. We saw little else, but sensed that there was not much else to see.

Colin, our boat broker in Mallorca, had told us that many Brits have second homes in Denia, but we saw no sign of a British invasion. We had no desire to spend more than an afternoon in Denia, but could understand why someone would find it a lovely place to live.

Seven years later we returned to Denia, now experienced Mediterranean travelers. This time we had a different reaction to the town. By then, the Denia Marina had been upgraded in dramatic fashion and was completely occupied by Brits, including Colin, who had moved his brokerage business to Denia from Palma. The food was excellent in the several restaurants within the marina and we thoroughly enjoyed our biking trips into town. We were sorry to leave.

Valencia

After a day in Denia, we were off again, cruising up the coast to Valencia, home of the original (or at least the best known) paella, and, allegedly, the original Biblical Holy Grail. The marina, another called Real Club Nautico, sits right next to the noisy, smelly, unattractive industrial port. It is cut off from the main part of town by the working port and the many large highways surrounding it, so we had to take a taxi to get to town. It was impossible to cover the short distance to town from the marina by bike or on foot because of the tight security, thanks to the Iraq War, leaving the busy highway as the only possible route. The actual Club had pleasant amenities, but the port that surrounded it was one of the least appealing places we visited in all of Europe. Even Livorno in Italy wasn't quite this grim.

We tried a paella restaurant on Paseo Neptuno, a street on the beach in Malverosa, the closest beach to downtown Valencia. There are dozens of little seafood restaurants side by side, right next to the street where large numbers of hookers congregate, a fact we learned from our cheery taxi driver, who pointed them out. Neither of us has ever been a paella (or hooker) fan, so we didn't properly appreciate the famous Valencia versions.

The city was interesting, especially the Holy Grail in the Cathedral. We naturally thought of the great Monty Python version of the search, but it appeared that the locals have taken the Holy Grail seriously for many centuries. Valencia is only one of several cities around the Mediterranean claiming ownership of the genuine "Holy Grail," the chalice that Jesus used at the Last Supper. Who knows? At least some historians seem to think Valencia's claim is strong. We were suspicious but impressed.

We visited the area north of Valencia by train. Upon boarding, the train conductor angrily stared at Roka and yelled at us in Spanish. Fortunately our Spanish wasn't quite up to understanding the word "muzzle" so it was only later that we figured out he was yelling because dogs on trains must be muzzled. We smiled and nodded politely, understanding there might be some problem with our dog on the train. I put her on my lap and the conductor finally gave up in disgust. Our goal was the local village of Sagunto and the hilltop ruins of the ancient Roman town of Saguntum. When defeat was certain during the siege of this town by Hannibal in 220 BC, the surviving townspeople threw themselves onto bonfires to avoid being captured. It's hard to imagine that a death by fire could be worse than capture by Hannibal, but I understand he wasn't a nice guy. The isolated ruins were high on the hill, reached after a long walk from the railroad station through the picturesque town market, where mushrooms, cheeses and tomatoes were artistically piled on carts by street vendors. The day was lovely. A gruesome death by fire in this place was hard to envision.

We left Valencia hoping to never return; the grim marina poisoned our opinion. Until our return to Valencia in 2010, we ranked it at the bottom of our list of Mediterranean cities. We had no choice but to return to Valencia on our way back to Mallorca. This time, it was a completely different experience. The difference was a new marina. Valencia was the site of the 2007 and 2010 America's Cup sailboat races and a new marina, the fancy but now nearly empty Marina Real Juan Carlos was built as a result. Unlike the old marina, the new one is adjacent to the town beach at Malverosa, home of the hookers in 2003. From the marina we could ride our bikes to town, although it was a long haul, or even better, hop on the newly built light rail line. We revisited the Holy Grail and enjoyed the Feria de Julio, a month-long town festival. The last day of the festival was marked by street fairs, dancing in the parks, and the most amazing fireworks display we'd ever seen, right on the beach where we'd eaten our paella in 2003. Our least appreciated city in Spain in 2003 became one of our favorites in 2010, an example of how impressions of a city can be drastically different depending on whether the visitor arrives by sea or land as well as the quality of the marina.

Vinaros, Morella, Peniscola

Up the coast from Valencia is a small marina in the miniscule town of Vinaros. We were certain that no tourist had ever before set foot in Vinaros. There were only a few restaurants, fewer hotels and no "establishment" car rental agency. We wanted to rent a car to drive to the local hilltop town of Morella where I had read about a wonderful restaurant, plus we wanted to visit the neighboring beach town of Peniscola with its well-preserved Knights Templar castle.

On our morning jog, we asked at a hotel where we could rent a car and were provided with the phone number of the town's only "rental car agency." We phoned. No one spoke English, but we somehow managed to arrange to be picked up at the marina. A friendly, middle-aged man arrived right on time and took us to his office, located at the back of a gas station on the edge of town. He had two rental cars, both old and battered, with ashtrays full of cigarette butts. Since there were no other options, we signed up. When we asked for a map we could use in our travels, he happily obliged by asking where we wanted to go, then drew a crude map on a piece of used Xerox paper, showing one or two roads that would lead to Morella, our desired destination. Hertz? Not exactly.

Morella is a well-preserved hilltop castle town built by the Knights Templar in medieval times. It was in Morella where Saint Vincent Ferrer performed the miracle of resurrecting an infant whose crazed mother had cut him up and stewed him to provide dinner for her husband. The distraught husband sought aid from the saint, who successfully brought the child back to life in one piece, except for one finger, which could not be found. No wonder – the mother had already eaten the finger to determine whether the dish was sufficiently salted. It was also in Morella that I had one of my favorite lunches in the Mediterranean: lamb stuffed with truffles at the Casa Roque.

The dramatic beach town of Peniscola was even better than the tour books claimed. Peniscola was where the papal pretender, Papa Luna, lived in a dramatic castle on a promontory bounded by the sea on three sides during the Great Schism of the 14th century.

In Vinaros the next morning, we took what is perhaps our favorite travel photo. On our morning jog around town, we found the gates to the local bullfighting ring open and the ring completely empty. We couldn't resist. We dashed back to the boat, grabbed a red pillowcase from one of our bed pillows and hurried back before the authorities could close the gate. In a classic shot, Bruce, the aspiring toreador, is fighting a smallish black bull (aka Roka) with his red cape. The photo was published in the Travel section of the Los Angeles Times. It was Roka's 15 minutes of fame.

Tarragona

From Vinaros we cruised up the coast to Tarragona, the Roman capital of Spain and home to many Roman ruins. In Tarragona, our friends, Wendy, a lawyer, and Bill, a business consultant, joined us for a few days to explore the area and travel with us to Barcelona. They were our first official visitors. It was the beginning of excruciating hot weather and Bill initiated the enjoyable routine of jumping fully clothed into the sea to cool off near the end of our morning runs. But beware: the water in the Mediterranean is so salty that a shower is a necessity as quickly as possible after a jump in the sea. The other big excitement was that the marina had a washing machine! Unfortunately, there were also late-night discos lining the harbor, which made for difficult sleeping before 5 a.m.

In the Tarragona marina, the comfortable Port Esportiu, we met Jacques, an elderly Frenchman whose boat was docked next to ours. After briefly chatting with him when we arrived, we invited him over to our boat for drinks that evening, a pleasant tradition in Mediterranean harbors. He reciprocated the next night by inviting us, including Wendy and Bill and a British couple, Harvey and Jean, who were docked nearby, to dinner on his boat. Such a feast! Jacques remained below decks cooking the five courses, insisting that his first love was cooking and he just wanted us to eat, talk and enjoy ourselves while he worked below. We were glad to oblige. The food was superb and very French, each course accompanied by a different French wine. Jacques was fascinating and mysterious; he told us tales of his fighting in Algeria with the French Foreign Legion, and then his adventurous life after the war in other African countries. We staggered back to *Avanti* many hours later, filled with thrilling stories and far too much food and wine.

When we returned to Tarragona seven years later, our British friends were still there. Tarragona was their boat's home and they never ventured far from their friendly port. They had kept track of Jacques for many years, but then he stopped responding. They sadly concluded that he had come to a bad end. Over drinks, we toasted Jacques and the memory of our dinner together.

Barcelona

Tarragona is 60 miles southwest of Barcelona – about five hours on *Avanti*. Between Tarragona and Barcelona is the upscale tourist town of Sitges, where we impulsively decided to stop for lunch. We maneuvered *Avanti* to the wharf beside the many elegant portside restaurants full of well-dressed Spaniards, all watching us. After lunch with a full bottle of wine, we staggered back on *Avanti* and headed to Barcelona. We were beginning to feel confident of our skills. Wendy and Bill seemed impressed.

Arriving in Barcelona is a treat. The city forms a dramatic crescent around a huge harbor lined with enormous commercial vessels. We felt a bit uneasy, like a sardine among dozens of giant salivating sharks, but we managed to maneuver our way through the huge port to the ancient Marina Port Vell, abutting the heart of the City in the Barceloneta neighborhood. After stopping and checking in at the temporary dock, as instructed in our Heikell book, we were sent off to Dock D, the best dock for visitors, close to the Museum of Catalonian History and the ever important bathrooms and showers. Marina Port Vell is a fun place to hang out – the icing on the cake of what would become our favorite Mediterranean city.

Barcelona is crazy, full of constant energy. Immediately adjacent to our berth in Marina Port Vell was a big multi-tent exhibition for seniors. Of course we appreciated this particular exhibition – it contained all the latest styles of hearing aids, for example. After that, in addition to a constant parade of people, dogs, bike-riders, ice-cream and soft-drink sellers and bench-sitters on the shore nearby, there were impromptu concerts we could enjoy from the deck of our boat and a most energetic, and loud, aerobics class that anyone could join ("Una vez mas! Uno, dos, tres, quatro!").

Musicians, flowers and human statues are everywhere in Barcelona. Las Ramblas, the famous pedestrian street in the middle of town, ends at the harbor a couple of blocks from our berth in Marina Port Vell. We could wander there any evening if we were willing to mingle with the glut of tourists. One day a swarm of middle-aged American Harley riders, all gregarious and highly tattooed, came roaring through town, part of the Harley World Tour celebrating the company's 100th year. In town, bands play everywhere. Brides wander the street on the way to and from their weddings. The street is a constant feast for the senses. The nearby La Boqueria open-air market is full of luscious fresh fruits and vegetables, nuts and dried fruit, and butchers with their wares. At lunch in the market one day, we watched with amusement as a vendor tried in vain to shoo away the many pigeons constantly attacking her fruits.

We came to enjoy all things Gaudí – his whimsical architecture dominates Barcelona, from the famous unfinished church of La Sagrada Família, still under construction after over 125 years, to his otherworldly apartment houses and the astonishing Park Gruell. Barcelona is home to an outstanding Picasso Museum – Picasso, like Dali and Miró, was born and raised nearby. There's something in the Catalonian genes that seems to produce great artists.

Barcelona is an easy place to visit by bike, except for having to navigate through the crowds and traffic. We rode our bikes up to the base of Tibidabo, the mountain behind town, where the amusement park at the top of the hill looms over the city. Together with our bikes, we climbed onto the tram at the base of the steep hill and ascended to the top the easy way. The fun part was coasting back down the 2 kilometers to the base, with Roka riding in her basket behind Bruce.

Surprisingly, we were able to watch the famous FC Barcelona soccer team play at their giant 120,000-seat soccer stadium, a metro ride away from the marina. Naively, we had assumed we could simply buy a ticket at the stadium. Little did we know – it was a miracle we got in. As we now understand the rules, only season ticket holders are allowed to attend, although they can bring "friends" if they have extra tickets. In order to get in, one must find a season ticket holder who is attending and has an extra ticket or two, and then actually enter the stadium with the season ticket holder. Fortunately, we found a friendly, elderly Spaniard looking to sell two tickets. We negotiated a bit, but soon realized we were on shaky ground. Fortunately, he was anxious to get into the stadium and his price didn't seem unreasonable. So we paid him the asking price and sat with him and his buddy. He got so excited during the game that we began to fear that he might actually have a heart attack. Fortunately, FC Barcelona won handily, and he lived to attend another day.

The food in Barcelona is delicious and interesting. There are many small outdoor *tapas* bars, perfect for a small meal, and filled with young, sophisticated Spaniards. The local El Cortes Inglés department store has a basement full of gourmet groceries and will deliver free to boats.

The beach at Barceloneta was only about a half kilometer from *Avanti*'s berth. This was the summer that so many grandmothers died from the heat in Paris. It turns out they had been left to fend for themselves in their non-air-conditioned apartments while their families went off to the south of France on holiday. It was a scandal in France, where the death toll was highest, but every part of Europe was affected. The insufferably hot weather started when we reached Tarragona, around June 15, and was brutal and unrelenting through the end of August. We were told that more electric fans were sold in Europe in one week in June than in the entire prior summer. We bought several. Going to the beach was a salvation from the incessant heat.

Bruce was completely enamored with the beach, although normally not a big fan of sand and surf. Perhaps the appeal had something to do with the hordes of bare-breasted women to be found there, packed, sardine-like, into the narrow strip of hot sand next to the water. The topless crowd included both young nubiles and sagging grandmothers. There were more topless women in Barcelona than on all the other beaches we visited the rest of the summer put together, including San Tropez.

The locals speak Catalan rather than Spanish whenever possible, in recognition of their antipathy toward Spain and Spaniards. They want to be independent from Spain. Most, but not all, Catalans are willing to converse in Spanish with visitors, but don't be surprised if it makes them grumpy.

We were lucky to find ourselves in town to help celebrate the Festival of San Joan, June 24, a national celebration filled with ear-shattering fireworks, colorful festivals and huge crowds milling through the local neighborhood by our marina and beach. We finally crawled back to *Avanti* and our cozy beds at 1 a.m., but thousands of people continued to cheer and blow horns until dawn.

One thing we did not like about Barcelona was the petty thievery. We took two hits from Barcelona's rampant petty street crime. The new red bike that I purchased in Palma was the first to go, stolen when we went to the beach one day. The locks on both our bikes were cut, but only mine was taken. Much to Bruce's disappointment, even criminals didn't want the ugly, bright pink bike that he purchased used in Palma.

The day after the tragic bike theft, just as I was recovering from my grievous loss, my purse was stolen from an elegant outdoor restaurant right next to the Museum of Catalonian History. I had carelessly put my purse on the ground beside me at dinner. When I was ready to go, I reached down for my purse, but it was gone. We decided the thief was likely the rose seller peddling his roses to the diners. While he distracted us, he must have grabbed my purse. It was another huge blow. I was carrying many valuable possessions – my cell phone, all my credit cards and ATM cards, my Blackberry and far too much cash, over $500. I was inconsolable, but mostly I was outraged at myself for being so stupid. I never again put my purse on the ground for any reason – it stayed on my shoulder or lap from then on, at least until I got to Croatia and Turkey, where petty theft is so rare that I started to let my guard down again.

But Barcelona was too much fun to keep me down for long. The next day I bought a new purse, a new wallet, a new phone and Bruce got money for me on his ATM card. I bought a new orange bike, even nicer than the old one. Fortunately, I had given my assistant at work all my credit card numbers, so I emailed her from our still functional computer Internet card (it died soon thereafter) and she notified all my credit card holders. I was also able to get my banks to send new credit cards and new ATM cards to me in Barcelona. Their policy, at least then, was that they would not send new cards except to a home address unless someone was available to sign for them. Our only address was the port, and we doubted port officials would agree to sign for anything. But we were in luck! Rodolfo came to our rescue.

A special attraction of Barcelona for us was our much-adored foreign exchange student, Rodolfo, who had spent his senior year of high school with us. Rodolfo is from Punta Arenas in Chile, located at the southernmost tip of the South American continent. After his year with us in California, he completed college in Santiago and moved to Barcelona to study economics in graduate school. Sadly for us, he was too busy with exams to hang out much with us, but we had a few meals together. He was able to provide us with the critical address for our credit cards. The secretary in his graduate department agreed she would sign for the cards. They arrived before we left the city.

After more than two weeks and the completion of some minor boat repairs, we left Barcelona and Rodolfo with heavy hearts, vowing to return. Wendy and Bill had already left for home, so the three of us were on our own.

Seven years later we revisited Barcelona – this time for over a week. Even better, we were joined by our daughter, Andrea, her husband, Jason, and our adorable 1-1/2 year old granddaughter, Sienna. We berthed again on Dock D. We watched Spain win the World Cup with hundreds of cheering Spaniards just two blocks from our marina. The Spaniards celebrated all night. Again there were many bare breasts on the beach, but this time we were in for a real surprise – naked men on the beach as well, and not only on the beach. One day while Jason and I were sitting on *Avanti* during Sienna's nap, Jason asked, in disbelief, "Is that guy naked?" Yes, he was. One of the naked men from the beach was headed along the marina towards the subway, completely nude. People were walking by him with no sign of surprise. Jason and I wondered if he'd ride the subway nude too.

Barcelona remains our favorite city on the Mediterranean.

Cadaques

Our next stop travelling north from Barcelona along the Costa Brava was Cadaques, a small whitewashed town surrounding a small circular bay, where we had to anchor in the shallow water since there was no marina. It took us several tries before we thought the anchor was secure. After each anchoring attempt, I dove in to inspect the anchor, using my snorkeling gear. When the anchor was lying flat on the sea floor because it hadn't caught in the sand, we'd start again. I was exhausted. It was fortunate we were so careful. The winds came up and howled for three days without stop, clocked by our Australian neighbors in the bay at over 50 mph. We hunkered down, glad to be in such a picturesque town, but still cursing our luck that the big wind had come up while we were hanging by our anchor rather than safely tied up in a cozy marina.

Cadaques is almost perfect. Salvador Dali thought it the most beautiful town in the world. It is a fisherman's town, an artist's town. The whitewashed buildings creep up the hill above the bay on a steep slope laced with stone paths.

The little town of Port Lligat, a 20-minute walk from Cadaques, is the location of Dali's summer home, a building as quirky as the artist. At the front door, visitors are greeted by a huge stuffed, bejeweled, polar bear. The bear failed to welcome Roka, so she had to wait patiently outside.

The nearby town of Figueres, Dali's birthplace, is home to the unusual Dali Museum, crammed with his creative, humorous paintings and artifacts. Don't miss it. The car we rented to get to Figueres, however, established a new low standard for rental cars. Sure it was cheap and small and had no air conditioning, but the fact that the windows didn't roll down came as a huge shock. The windows weren't broken; they were simply not designed to roll down. Fortunately, we rented the car in the late afternoon and left Roka on the boat. Otherwise we would have been roasted alive and Roka would clearly not have survived. From then on, when we rented a car, we always asked if the windows rolled down. The rental agents thought we were idiots for asking such a dumb question. No one else had ever heard of a car with windows that didn't roll down.

Finally our impatience made us decide to leave Cadaques, even though the wind, while it had slowed, was still blowing. We pulled up anchor and took off up the coast, trying to make it around rugged Cape Creus to the northeast. But the wind didn't die and the swells got bigger and bigger. We panicked and turned back. In the process we learned two lessons. First, there was no need to worry about the sea-worthiness of our boat – we would chicken out long before the boat did. And second, impatience doesn't pay. The next day the wind was gone, the sea was flat, and the cruise around the cape into France was delightfully free from trauma. We learned that if we just wait patiently, the bad weather will surely change for the better in its own good time.

We had reached the Gulf of Lion. It was time to bid Spain adios and head for new adventures in France.

CHAPTER 3
FRANCE: CULTURED, GOURMET, DOG-LOVING

Bruce and Roka on the
Pink Monster

Biking and wine-tasting in
the vineyards in Cassis

Noisy cicada toys are sold all over the south of France

Respite from the heat near Antibes, waiting for the ice
cream boat

Morning run in Antibes for
breakfast croissants

Small coastal town of Bandol
offers tea dancing for seniors in
the afternoons

Every child on French
beaches sports water wings
and a paddleball set

Pétanque player awaits his turn in a
international tournament in Nice;
pétanque is a French mania

We'd been to France before. A couple of trips to Paris, a drive from Italy to Switzerland through the French Riviera and the wine country, a biking trip in the Dordogne. We both speak a bit of French. Still, we didn't know what to expect.

France was remarkably different from Spain. Suddenly Roka was welcome everywhere and doted upon. The bread was fabulous, the croissants to die for. People were noisier than in Spain, although not extravagantly so (wait for Italy). There was a whiff of arrogance in the air, but generally the French were friendly and helpful. The ceramics were exquisite. The food was delicious. Duck and lamb were on the menus, as well as lovely quiches. The weather was hotter, but that was expected since it was late June, pushing into July.

Leaving the terrible winds in Cadaquez, Spain, behind, we arrived in France in only a few hours. We soon concluded that there are no appealing marinas along the east coast of France north of the Spanish border, but we had to stop somewhere. We ended up at the "new tourist town" of Cap d'Agde. Our advice: avoid it. It is ugly and packed with French tourists. On our way home in 2010, we were stuck here for five days when *Avanti* had a major repair issue and we hated it even more the second time. We left as soon as possible on both visits.

The Rhone

Between Cap d'Agde and Marseille, on the north side of the Gulf of Lion, lies the mouth of the great Rhone River. We bypassed it in 2003, but couldn't resist visiting on our way home in 2010. We found river cruising to be dramatically different from cruising at sea. In many ways it is easier – no surge, no banging into rough seas, no tricky wind changes – but in other ways more difficult. The strength of the river's current is a big surprise. Our only damage to *Avanti* in our entire Mediterranean adventure occurred on the Rhone. A record heavy rainfall in France had made the Rhone run faster and higher than normal. Upon leaving our quiet marina in Valence, Bruce misjudged the current. *Avanti* moved into the speeding river and slammed into a fixed pole. Cost to fix: 10,000 Euros. Good thing we had insurance.

Travel on the Rhone entails managing its many locks, which required that we pull *Avanti* up to crumbling docks to await each lock opening, then slowly drive into the lock and tie up on slimy posts that move up and down the lock as the water goes up and down; the boat rises as water fills the lock and descends as the water is expelled. The high lock walls looming over us were unnerving, but the process soon became boring and we came to resent the long waits and interruptions of our days.

Our travel up the Rhone took us from our winter port, isolated Port Napoleon at the mouth of the Rhone, past Arles and Avignon as far as Valence. To the west of Port Napoleon lies the Camargue, a rarely visited part of France, a vast delta home to flocks of birds and famous white horses. To the northeast is Provence, full of good wine and food. We spent several entertaining days driving through Provence and the Camargue when high winds delayed us in Port Napoleon.

Avignon was our favorite Rhone city, a small town surrounded by a massive stone wall. Avignon was the official papal seat for much of the 14th century, moved there when Pope Clement V abandoned unruly Rome. When the Popes returned to Rome, a rebel group remained, claiming to be the true Popes. This schism lasted into the 15th century. An enormous palace, dominating the town's main square, was built for the Popes and remains the town's main tourist attraction. Crowds are lively and even raucous. And food is superb – it's the heart of southern France after all.

We had intended to ascend the Rhone to Lyon, but we were thwarted by foul weather, those same storms that created the flood waters that caused *Avanti's* accident. The storm was ruining our fun, so we decided to stop torturing ourselves and just settle in to a quiet marina and wait out the weather. We pulled into Valence, a river town just south of Crozes l'Hermitage, location of the vineyards producing the wonderful Crozes Hermitage wines. Nearby is Tain l'Hermitage, home of the Valrhona chocolate factory. What a find! Chocolate shops like See's back home might offer a single bite of chocolate, maybe two, as a sample. At Valrhona, a dish brimming with samples sits beside each of the dozens of varieties of chocolates – try as many as you like. We pigged out. And when we actually purchased some chocolates, even more samples were piled into our bag. That stop was not good for our expanding bodies. The food around Valence was some of the best we found in France, especially the little sleek restaurant Umia, nestled in a local vineyard, serving fusion French and Japanese food (French chef, Japanese wife). Once we stopped fighting the weather, even the rain seemed delightful.

Marseille

Across the scary Gulf of Lion, east of the Rhone, lies Marseille. The violent mistral wind is reputed to come up quickly without warning in the Gulf of Lion to flatten boats in its path. We crossed the gulf twice and worried both times, watching the sky nervously. These were "blue-water" days, when no land was visible, which always makes us feel vulnerable. There's something about seeing land that brings comfort. But both crossings were calm with not even a hint of breeze.

I'd been to Marseille in the 1960s and remembered it as a dirty place that I could hardly wait to leave. But, as we learned again, cities are remarkably different when approached from the sea. Arriving by car, bus or train takes you through the dirty industrialized outskirts of town before dumping you into the tightly packed downtown/marina area where there is no place to park your car. Approaching by sea, however, is an adventure. After passing the dilapidated ruins of the Chateau d'If, a castle on an island off the harbor entrance where Dumas' Count of Monte Cristo was imprisoned for 14 years, the city's dramatic panorama opens, displaying cathedral spires, bulky forts and houses climbing up the hillside to the south, crowned by the Basilique Notre Dame atop the hill. Entering the harbor can be intimidating since giant ships loom nearby. But they all veer off to the left into the unattractive commercial area, while the small pleasure boats and fishing vessels stay right to enter the historic old port, the Vieux Port, passing by Fort St-Jean and Fort St. Nicholas, built by 13th-century knights.

Dockhands shouted to us as we pulled into the port, welcoming us to their town. After settling into the cozy marina, the sun went down and lights appeared around us, lighting the forts we had passed, as well as the Town Hall, the Abbaye St. Victor, the Nouvelle Cathedrale de la Major and, at the top of the hill, the Basilique Notre Dame. We love Marseille. It is one of the most delightful harbors in the Mediterranean. Everything is within walking or biking distance. We rode our bikes along the oceanfront road running along a cliff south of town, the route the Tour de France bicyclists would sprint over the following week. We ate dinner on board, our delicious canned confit de canard that we'd bought in Barcelona, with our new Ikea candles glowing, and medieval monuments lit all around us. Later we dined at the highly recommended Chez Fonfon where the bouillabaisse was allegedly the best in France. We certainly paid for the best – 140 euros. Other than the picturesque setting on the edge of a tiny harbor crammed with fishing boats, the experience was terrible. The service was atrocious. We asked for water and it never came, even after reminders. And the food was so bad we ate only a few bites. Think leftover fish in tomato dishwater with a couple of potatoes thrown in. Don't go there! To add to our expensive misery, we had to pay a taxi to get there and back. Our canned confit de canard on board *Avanti* was so much better.

Cassis

East of Marseille, the famous white-cliffed calanques rise up – narrow inlets that appeared far too small for any self-respecting boat to enter. At the end of the white-cliff area, the tiny fishing town of

Cassis appears. Here we found a marina that was almost too tiny for *Avanti,* crowded with a jumble of small boats. We thought we might have to turn back, but a dockhand waved us to a berth and we shoehorned in.

Downtown Cassis isn't big: a few small shops, trees full of chirping cicadas, and loads of French tourists. The shops sell fun and interesting gifts from the surrounding area, including ceramic cicadas that chirp wildly.

The countryside within biking distance of Cassis was the best part – bucolic, dotted with vineyards and wineries. Just outside of town we encountered the Clos Sainte-Magdeleine, a fancy wine chateau behind imposing gates. We peered in, wondering if visitors were welcome, then rang the bell. Out popped a suave, nicely dressed Frenchman, speaking excellent English, eager to share his wines in his elegant tasting room. He hoped we might have connections with wine importers in California. The best we could do was to buy six bottles of excellent wine. The next winery was Domaine Caillol. Sounds elegant, doesn't it? But the winery was no more than a dilapidated barn. We saw its roadside sign and followed the arrow up a narrow dirt road ending at the barn. We and Roka hopped off the bikes and looked around. No people, no bell. Finally an older gentleman appeared, dressed in wrinkled shorts and an undershirt, his head topped by a jaunty cap. He spoke no English. His tasting room was a bench in his garage where he poured us wine from a large vat. It wasn't great wine, but we couldn't leave such a sweet scene without buying a couple of bottles. *Avanti* was starting to fill up with French wines.

Iles d'Hyeres

A short voyage from Cassis brought us to the Iles d'Hyeres, three pine-covered islands outside of the Bay of Toulon. Like so many of our stops, we had never heard of this place. The biggest island, Ile de Porquerolles, is a national park fringed by a couple of towns and some crowded beaches. The island was packed with French tourists celebrating Bastille Day. Alas, no fireworks are permitted on the island, so our celebration was a bit of a bust, other than dancing with other celebrants in the town square. We swam at a crescent beach where the water was just starting to get warm and everyone was playing paddleball. Beach paddleball was popular in Corona del Mar when our children were small, but then seemed to disappear. Apparently all the paddleball sets were shipped to France. Any child not playing paddleball sported water wings instead – another French obsession.

To the east is a second island, Port Cros, with a marina so tiny that we had to anchor a few hundred yards from town. We motored into town on our dinghy for dinner, without Roka since we had read that dogs were not allowed on the island. We planned to motor her to shore for her evening pee when we returned. There proved to be lots of dogs in town, but it was too late to go back for her.

All seemed perfect; but it wasn't. By the time we returned to *Avanti*, the wind had come up – too windy to take Roka to shore. She'd have to relieve herself on the boat if she got desperate. During the night, the wind grew stronger and waves pounded and bounced us around. We awoke in a panic. Unlike in Cadaquez, we were anchored near rocks. By early light it was clear that staying was not tenable. Our neighbors had all left and we had no idea when or where they'd gone. The wind howled; the rain poured down. We quickly pulled up our anchor and lurched off, out of the poorly protected bay, seeking a quieter anchorage. We failed to batten down, assuming we'd move only a short distance. But we found nothing quieter. We realized with increasing dread that our only choice was to head out across the open sea to the mainland. We were not prepared. The windows in our main saloon were open; our big saloon table was not tied down. Papers and books were scattered about. My new mobile phone, just purchased in Marseille, was sitting on a shelf. By the time we realized our mistake, the sea was far too rough to risk trying to go below to tie things down. We were stuck on the upper helm. Tense and afraid and pelted with rain, we banged into the swells, water spraying into our faces. Poor Roka was tied to the captain's chair, skidding from side to side on the deck of the upper helm each time the boat lurched.

This was my first genuine scare at sea. I felt like a small child in the back seat of the family car, asking Bruce every few minutes, "How much farther?" "Are we almost there?" As if he knew. Finally, gratefully, in the distance we saw the marina at Le Lavandou, on the mainland. We glided into calm waters, exhausted. When we tumbled below decks to look around, we were aghast. It looked like a cyclone had hit. The big saloon table had fallen on its side. The floor was covered with papers and books, all soaked. My new mobile phone was drenched on the floor, ruined. How stupid of us! Only Roka was happy. She had not visited land since early the previous morning and was ecstatic to reach dirt; she had held in everything for over 24 hours.

Le Lavandou turned out to be a pleasant town named for an ancient "washhouse" at the town site, not the huge lavender fields nearby, though the town encourages the romantic but incorrect translation. But there wasn't a single mobile phone store in town; we had to rent a car and drive to the next town to buy a new one.

St. Tropez

St. Tropez is a short day's cruise from Le Lavandou. We had low expectations. We knew we'd hate it, with its mindless glamour, shallow ostentatious wealth and glitzy jet-setters. After all, St. Tropez was where Brigitte Bardot was discovered.

St. Tropez has a tiny but popular marina and we were lucky to get a spot. The giant glamour boats are directed into the ancient, but miniature, port in the middle of town. We were left to jostle with the rag-tag smaller boats in the outer harbor where we were directed to a berth. Our next-door neighbor proved to be a first-class, type-A jerk from Italy. He ran up on his deck as we pulled in to yell at us because he thought our boat fenders weren't properly inflated. Then he went wild when a few drops of fresh water hit his boat as we washed *Avanti*. All our negative feelings about St. Tropez seemed justified. We left *Avanti* quickly, heading off to see the town. Our initial glance reinforced our bias. The wannabes in town were wearing tight pants, skimpy tops, high-heeled shoes, and plenty of make-up, in tune with the all-night nightlife. Lining the ancient port were the most obnoxiously ostentatious pleasure yachts we'd ever seen. The town resembled a zoo; the wharves running beside the boats were jammed with gawkers, staring at the mini-ocean liners and the rich people on them as if staring at monkeys in the zoo, while the wealthy owners and their guests lounged on board, being served exotic food and drinks by their zookeeper crew. We were appalled at the unbridled wealth. When we returned in the evening, the boat show was even more garish. The oglers were watching the many giant-screen TVs glowing from inside the boats. The water in the harbor was brightly lit by the universal multi-colored underwater lighting along the stern of each giant yacht. This was the St. Tropez we expected.

But we also found another side to the town; just walk a block from the harbor to see a typical small French town, full of patisseries, boulangeries, vegetable markets, and old men playing *pétanque*. On the hill above town is an ancient Citadel. We walked up the hill and wandered in, although it appeared to be closed and populated only by roaming peacocks. From the Citadel through the pine trees covering the hill, we could watch the quiet sea in the distance. This place was actually likeable.

The other surprise is that this famous beach town has no beach. Who knew? To reach the beach, we had to bike several miles across a peninsula to the Bay of Pamplonne. Here, again, the wealthy, off-putting St. Tropez made an appearance. Gaudy beach clubs stand cheek to jowl. These ultra-chic nightclubs are reserved for the truly trendy. A wide sandy beach stretches out in front of the clubs, filled with chairs and umbrellas, but the real action is far back from the water, behind high walls, where there are bars and large swimming pools. Each club has its own set of identical striped chairs and umbrellas in its signature color lining the sand, each set of two chairs and one umbrella packed tightly against the next two-chair set, row after tightly-packed row from the back of the beach to the front. Being a Southern California girl where umbrellas are rare at even the nicest of beaches and everyone just throws out a towel, this set-up looked exceptionally dreary. Plus it cost some real bucks, around ten euros per chair for the day, with extra for the umbrella. On our first visit, we walked the length of the beach, past the Plage Tahiti where all women are reputed to be gorgeous – naturally I felt at home there – to the low class, non-club section, where we plopped ourselves and Roka and swam among the low-life locals.

On a later visit, at the end of a long bike ride, we randomly picked a side street to take us from the main road to the beach. Upon our arrival, we noticed that the sunbathers looked different. What was this? Aha! They were nude. At least half of the people on the beach were entirely naked, including three extremely elderly men standing and chatting, looking like aging Shar-Peis. They were not attractive. Bruce is a bit of a prude, but I immediately joined in and stripped off all my clothes. Roka of course was already nude. It was all quite surprising.

The hill towns near St. Tropez are the best in southern France, Ramatuelle, Gassin and Grimaud being our favorites. They are full of tiny cafes and the odd art gallery or pottery shop, with amazing views over the sea and valleys. The hilltop town and castle of Grimaud constitute a fief given to the Grimaldi family, now the ruling family of Monaco, by William the Good of Provence, in the 10th century as a reward for the family's assistance in driving out the Saracens. The Grimaldi family controlled much of the French Mediterranean during the middle ages and there are Grimaldi castles and chateaux in many of the hilltop towns.

We visited Ramatuelle on our bikes, learning the hard way that the term "hill town" is not a euphemism. We rode our bikes up and up and up. Poor Bruce had 15-pound Roka in her box on the back of his bike. We arrived cranky and dripping with sweat. We were cheered by the colorful little town, a picture-perfect walled village with narrow streets lined by homes and bougainvillea-covered shops. Outside the walls is a panoramic view over the Pamplonne Bay, as well as the best ceramic shop in all of Europe. We looked and salivated at the shop, vowing to return to buy, which we did the next day, this time by rental car. We thrilled in the fast bike ride back down the hill – far more fun that struggling up.

As much as we enjoyed St. Tropez, we ended up being kicked out of the marina, not because of the disagreeable Italian, but because there was a three day limit in the marina. We headed a few miles up the coast to Antibes, settling in for a couple of weeks, waiting for our adventuresome Australian friends.

Antibes

Our initial reaction to Antibes was negative. The air was hot and oppressive inside the town walls. The incessant, unbearable heat exacerbated our low opinion. However, within two weeks, we were big Antibes fans.

Antibes is a sister city to Newport Beach, a surprise to us. The old town sits next to the port inside 17th-century ramparts. Dotting the requisite narrow streets were a 12th-century church, a Grimaldi chateau that now houses a Picasso museum (Picasso spent much of his life in and around Antibes), a bustling daily vegetable market and a big clothing-plus-everything-else-you-can-ever-think-of weekly market.

Antibes is a working class city, but it abuts the town of Juan-les-Pins, home to the very rich. Antibes and Juan-les-Pins are located on each side of the neck of a peninsula that extends down to Cap d'Antibes.

We biked down the peninsula past large mansions and expansive trees until we reached the exclusive Hotel du Cap Eden Roc, the hotel so snooty that it wouldn't even accept credit cards until 2006. We strolled around the hotel grounds until we were ordered to leave; we were not even allowed to walk the grounds. We figured it was because Roka isn't a purebred. Cap d'Antibes is the place where "summer on the Riviera" was invented by Cole Porter and his friends in the '20s when they cleared away the seaweed from Plage Garoupe to swim, declaring that they would henceforth return each summer. Prior to then, the Cote d'Azur was only a winter resort and people didn't sunbathe; a suntan was viewed as an undesirable characteristic of the "working class."

We learned to handle the oppressive heat by taking *Avanti* out of the stuffy marina during the day to anchor off the Plage Garoupe. This was the Riviera at its best. I'd dive off *Avanti* and wiggle into the big blow-up ring we tied to *Avanti* by a long rope and then float in the cool water. We found our favorite treat – the ice cream boat. Normally manned (womaned?) with scantily clad young women, these boats zipped by every few minutes to sell Dove-bar clones, or beer or wine if you preferred. How civilized.

The marina at Antibes is so huge that it took us fifteen minutes to jog to the closest boulangerie. We ran there each morning for our breakfast croissant, hoping the run would use up all of the croissant calories.

We rented a car to explore the hills and stopped for lunch at a recommended restaurant, Auberge de Mole, in the non-town of Mole. The place was clearly a dump, charmless to say the least, located right on a busy highway in an old gas station. Plus it was outrageously expensive, at least in our view, with a fixed price of 25 euros per person just for lunch, excluding wine. But we stayed and had our best, most fun meal in Europe. The lunch was served family style, except for the main course, which was ordered off the chalk board. For the first course, the friendly waiter left several platters of appetizers on our table for 15 or 20 minutes. We took what we wanted. It was all delicious and the style of serving allowed us to try many French dishes we wouldn't normally order. Then the platters were whisked away to the next table and the platters for the second course, more delicious appetizers, were brought and left for another 15 or 20 minutes. After our ordered main course was brought, dessert reverted back to many platters of delicious sweets, plus dozens of cheeses. The food was glorious and the variety amazing. We could barely waddle out of the restaurant and had to return immediately to *Avanti* for a nap.

Iles de Lerin and Cannes

Our adventurous Australian friends finally arrived in Antibes to join us: Jan, a sociology professor with an expertise in domestic violence, and Malcolm, a geophysicist and earthquake expert with the U.S. Geological Survey. We headed east again, stopping at the surprisingly pristine Iles de Lerin, small islands just off the coast of Cannes. We avoided Cannes, thinking it must be an insipid spot full of shallow starlets, like St. Tropez. The Iles de Lerin were quiet and isolated. The "big" island, Ile Ste-Marguerite, is perhaps a mile long and half-mile wide, containing not much more than one restaurant, a few ramshackle houses, and an ancient fort where the mysterious prisoner known as the "Man in the Iron Mask" was held in the 18th century. These days the fort houses teenaged summer-campers who are learning water sports. The extensive running trails through the woods on the island were pristine and our over-achieving friend Jan actually swam to shore from *Avanti*, running shoes tied to her back, to take her morning run. The rest of us sipped coffee.

The "small" island, Ile St-Honorat, contains only a monastery for Cistercian monks. There has been a monastery there since the 4th century and it produced, among others, Ireland's St. Patrick. A dramatic sea-side fort was built there in the 11th century to protect the monks. They currently number about 30, down from the 4000 living there in medieval times, and they now live in a "new" 19th century monastery, happily greeting visitors and selling wine, soap and the other monk-made products. The woods on the island are quiet and empty, other than a few ancient chapels still used by the monks.

Our negative stereotype of Cannes, like St. Tropez, proved to be off the mark. On our return in 2009, we were forced to stop in Cannes when an engine died as we were attempting to anchor in the Iles de Lerin. We limped to the town marina where we summoned a repairman and then waited and waited. He promised to come the next morning, then neither appeared nor answered his phone. When finally reached by phone, he promised to arrive in the afternoon, but again failed to appear. This went on for several days. We thought his behavior was suspiciously Italian, so we weren't surprised when we realized that, yes, in fact he was an Italian. Bruce finally fixed the problem himself. Meanwhile we were stuck in Cannes for several days. Surprisingly, we concluded that it is a fabulous town. The smarmy movie part of the town was off to the east and we avoided that. Directly beside our marina was the medieval village, a warren of streets with typical French (meaning delicious) restaurants and lots of street musicians, plus a daily fruit and vegetable market.

Cap Ferrat

The most glamorous part of the French Riviera is located east of Cannes and the Iles de Lerin, and past Monaco and Nice. We visited both Monaco and Nice, but neither was a stand-out for us. The best part of Monaco is its amazing aquarium. Monaco was the site of Bruce's "accidental" dumping of his garish pink bike off the dock into the water, where it sank. He said it was only a coincidence that he had just returned from visiting the nearby Decathlon store where he admired the shiny new bikes. Right. Not surprisingly, immediately after the dumping, he bought one that was shiny and bright blue.

The most glamorous place in the South of France is Cap Ferrat, the peninsula where Earnest Hemingway, F. Scott Fitzgerald and their

Lost Generation friends spent drunken and decadent holidays. The water is a crystal-clear turquoise blue; the snorkeling was some of the best in France. Naturally, the food was amazing.

A Rothschild heir built the serene Villa Ephrussi de Rothschild in Cap Ferrat in the early 20th century. The view is reason enough to visit, but the mansion and the amusing gardens make it a highlight. The peninsula sports another super-pricey old hotel, but we'd learned our lesson in Antibes and didn't even try to visit.

We berthed at the marina at St-Jean-Cap-Ferrat, and later at the nearby marina at Beaulieu sur Mer, Bruce's favorite French town. St-Jean-Cap Ferrat sits on an inlet just below the famous hill town of Ezes. During our 2003 visit, the intense heat produced hill fires all along the coast, creating smoky skies and brilliant sunsets. On the hill just below Ezes, we watched a small fire start on the hill, perhaps 200 yards below the town. The flames crept up the hill toward the town, starting to gain speed. The town was in danger. Suddenly the fire planes appeared. Brightly painted red and yellow, they scooped up water in front of *Avanti* by skimming the surface of the sea, then soared upward, circling. When they reached the right altitude, they dropped their loads of water on the flames, then quickly returned to refill. The fire reached the base of the town before it was extinguished. We saw many fire planes during the summer of 2003, but the best show was in Cap Ferrat where we sat on *Avanti* hour after hour, watching the fire planes reloading with sea water.

When Jan and Malcolm took off, new friends arrived: Susan, an accountant, and Winston, a wildlife veterinarian. They took the train from Genoa, Italy where they had landed, but we had flawed communications and we weren't sure when or how they would appear in Cap Ferrat. We guessed that they might take the late train from Genoa to Beaulieu sur Mer, so we took the taxi to the station, hoping we'd guessed correctly. The station was empty – no one either working or waiting. It was midnight. The train finally pulled in and there they were, the only people to disembark. Most of our connections with friends were less random.

The next morning we left Cap Ferrat and headed east, stopping at Mentone, the last town before the Italian border, a town frequented by elderly Brits. Then the winds rose. We were planning to stay one night, but by now we had learned that plans meant little. The wind howled for days, churning the seas and bringing colder water to the surface, making the water too cold for swimming for the rest of the year. There were no available berths inside the marina, but a makeshift spot was found for us at the marina entrance. It wasn't pleasant. The winds and sea surges bounced us around unmercifully. We begged for a better spot, but no boat was crazy enough to leave the marina in such high winds. No protected berth opened for us. We lingered, quickly getting bored with sleepy Mentone. We triggered Plan B, a quick trip on the train to Nice, less than a half-hour away, to visit its fabulous Chagall museum, well worth the effort.

Finally the wind died and we were off to Italy.

CHAPTER 4
ITALY: DIVERSE, NOISY, READY FOR A GOOD TIME

Of course he's smiling; our mechanic Pumpellyo just finished pricey rebuild of *Avanti's* engine

Italian women are always fashionable

We could walk on burning sulfur on the island of Vulcano just off the coast of Sicily

The coastline of Corsica is dramatic and tinged with glowing red rocks

Remains of 14th-century martyrs in wall of Otranto cathedral

Scary! Even little kids race motorscooters in Naples

Corsicans black out all French language names on road signs

Our marina in Venice looks directly over to St. Marks

In Mentone we could feel a change. Unlike the reserved French, who are generally well-behaved, the Italians yell and wave their arms with gusto in normal conversation. Border towns like Mentone tend to have both cultures, although Mentone still looks like France. But now and then we'd run into people screaming at each other. Clearly Italians.

We immediately noticed many differences between France and Italy. The quality of croissants and bread fell precipitously. Pastas and pizzas appeared. There was more noise and clutter. Towns were more lively and colorful. Italians were more talkative, friendly and outgoing than the French. There was always something astir. But nothing runs particularly efficiently in Italy and when things go wrong, the Italian response tends to be a shrug and a sigh. The often irresponsible Italians frequently fail to show up for appointments and sometimes aren't as careful as one might hope. They can make a boater's life miserable. Still it's a congenial, diverse country, the more cultured north with its exquisite cuisine counterbalanced by the more disheveled south where the Mafia flexes its muscles and life is edgier.

After leaving Mentone, we bounced along the Italian Riviera until we arrived in the big industrial city of Genoa, where Susan and Winston left us. Our daughter, Andrea, and her best friend, Megan, arrived a day later.

Genoa

Who would choose to visit Genoa? It has a miserable reputation. Travelers are forced to go there because its airport and sea port are gateways to Cinque Terre and Portofino. They arrive in Genoa by plane or boat and leave immediately for the "good" places.

In our opinion, Genoa is the most underrated city on the Mediterranean, the sea it once dominated. Ancient Genoese towers dotting the entire Mediterranean coastline evidence Genoa's glorious history, a history of violence, political turmoil, and huge fortunes stemming from the city's centuries-long role as the bankers of Europe.

In both 2003 and 2007 our marina in Genoa was Porto Antico, the ancient port. Porto Antico is a block from the core of the city, the oldest and most interesting part of town, where the confusing warren of narrow, dark medieval alleys radiates an edgy, sinister air. The streets teem with jostling immigrants. Shops advertise cheap overseas calls and crowded African restaurants abound. And then there are the hookers. A glance down almost any of the dark alleys reveals red light bulbs glowing above doorways. Venturing down one of these narrow alleys to a door with a red light, we peeked through an open door where we saw a heavily made-up middle-aged woman sitting on an old steel bed in an otherwise barren room waiting for a customer. The streets of downtown Genoa are lined with scantily dressed women, awaiting work, some only a few doors away from one of the city's most highly touted restaurants, The Three Crows, and a half block from the stately Renaissance-era palaces on Via Garibaldi, once known as Genoa's "Millionaires' Row."

The elegant old palaces show off the wealth and grandeur that existed when Genoa was the financial center of Europe in the 16th and 17th centuries. Now they house impressive art collections as well as musical programs in the evening. These homes belonged to the elite families. These rich and powerful neighbors, living only a few feet apart, were involved in hostile feuds that divided the city into warring factions. Rancor was so extreme that murder might well be the fate of anyone foolish enough to walk by his neighbor's house. This disruption and turmoil in the city eventually cost Genoa its dominance in Europe.

Upon arrival at Porto Antico, we were directed to a berth directly in front of one of Genoa's trendiest restaurants, Da Toto. Diners at Da Toto ate on a small outdoor patio with a direct view into our slovenly boat, more often than not decorated with drying laundry hanging only feet from their tables. Shamed and embarrassed, we actually cleaned up a bit and put the laundry on the upper helm where it wasn't so obtrusive. We ate lunch one day at Da Toto – inside to avoid having to look at *Avanti* – and found the food good, but way beyond our budget. A half block from our marina is the city's modern aquarium and a large park where Genoese and tourists parade in the evenings. We attended a rock concert at the nearby outdoor theater where we sat so close to the water that we could see the smiles on the faces of passengers waving from the gigantic ferries passing by. There are good marine shops in the harbor and mechanics were eager to fix *Avanti*'s various problems. The compact town is ideal for walking and biking. Genoa became one of our favorite cities.

Cinque Terre

Just south of Genoa lie two of the most famous tourist regions of Italy – Cinque Terre and Portofino. They deserve their fame. The villages along Cinque Terre are too small for boats like *Avanti*, so we headquartered in La Spezia, a nondescript naval town with an expensive marina complete with an infinity swimming pool and a fancy restaurant. From the marina, a fifteen-minute bus ride took us to town and after another fifteen-minute train ride, we were at Cinque Terre. The train stops at each of the five towns that make up Cinque Terre so visitors can either ride by train to each town or walk on the footpath from one town to the next. We were here in 2003 with Andrea and Megan, and again in 2009 with my college friend Jean, a TV journalist, and her biomedical entrepreneur husband, Bruce.

The northernmost path between the towns of Monterosso and Vernazzo is our favorite. It is not paved and can be hard going in spots, but the hardships keep the foot traffic down. When hiking from north to south on this path, the panorama suddenly opens to one of the most dramatic views in Italy – the seaside town of Vernazzo, our favorite of the five towns. In contrast, the southernmost path between Riomaggiori and Manarola is a wide, dreary paved road packed with chatty walkers. Each path between the small towns is different. Between Manarola and Coniglia, trekkers pass a small inlet with rough seas where the brave and crazy can swim. My friend Jean took a dip there after stripping down to her bra and panties. She was thrilled.

Portofino

Just south of Cinque Terre area is the tiny village of Portofino. It is far too small for the hordes of tourists deposited daily from cruise ships, but there are lovely, quiet walks in the local hills and the crowds are gone in the evening. On our first visit, we tied up in neighboring Santa Margherita Ligure, assuming that actually taking *Avanti* into the diminutive harbor at Portofino was not possible. We hiked to Portofino on a scenic path – a walk of an hour or two through fields and past farm houses, a monastery, several small churches, superb villas, olive and lemon trees, views of the shining blue sea and an occasional motorscooter. The path was mostly deserted. When we reached tourist-packed Portofino, we chatted with a young Italian hanging out by the boats and learned that he was the "official" harbormaster. He pointed to the one or two boats at the wharf and said, "Sure there's room," only in Italian. The spaces were first come, first served. We quickly hopped on a bus back to Santa Margherita Ligure, powered up *Avanti*, and headed for Portofino, where we nestled into one of the berths with a boffo view over the tiny harbor and town. It was heaven. Well, not quite. As the day progressed, the sea got rougher and we discovered Portofino's nasty little secret – the harbor offers almost no protection from the churning sea. *Avanti* bounced and rolled during a stormy evening and night.

The next morning dawned even stormier and the sea was rougher, so we downed a hasty breakfast, battened down and nosed *Avanti* out of the harbor through a driving rainstorm. We checked Santa Margherita Ligure for space but there were no empty berths. We had no choice but to head through the storm to the next marina south,

Chiavari, where a giant and mostly empty marina greeted us. By then the sea was raging and we were grateful for any protected waters, regardless of how unappealing the town. Chiavari turned out to be a surprisingly interesting town, so we were doubly fortunate.

Oddly enough, the exact sequence happened the next time we were in Portofino, this time with Jean and Bruce. Even though it wasn't stormy, the chop in the harbor was unacceptably rough. We worried that *Avanti* might be damaged by smashing herself against the neighboring boats. Again, we left after one rough and bouncy night and scurried down to Chiavari. Still, even given our problems there, we love Portofino. We wouldn't have missed it and would brave the rough harbor a third time if given the chance.

Livorno and Tuscany

The west coast of Italy near Tuscany is neither interesting nor attractive. We stopped at the smelly, dirty port town of Livorno because there was nowhere else to stay. One small corner of the giant port is set aside for small yachts. The rest is full of enormous commercial vessels. Because Livorno is so close to Tuscany, it makes a good jumping off spot for visits by train to Pisa and Lucca, each an easy journey. We visited both towns, taking Roka with us, which meant we had to take turns going into various churches where dogs aren't allowed. She rewarded our slavish attention by wandering away from *Avanti* in the Livorno marina while we weren't paying much attention. After searching for about an hour, we feared we had lost her forever. We found her eventually, scrounging for tasty morsels among some nearby trash cans.

Elba

Elba: we've all heard the name. It was Napoleon's island of exile. That's about all we knew before we arrived. The island lies about fifteen miles southwest of Livorno. We landed in the historic harbor of Portoferraio, a small, protected port that's full of life.

Portoferraio is where Napoleon lived when exiled in 1814. The small harbor is tucked below a steep hill, crowned by a 16th-century castle and Napoleon's "town" home. The town is laced with narrow streets, steep steps and majestic hilltop views. Each visiting boat in the busy harbor at Portoferraio is tied with its stern only feet from the main street, where noisy Vespas, cars and pedestrians pass by, often on their way to the shops, trattorias, gelaterias and bars on the other side of the busy street. The ruckus continues well into the night.

It's surprisingly easy to reach Elba from the Italian mainland. Dozens of ferries take less than an hour to reach Portoferraio from towns on the mainland; they run day and night. The ferries are big and modern and, oddly, many sport giant cartoon pictures of Moby Dick, Taz, Daffy Duck and the Road Runner on their hulls.

Elba turned out to be a happy surprise. After visiting the dreary Tuscan coast, we weren't expecting such an interesting, entertaining island. To the west of the lively town of Portoferraio, mountains rise abruptly, adorned with green fields, small terraced vineyards and miniature villages. A rocky shoreline dotted with small pristine sand beaches rims the entire island. Iron mining was the historical base for the economy, carried on from Etruscan times until well into the 20th century. Evidence of the old mines covers the eastern part of the island in the form of giant quarries and huge waste piles, partly overgrown with new vegetation.

Today tourism is Elba's main source of income. Most tourists are Italian, French or British, all searching for the ideal beach during the summer months. We were there in September, a quiet month, too cool for the beach and without the summer crowds.

There were four American boats along the wharf in Portoferraio, including *Avanti*, an unusually large number. In most ports, *Avanti* sported the only U.S. flag, at least until we arrived in Turkey where, for tax reasons, Turks sometimes register their boats in Delaware. It was always interesting to find out who was on board the boats with

U.S. flags. One U.S. flagged boat in Elba was owned by an Italian couple from Pennsylvania to whom we took an instant dislike after they started to extol the virtues of Silvio Berlusconi. A French couple from New York lived on another American boat. The third, the lovely sailing yacht Grace, was owned by blond, exuberant Ellen and her retired airline pilot husband, Jerry, from Las Vegas. We met up with Ellen and Jerry again in Porto Ala, our next stop, then in Rome and years later in Kemer, Turkey. We still stay in touch.

Getting around Elba is easy. There are a half-dozen car and motorscooter rental agencies at the ferry dock, with motorscooters available for around $15 per day and cars around $40. We explored the island by car, motorscooter, bike and on foot. Most roads are narrow with no shoulder, so they were scary on bikes. The locals may be laid-back islanders, but they're still crazy Italian drivers. We ventured out on a Vespa one day, rented from the local "Baby Rents" shop. We spent another full day circumnavigating the island's winding roads in a "Baby Rents" car. We regretted not spending a night in one of the little island towns along the way, but it seemed unwise to leave *Avanti* unattended in the busy Portoferraio harbor.

The small hilltop towns on the north side of Elba are alone worth the visit to the island. Situated high above the wind-blown sea and green vineyards, they look out over the entire island to the mainland. In the tiny hill town of Poggio we discovered Da Publius, our favorite restaurant in all of Italy. The food was so good that we felt obligated to rent a car for a second day for the sole purpose of eating there again. The town of Poggio can be thoroughly explored in ten minutes or less; in addition to the restaurant, it has one interesting church, a few houses, a hotel and a tiny grocery store. Although the restaurant is the highest rated on the island, it was almost empty on both our lunch visits. On our second visit, the owners, a young couple, remembered us, and seated us at "our" table. Our favorite dish was their wild boar, *cinghale* – a specialty in Elba – along with a fabulous dessert, *formelladi gelato alle merenge*, a delectable combination of ice cream, meringue and dark chocolate. We lunched on exactly the same food on our second visit. From our table, we looked down the steep green mountain out to the white-capped sea. We enjoyed the intimate tableau of an elderly woman washing pink napkins by hand in a basin in the yard downstairs while a small child played at her feet; she was the grandmother of the family, washing the restaurant's daily supply of fine pink napkins while she babysat her small grandson.

Poggio lies at the foot of Mt. Caponne, the highest mountain on Elba, where the fearless can take a rickety stand-up gondola from the end of the road to the mountain-top. There a dramatic view unfolds to mainland Italy to the east and the French island of Corsica to the west. The gondola is no more than a small wooden platform large enough for two, enclosed by a wire cage and suspended from a rusty cable.

We had always thought that Napoleon's exile in Elba must have been confining and miserable – that's how exiles are supposed to work – thus explaining his hasty escape and return to France. But it turns out he had a fabulous life there, at least by any rational standards. He was made the Emperor of Elba and given a staff and army of 600. He was provided two big houses by the French government, one in Portoferraio and a country home about 20 miles outside of town. The main house sits high on the hill above the port with views over the island and to the mainland. A fascinating museum of Napoleon memorabilia is now housed in his spacious country home. During his short nine-month rule on the island, Napoleon was a whirlwind of accomplishment. He reformed the Elban government, set up a modern school system and built roads and irrigation systems that are still in use.

Personally, I would have been totally content to be Napoleon on Elba and would have quickly forgotten about the glories of France. But Napoleon had been the Emperor of France and had lived in the Palace at Versailles. He had bigger visions for himself than ruling 100,000 Elbans. He soon set sail for France with his small army and marched with little opposition back to Paris, picking up supporters along the way and forcing the king to flee. Napoleon again achieved the exalted title of Emperor of France. But the exasperated leaders in the rest of Europe refused to tolerate his return and sent their armies against him. He was defeated at Waterloo less than six months after his return to France. This time he was exiled to a small island out in the Atlantic where his exile truly was miserable, unlike on Elba, and he soon died.

After a month in Italian waters, we left Portoferraio for Corsica, directly west of Elba.

Corsica

I know, I know. Corsica is part of France, not Italy. Yet here it is, right in the middle of the Italy chapter. Other than the language and the quality of the croissants, it just feels like Italy and we landed there in the middle of our Italian visit. It lies right off the coast of Italy, visible from Mt. Caponne on Elba on a clear day. It was controlled by Genoa or Pisa throughout much of the last millennium. It never felt particularly French to us.

Corsica is a special place, our second favorite Mediterranean destination, Turkey being the first. Why were we so smitten? Our love of Corsica probably reflects badly on our personalities. While the south of France and the Italian coast have an upbeat, cultured feel, full of cheerfulness and warmth, Corsica feels primitive, dark, ominous. It doesn't belong in the 21st century. The cities are small and unsophisticated; most of the island is either uninhabited or dotted with tiny, isolated villages. A sense of danger permeates the air, perhaps due to the violent history of the island. Corsica has been ravaged by massacres by Saracens and pirates, constant warring among Genoa, Pisa, England and Spain for control of the island, internecine vendettas between families, and the extreme and violent independence movements that continue to this day. Due to its ruggedness, there is little agriculture other than vineyards and some grazing land. Without constant vigilance, our rented car would likely have hit a pig, and maybe her babies as well, or a cow or goat, standing or lying in the middle of a road. These animals are genuinely "free-range." There are no fences. The excellence of Corsican sausage may result from the wild chestnuts the pigs eat in the fields and along the highways.

French is the official language of Corsica, but the inhabitants consider themselves Corsicans, not French. The inhabitants have voted against independence, yet their intense dislike of all things French is obvious. As in Canada, official signs in towns and highways in Corsica are bilingual, in this case French and Corsican. Almost uniformly, the French names on these signs have been obliterated with black spray paint.

Corsica is a land of centuries-long vendettas. Most towns, however small, boast stories of long-standing violence between families, usually generated over a hundred years earlier by some wife's infidelity – we all know how much trouble women can cause. Huge forest fires break out regularly in the Corsican wilderness. We were told that most are deliberately set by renegade owners of cows who own no grazing land themselves. They burn down the vegetation on government land and then let their animals loose to graze on the new grass that grows in the burned-over areas the following spring. There are apparently no consequences for these acts.

Corsica's wild mountains are covered in snow in the winter. The mountainous backbone of the island makes crossing Corsica from east to west difficult and slow. We drove south to the unusual and striking town of Bonifacio, a town that sits on a white cliff that extends out over the turquoise waters below. This was where the Laistrygonians threw stones from the cliffs at Odysseus' ships and sank all but one. These Homerian giants were likely the people who lived in Corsica from about 6000 BC to 1500 BC and who built the stone monuments, known as menhirs, found throughout Corsica.

Menhirs stand in long rows, lined up like soldiers, human-like figures with barely visible eyes and mouths.

We used the brooding harbor of Bastia in Corsica's northeast as the base for our visit, venturing out in a rental car for a day or two at a time. We circumnavigated the island, which stretches over 100 miles in length and about 60 miles in width. In addition to our visit to Homerian Bonifacio in the far south, we stopped for dinner in the grim, gloomy city of Sartene, described by one German writer as a "town peopled by demons," once an asylum for criminals seeking a refuge from Corsican authorities, and home to an infamous bloody 19th-century vendetta. We were struck by the cold harshness of the town. We found only one restaurant open. As we ate, a thunderstorm raged and extinguished the town's electricity, plunging our world into darkness. Candles were lit. When we stumbled out of the restaurant, we were enveloped in total gloom punctuated by flashes of lightning and an occasional candle glowing in the dingy buildings that closed in around us. We had been transported to the demonic Sartene of the 14th century.

Our favorite place in Corsica was the west coast near the small town of Piana, where stunning red-rock fjord-like calanques mark the coast. We stayed in a 1920s grand palace style hotel, Les Roches Rouges, with a fin-de-siècle ambience and expansive views over the calanques and the sea. The main "highway" from Piana up the west side of the island consisted of one lane and so many hairpin turns that only first and second gears were useful. Cows, pigs and goats, and infrequently a car, were our fellow travelers. The views of mountains and sea were worth the many hours of hard, slow driving.

We spent several days on *Avanti* in the harbor in Bastia. Unlike most of the brightly restored ancient harbors around the Mediterranean, Bastia's harbor is ringed with tall, gray, crumbling buildings, so crowded together that the air is oppressive and claustrophobic, interrupted now and then by a small splash of bright paint indicating that a restaurant had managed to wedge itself into the gloom. The town's grimness is exacerbated by unrepaired damage to the decaying buildings caused by an unfortunate American bombing of Bastia in WWII. The Germans had actually retreated and no Germans were left on the island, but the Americans didn't get that news. The locals were in the midst of celebrating the German departure when the American bombing started and many Corsicans were killed. We learned that the 60th anniversary of the bombing was coming up in a few days and wondered how Americans might be treated on that day. We decided not to chance it and left the day before the anniversary.

Down the Italian Coast to Rome

Upon returning from Corsica to the mainland, we ventured into the luxury marina at Porta Ala, an upscale development of huge mansions, a well-maintained golf course, tree-lined bike lanes, groomed beaches, a polo center, a modern marina, and no people anywhere. We felt like characters in the novel *On the Beach,* that chilling Nevil Shute novel of life in an empty Australian town after almost everyone had been killed in a nuclear holocaust. The weather was warm, but the season was clearly over and the rich Romans had returned home for the winter. Hotels and restaurants were closed, shops were shuttered, and houses were boarded up. We had no choice but to cook dinner on board, picking from the meager selection at the convenience store near the marina, a small grocery where everything looked months old. A rising wind kept us in port. Our small silver lining was the golf club, within biking distance, where there were real people and a small open restaurant at the clubhouse. The clubhouse was so deserted that our dog-loving waitress allowed Roka to come inside so long as she hid under our table where the manager couldn't see her.

South of Porta Ala is the elegant Argentine peninsula, a posh enclave where Sophia Loren has a home. The only marina with any space available was the soulless Marina Cala Galera. Its only saving grace is the attractive town of Porto Ercole, a short walk away. On our daily bike venture, we found an upscale resort and stopped for lunch; the resort hotel was Il Pelicano – the Pelican – amazingly named after the pelicans in California. There are no pelicans in the Mediterranean. This idyllic inn was built in the '60s by a California woman and her British adventurer husband as a romantic retreat. We stopped for lunch and loved every minute there, but we could barely afford our small meals and Roka was unwelcome – she was forced to wait unhappily outside in the parking lot. We've since found Il Pelicano listed as one of the top ten resort hotels in Europe.

Just off the tip of the Argentine Peninsula is the now infamous island of Giglio, location of the disastrous Italian cruise ship demise. We visited this island to satisfy the fervent desire of my best high school buddy, Jan, a teacher, who was visiting with her partner, John, a nuclear physicist. The small island consists of a village where ferry boats land and disgorge hordes of Italians, a castle or two and a few crowded beaches. Gilgio has no marina and the small town wharf was full, so Bruce and I anchored in rough seas while John and Jan rowed our then motorless dinghy into town to spend the afternoon. When it was time to anchor for the night, we headed to a small cove on a quieter side of the island where we could swim. The next morning, Bruce and I rowed the dinghy to the rocky shore from our anchorage, scrambled up a steep cliff, maneuvered through a wire fence, and finally reached the town. The warm breakfast rolls we found there compensated for the difficult hike.

Rome

Most visitors to Rome by boat land in Civitavecchia. This is where all the cruise ships stop. Don't come unless you must or unless you'd like to visit an unexceptional industrial town. We berthed there both to meet our friends Jan and John and to take a needed week off from *Avanti* to drive through Tuscany and Umbria. Everyone needs a vacation from a boat now and then. We reached Civitavecchia after a grueling day in a churning sea that was growling in anticipation of an approaching storm. We were lucky to make it – the next day the winds howled, the rain poured and thunder and lightning rolled around us. The marina, just south of town, is huge and pleasant with good restaurants and a large grocery store within biking distance.

When visiting Rome proper we stayed in Porto di Roma, a fairly new marina disguised as an outlet mall. We were stuck there for several weeks, mostly waiting for boat repairs. Life in the outlet mall soon became tedious. The marina was a ghost town during the week, but on Sunday thousands of people poured in to walk and window-shop at the "outlet shops," in appearance identical to outlet shops in the U.S., except these shops were stunningly expensive. Life was so boring at Porto di Roma that I was finally driven by desperation to buy some of the pricey Italian clothes in the shops. The marina itself is designed so badly that a constant surge from the sea disrupts much of the marina, banging boats around. We were placed in a berth near the entrance to the marina, where we rocked and rolled uncomfortably right beside a lovely German couple, Gisela and Günter, who had actually purchased their berth and were doomed to experience continual rocking forever. We shared drinks and meals and later visited them in their hometown of Frankfurt.

We were thrilled to find a Chinese restaurant near the marina where we could escape the constant sameness of the marina's mediocre Italian restaurants. We ate there with friends Ellen and Jerry from Portoferraio and were rewarded for our patronage with a cheap plastic Buddha statue which we placed in an honored spot on *Avanti*.

In Porto di Roma, we experienced our first *Avanti* haul-out. As we came to expect in Italy, things did not go smoothly. One of the pieces of haul-out equipment was broken and the replacement was scheduled to arrive from Milan. Every day, day after day, we were assured that the missing piece was "on its way" and would arrive that afternoon. We learned that Italians don't like to give bad news and will just make stuff up to avoid it. After five days of "it's on its way," we offered to drive to Milan to pick it up ourselves. Our offer was politely declined. The part finally arrived and *Avanti* was hauled out of the water to a large parking lot where she joined others of her kind to spend the Italian winter.

When we returned to Rome the following spring, a major engine repair kept us in port for a couple more weeks. Everything in Italy moves at a frustratingly slow pace. We were lucky that Rome was only a half hour away by train. Bruce and I had passed through Rome before and the city had been so overwhelming that we genuinely believed we didn't like the place. We learned better. Now we were close enough to take short day trips and go to only one or two places each time – Coliseum, Forum, Capitoline Hill, Baths of Caracala, Etruscan tombs, Piazza Narvona – plus have a leisurely lunch. We ran in the Komen Race for the Cure with Roka, starting at the Baths of Caracala, along the Circus Maximus, by the Forum and the Coliseum, then back to the Baths. Italians don't seem to understand the importance of race-day water stations on a hot day. There was no water anywhere. Finally one kindly street vendor by the Coliseum started giving away huge liter bottles of water. They were heavy, but still appreciated. The other entertainment in Porto di Roma was close-by Ancient Ostia, the remarkably-preserved coastal city that predated the Roman civilization. The ruins there are voluminous and well-preserved, and well off the normal tourist path.

Sardinia

Avanti didn't make the trip to Sardinia; she was still undergoing expensive repairs in Porto di Roma. More important, Sardinia was too long a slog from the mainland for *Avanti*. We took the overnight ferry. No dogs allowed, so Roka sneaked in as a stowaway. When Roka is in her airplane carrier, no one knows she's there; her carrier looks like just another piece of carry-on luggage.

Sardinia is a bit like Corsica, but more serene, less brooding. Like Corsica, it has changed hands many times over the last 1000 years. The longest period of domination was by the Catalans from Spain, so there is still much Catalonian culture and architecture on the island.

71

The weather during our visit in May was a disgrace – lots of rain and high winds – but the colorful wild flowers were dazzling.

Sardinia is covered with nuraghes, cone-shaped rock structures built as a combination house and fortress by the prehistoric Sards, a goddess-worshipping culture. Seven thousand nuraghes dot the island. Many are several stories high with complex interior rooms and both inside and outside staircases. Scattered throughout the countryside are large burial tombs, known as "tombs of the giants," together with prehistoric caves dug by the Nuraghic people. Sardinia also has Greek and Roman ruins, but the nuraghes are more interesting and unusual. And how could one not be appreciative of a culture that worships women?

By good fortune and dumb luck, the major Sardinian festival started the day we arrived in the capital city, Cagliari. The festival honors Sant'Efisio, a Spaniard living in Sardinia who was martyred after converting to Christianity in the 4th century. He returned in the 16th century to intercede and save Sardinia from the plague, the event celebrated by the festival. Families in their native dress come from villages throughout southern Sardinia to make the two-day journey from Cagliari to the Church of Sant'Efisio in their ox-drawn wagons extravagantly decorated with flowers and produce from their regions. After the two-day journey, the procession turns around and comes back. Grandstands are set up in town so viewers can watch the floats go by – a bit like the Pasadena Rose Parade, but without the Rose Queen. The parade stops often for no apparent reason while on-lookers rush into the street to have their photos taken, pat the oxen and chat, while participants aimlessly meander. It's a big TV draw around Sardinia, and the grandstands give it a festive feel, just like on Colorado Boulevard.

Horse races occur the following day. Buff young Sardinians race their horses bareback, some wearing brightly colored racing silks and some wearing ragged t-shirts. Before the races, groups of costumed riders gallop by, standing upright on their horses' backs while hanging on to each other. Some fall off. As with the parade, on-lookers feel free to wander onto the track at any time. Without the festival, Cagliari would have been disappointing – it's rather drab.

The northwest corner of Sardinia is a different story. We were entranced with the Catalonian town of Alghero where, during Catalonian rule, an early form of ethnic cleansing was practiced. The number of Sardinians allowed in town at any one time by the Catalonians was strictly limited, and even those permitted in the town were required to leave when a trumpet was sounded.

We treated ourselves in Alghero by staying at Villa Las Tronas, a 19th-century palace surrounded on three sides by the raging sea. The day was stormy so we hunkered down in our fancy palace waiting out the rain, wind, lightning and thunder. The hotel was so up-scale that breakfast included "made-to-order" eggs, a real change from our normal breakfast offering. Typically in Italy, "made-to-order" refers to whether butter should or should not be put on the cornetti, the pale Italian replica of the soft and delicious French croissants.

The most well-known area of Sardinia is Costa Smeralda in the northeast corner of the island, the infamous den of iniquity where Dennis Koszlowski put on an extravagant birthday party for his wife, flying in their friends at his company's expense. He went to jail for misuse of company assets. The community was developed by the Aga Khan in the 1950s. The buildings are reminiscent of Disneyland, with newly built hotels, homes and shops desperately trying to look old and charming. The only shops in the area are of the Gucci/Prada ilk. We were glad to leave. Don't bother visiting this area unless you like fake ruins and designer shops.

Naples and the Bay of Naples

Two places are worth a visit when traveling between Rome and Naples. The first is the little marina town of Nettuno where you can visit next-door Anzio, home of the emotionally powerful World War

II American cemetery. Over 7000 American soldiers killed in Italy are buried there, representing about a third of the Americans killed in the battle for Italy in 1943/44. The battle started in Sicily and worked up the Italian peninsula until Rome was finally taken in the summer of 1944.

The second, thirty-five miles off shore, is the island of Ponza, about the size of Giglio. We arrived just as the island was preparing for its annual summer solstice festival. Likely because of the festival, every dock and marina pontoon was closed off. We dropped an anchor in the bay to scope out the scene and our overnight options. There were big uncomfortable swells on the open sea and wind-driven chop in the bay. We wondered if we'd made a huge mistake coming all the way over from the mainland. Fortunately, the sea quieted after a couple hours and we took our dinghy in to visit the colorful village, not more than two blocks long. Our biggest problem occurred the next morning when we discovered that our anchor had caught on a mooring chain tied to the sea floor. As the official *Avanti* diver, I had to solve the problem. In I went, decked out in fins, snorkel and mask. After several failed attempts, I managed to free the anchor with a fancy combination dive-and-hook maneuver. Bruce awarded me a score of ten, but I was exhausted for the rest of the day.

Entering the Bay of Naples is a thrill, especially when threading your way among all the ferries that whip across the bay at high speed – sort of like trying to avoid Italian drivers on the Autostrada. Mount Vesuvius towers over the bay, and the houses built up its sides are a grim reminder that there might be even more dangerous places to live than California. On a clear day the entire bay comes into view, from Capri and the Amalfi peninsula to Ischia.

Naples itself is a wildly chaotic town where crossing the street on foot is an adventure and driving is suicidal. *Avanti* settled into a spot in Santa Lucia, a miniature marina beneath both a huge castle and the Grande Albergho Vesuvio Hotel, where Bill and Chelsea Clinton stayed during his presidency, and where Caruso died. The marina has no facilities (meaning toilets and showers), and the dockhands (ormeggiatori in Italian) ferried us from the boat to shore and back. Naples' pizzas are more like the ones we're used to than the extremely thin-crusted ones in Rome. We settled on the basic Margherita version with tomato, mozzarella and basil. One a day is about right.

Our climb to the top of Vesuvius along with the 80-year olds and thousands of school kids is exhilarating and was especially exciting for Bruce since it is a geological "classic." The volcano is mostly quiet, with just a few puffs of sulfurous steam wafting out of random cracks. You know a volcano isn't dangerous when the tourist shops are set up right at the rim. Both Herculaneum and Pompeii were buried by the ash flow from the eruption of Vesuvius in 79AD. Both towns have been unearthed and are endlessly fascinating. A surprising fact for us was that as few as ten percent of the citizens in Pompeii were killed; most managed to escape. The amazing thing about Vesuvius is how well the ash preserved what it buried. Pottery, frescoes and buildings in Herculaneum and Pompeii are emotionally moving, capturing the day-to-day routine of those whose lives ended so abruptly. We were most disturbed by the cast of a person, crouching in terror and fear at his death, and another cast of a dog, unable to escape due to his heavy collar and chain, frozen forever in the ash as he writhed in pain.

There are three notable islands in the Bay of Naples: Capri, Ischia and Procida.

Most famous is Capri. We found Capri too touristy: too many people and too many tourist shops, even in off-season September. But we were glad for the magnificent walk from the town to the former palace of notoriously evil Tiberius, built in 27AD for his retirement from being Caesar. When he retired, he moved to Capri with some of his boys – he was big on pedophilia. He enjoyed the location of the palace due to the nearby steep cliff which made it easy for him to throw his enemies to their deaths. He was not a nice guy.

The second island, Ischia, is larger and livelier than its neighbor, Procida. We spent one night in Ischia in an enormous convent, converted from a castle in the 14th century, and perched dramatically on the top of a massive rock jutting into the sea. Bruce complained of the lack of air conditioning and the size of our room, a former nun's chamber, but I loved sitting at our window gazing over the countryside, imagining the life of the nun who once lived there. We spent a second night on Ischia with our friends Susan and Winston on *Avanti*. They agreed to visit once again, having foolishly failed to learn anything from their prior visits to *Avanti*. We berthed *Avanti* in the small main Ischia port where there was loads of action – ferry boats, music, crowded restaurants and fun shops. Best of all were the six young, buff Italian men on the boat next to us. Susan and I watched with appreciation as these scantily dressed stallions spent the entire afternoon cleaning their boat. I'm not sure which was better, the buff bodies or watching men clean. But, alas, there was more action in the port than we bargained for. At about 11 p.m., loud music started to blare from the closest bar, only one boat away from *Avanti*. The good news is that the racket ended at 3 a.m., two hours earlier than bar music normally stops in Italy. The bad news is that there was no possibility of sleep while the partying went on. The cool guys on the next boat were loving it; by party time their boat was filled with gorgeous women. Bruce pointed out that their boat was both bigger and newer than his, which was his explanation for why the women went there and not to *Avanti*.

There's more than partying on Ischia. Its size is manageable, dotted with postcard-ready seaside towns and an exotic garden and museum, the Giardini La Mortella, created in the mid-20th century by a famous British composer and his wife.

Procida, five miles across the Bay from Ischia, is a subdued family island. This was a big relief after the party life in Ischia. It's possible to walk the entire island in only a few hours. Actually we found it too quiet for our taste, best for someone desperately needing an extremely calm rest.

Amalfi Peninsula

Naples is so exhausting that it requires a visit to the nearby peaceful Amalfi Peninsula for unwinding. We first attempted to stay in the harbor in Sorrento and even called ahead, but when we arrived we were told that nothing was available and that we should come back later, a response that is probably the true origin of the famous Frank Sinatra song, "Come Back to Sorrento." We rejected the suggestion and never returned. The town of Amalfi was happy to take us. We were told we could stay only two to three days, but the marina was not crowded and we were eventually allowed to stay longer. Perhaps there are no crowds because the harbor is not well protected and subject to an uncomfortable surge. But there are no other places to dock on the Amalfi Peninsula other than Sorrento, which is small, and Capri, which is both small and outrageously expensive.

Amalfi is a classic Mediterranean coastal town surrounded by mountains and dripping with charm and ambiance, at least once you turn inland from the docks and walk a couple of blocks. The block adjacent to the water is a horror – packed with tourists just off their buses or cruise ships. It's interesting how those folks rarely stroll deeper into a town than that first block. After the first block or two, the little village is nearly tourist-free.

Outshining even Amalfi is the nearby mountain town of Ravello, a scary bus ride from Amalfi over narrow hairpin turns up the side of the mountain. Ravello, like Amalfi, can be flooded with tourists during the day, but both settle down to their local roots when the tourists get back on their buses or ships. Ravello is famous for its evening outdoor concerts in the Villa Rafalo, a villa where Wagner wrote part of Parsifal. Gore Vidal claimed the view from Ravello to be the most beautiful in the world; it's hard to disagree. I was so taken with Ravello that I decided this is where I will come to die. Our visiting friend Susan agreed, so when we're both exceedingly old and totally deteriorated, we'll come together. It is a magnificent spot, utterly quiet since no cars are allowed, only donkeys. The views are the most magnificent in Italy – up and down the Amalfi coast over the nearby lemon groves, where lemons are grown for the ever-present limoncello liqueur. The main and only street is filled with little restaurants perched on the cliff overlooking the sea and small shops selling olive oils and high quality ceramics. We hiked from Ravello down to Amalfi past small villages, waterfalls and prolific wild flowers. Some foolish people actually hike *up* the mountain, and then take the bus back down.

Agropoli and Paestum

Agropoli has one of the best marinas south of Rome. It is an exceedingly quiet town with a small medieval castle, but it's real claim to fame is that it is a short ten kilometers south of Paestum, home of three enormous Greek Doric temples, some of the best-preserved Greek temples in the world, as well as a National Museum containing unusual 5th-century BC painted tomb frescoes taken from nearby burial mounds. The easy coastal bike ride from Agropoli to Paestum passes olive tree orchards and buffalo ranches, home of those famous Italian buffalos that are the source of real Italian mozzarella. Roka was wary of the buffalos, but they seemed overjoyed to have her visit. Locals flock to the ranches to buy fresh buffalo mozzarella.

Sicily

It's a long slog from Agropoli to Sicily, but there are some hidden gems along the way. The best is the isolated hill town of Maratea, a short bus ride up the hill from the excellent marina, where we sipped limoncello in the garden of the lovely La Locanda Delle Donne Monache, a former convent that's now a hotel.

We also enjoyed the friendly marina at Vibo Marina, owned by a Canadian woman. The town isn't much, but the next town east, Pizzo, high on a cliff, is a worth a visit. We visited Vibo Marina with our friends, Loretta, a congresswoman, and her now-husband, Jack, a lawyer. We were happy to settle into quiet Vibo Marina. The prior day was so threatening and terrifying, with rain and high wind, that we made an unexpected and undesired overnight stop at the huge, barren shipping port of Gioia Tauro. The small-boat marina at the port was not open to transients and we had to argue vehemently with boaters who were shouting at us to leave. We insisted that returning to the open sea would be too dangerous. They reluctantly allowed us to stay. We learned later that this is a genuinely scary place, likely run by the mafia, where 80% of Europe's cocaine arrives from Colombia, as well as many illegal arms. No services were available. Jack had to climb a fence to open the marina gate so we could walk along a half mile of desolate highway to reach a local restaurant for dinner.

Vibo Marina seemed safe compared to Gioia Tauro, but the next day the weather was still terrible and wild wind gusts blew *Avanti*'s upper bimini frame out of its canvas bimini cover. One of the ends of the loose frame smashed into a saloon window below. Loretta was sitting beside the window and saw the metal tubing come hurling directly at her. Her life flashed before her eyes, but fortunately, saloon windows are strong. The window cracked but did not shatter.

We traveled much of Sicily by car – the weather was too rough to take *Avanti* out of protected Vibo Marina. When the weather was better, we ventured on *Avanti* to the ports on the east coast of Sicily, maneuvering her through the tricky Strait of Messina, where Scylla and Charybdis tormented Odysseus.

We weren't all that impressed with Sicily. Perhaps our expectations were too high. Sicily did have some highlights, but the island ended up in a low position on our list of best Italian islands. The volcanoes fascinated us: we visited Vulcano, actually an island making up part of the Aeolian Islands north of Sicily, as well as Mt. Etna. While Vesuvius was impressive for its historic destruction, the reality of the continuing threats from volcanoes was dramatically clearer at

Vulcano and Etna. We trekked to the top of Vulcano's sole volcano, where there are no fences or other markers keeping tourists from danger. The soil was almost unbearably hot, our lungs burned from sulfuric acid and we were unable to avoid stepping on smelly, sulfuric vents belching scalding steam. Even Roka hated walking on the hot ground. Mt. Etna was intimidating in a different way. We drove up the mountain until the road was no longer passable due to the streams of now-hardened fresh black lava that spewed forth in a big 2002 eruption. Realizing how many small and large Sicilian towns sit in the path of inevitable future Etna eruptions made events at Pompeii even more chilling.

We also liked Palermo, a mad-house city where walking across the street is dangerous. The Norman churches, built in the 11th and 12th centuries, were our favorite sites. On the hill above Palermo sits the cathedral of Monreale, one of the most imposing churches in the world, rivaling Hagia Sophia in Istanbul and the great churches of France. Gold mosaics of stunning richness and beauty cover its walls, columns and ceilings in an excess of radiant golden glory.

We saw an abundance of poor but productive land in Sicily's interior. We were surprised that so little is cultivated given Sicily's gentle topography. Perhaps lack of water is the limiting factor. The Sicilian hills are still green in early June, but they dry out during the hot summers. Wine grapes do well here – for centuries Sicily provided most of Europe's inexpensive table wines. Now the winemakers are upgrading and some good, but not great, wines are produced.

Syracuse was our favorite Sicilian city, with its gracious historic center located on an island attached to the mainland by a small bridge. A rival of Athens in ancient times, Syracuse has preserved its sense of rich history without the tacky overlay of tourist kitsch that spoils many historic places. At a large ancient Greek theater, located on a hillside a few kilometers inland, we took in Euripides' *Medea*, a play that absorbed us completely even though we understood none of the Italian. As goddesses often do, Medea left behind all her sorrows by flying off with the sun.

We also stopped at Taormina, allegedly the most popular town in Sicily. We were able to berth *Avanti* in the village of Naxos just south of Taormina, at the foot of Mt. Etna. The views of Etna from Taormina are stunning. We noticed that when clouds hanging over Etna all morning finally disappeared, one little cloud remained, hovering at the top of the crater, never moving, only growing larger or smaller. We finally realized that the cloud was actually smoke from the volcano. It was an alarming realization that Etna is still a threat and could erupt at any time. We found Taormina, unlike Syracuse, to be a once-lovely city now overrun with tourists and the bric-a-brac created by the tourist industry. Although it is Loretta and Jack's favorite Italian town, we didn't warm to the place. We were glad to get back to Naxos, a working town not much impacted by the tourist behemoth on the hill above it.

Otranto

Traversing the bottom of the boot of Italy is long and dreary. Sadly, it must be done. Bring something to read. The first interesting town on Italy's east coast is Otranto, which still identifies itself almost entirely by its 15th-century history, when the Turks invaded the town, killing 12,000 Otrantans. The 800 souls left alive in the town were told by the victorious Turks that they had two choices: convert to Islam or be beheaded. I know which I'd choose, but religion was big in Otranto then, so all 800 chose beheading, and today they are known as "The Martyrs." Their names are inscribed in the church built atop a wooded hill where the beheading was carried out, and their skulls and bones are "tastefully" displayed in glass cases in the town cathedral. Otranto's attractions include an impressive castle, small medieval streets, and some trendy shops where we both went to buy clothes to make us look more fashionably Italian (fat chance, you're likely thinking).

After Otranto we visited Brindisi and Bari. If you've been there to catch a ferry to Greece or Dubrovnik, you'll recall that neither town is anything special. We found Bari the more interesting of the two, especially its extremely fashionable main drag with one of the liveliest "passagiatas" we've seen – everyone walking in the evening dressed in their finest (and often skimpiest) clothes, parents pushing baby strollers, teens eying each other coyly, everyone chattering incessantly. It was in Bari that the Italians bested the Turks, unlike in Otranto. The patron saint of Bari is none other than old St. Nick, who turns out to have been a native of Myra, Turkey. In the 11th century, the locals from Bari stole the bones of St. Nicolas from Myra for their own cathedral. In the dark basement of the church we found an Orthodox priest chanting in front of St. Nick's bones, which, for some incomprehensible reason, were sitting in an open vault directly beside a tacky plastic shopping bag – maybe it had something to do with shopping for Christmas presents.

Gargano Peninsula

The Gargano Peninsula is known as Italy's "spur." Our son, Adam, visited us here, joining us at the village of Trani just south of the spur and traveling with us to Vieste, at the tip of the spur.

Gargano is a huge magical oasis of thick forest, rocky inlets and blue sea in what is otherwise a dreary part of Italy. Dramatically eroded limestones along the coast have formed caves and grottos large enough to enter with a small boat. The three of us, plus Roka, rented a grotto boat for the day from our marina in Vieste to explore the carved rocky coast. We also spent a couple of days anchored in the Tremiti Islands, a group of four tiny islands about 30 miles off of the Italian mainland, isolated enough to be a traditional place of exile and punishment beginning in Roman times. Tremiti is surrounded by the clearest water we saw in Italy and the snorkeling was good, though not to be confused with, say, Hawaii. On one island stands a massive 9th-century monastery fortress where monks welcomed knights on their way to the Holy Land and where later rulers, including Mussolini, locked away political prisoners. It is said that the Trojan War hero Diomedes was buried on these islands and that his grieving followers were turned into the crying sea birds that now inhabit the area. That seemed a bit far-fetched, but there were a lot of birds and their cries were in fact especially doleful. We highly recommend a visit. There is no marina in the Tremiti Islands, but the anchoring is peaceful and not crowded.

Most nights in Trani and Vieste we could sit outside with the crowds at a local cafe in front of one of the many big TV sets set up for the big Euro 2004 soccer tournament. Italy lost in the first round, but the Italians still came out to watch – they are obsessed with soccer.

Venice

After spending a month in Croatia (see Croatia chapter), we headed northwest to Venice, a half-day of cruising from Croatia. We didn't know what to expect since Venice is such a tourist town. As we neared Venice, a huge storm hit us with massive and scary thunder and lightning - the type of weather we try to avoid. But by the time *Avanti* reached St. Mark's Basilica and the Grand Canal, the sky had cleared and the normally hazy skies over Venice had turned a bright blue. We could even see the southern edge of the Alps to the north of the city.

We had read about a private marina on the island of San Giorgio, directly across the channel from Piazza San Marco and the Doges Palace, where visiting boats are allowed to stay if a spot has been vacated by a permanent resident. We cruised up to the marina and, sure enough, there was an open berth there for us. What good luck! From the marina we had a close-up view of the heart of Venice and the Grand Canal, plus easy access to town since San Giorgio is on the route of the vaporetto, the Venice canal bus. The canals and bridges of Venice are visual marvels as well as vital for transportation and shipping. Venice is surely unlike any other city in the world. We walked and walked, always entranced at the beauty of this old and collapsing city.

Several times when we ate at outdoor restaurants along the Grand Canal, we could barely stand the stench. The sewer system in Venice is practically non-existent since so much of the city's sewage is released directly into the canals. The Venetians rely on the cleansing power of the twice-a-day tides that sweep in from the Adriatic. In addition to producing damaging floods, rainstorms disrupt the tidal effect. Not surprising, the worst smells occurred right after a rain. But even when it smells bad, Venice is glorious. If you can get a spot at the San Giorgio marina, you'll find that your accommodations are finer than the $1000 per night Hotel Danieli just across the canal.

CHAPTER 5
CROATIA: BEAUTIFUL, COMFORTABLE, FRIENDLY

View from walls of
Dubrovnik down the coast
toward Montenegro

In downtown Dubrovnik, bullet
holes from the 1991 war are still
visible

James Joyce's favorite plavic
wine from Vis

Roka enjoys the view from
the citadel on Hvar

Croatia is a center for "naturists"

Toni's supermarket
boat near the Kornatis

This strawberry seller has to
explain her prices to us in writing

Bruce negotiates hard in
Rab for a garlic string

Typical isolated taverna/marina
in the Kornatis

Well-preserved Roman amphitheater in Pula

"On the last day of Creation, God desired to crown His work, and thus created the Kornati Islands out of tears, stars and breath."
— George Bernard Shaw

Croatia is home to wonderful but still undiscovered towns – Trogir, Pula, Split, Rab, Primošten – as well as the haunting Kornati Islands immortalized by George Bernard Shaw. Travelers visiting only Dubrovnik miss the heart of this Balkan country. Conquered and ruled by Greeks, Romans, Saracens, Venetians and Austrians before finally gaining independence from Yugoslavia in 1991, Croatia is a treasure of well-preserved castles, churches, walled cities and other vestiges of a long, complex history.

We traveled the coast of Croatia for about five months, leaving *Avanti* one winter in a top-notch marina on the coast just south of the little walled town of Primošten. The coast and the over 1000 Croatian islands make this part of the Adriatic a boater's paradise. We arrived in Croatia from Vieste, Italy in a long day crossing – another one of our tense "blue water" days – landing on the island of Korčula. From Korčula we traveled south to Dubrovnik, then back north all the way up the Croatian coast to Slovenia and Venice. Then we cruised back down the coast to Korčula and retraced our path to Italy before heading south to Greece.

We had visited Croatia before, in 1970, when it was part of Yugoslavia. Through our rose-colored glasses, we thought it heartwarming that Tito had so successfully joined the various ethnic groups that constituted Yugoslavia – Catholics, Eastern Orthodox Christians and Muslims, with various languages and two alphabets. We were oblivious to the tensions among the ethnic groups that would lead to turmoil, massacres and war before Yugoslavia split back into its ancient tribes: Slovenes, Croats, Bosnians, Montenegrins, Macedonians, Serbs and Kosovars. Croatians, like Slovenes, are mostly Roman Catholic, distinguishing them from some of the other parts of the Balkans where Orthodox Christian or Islamic faiths dominate.

In 1970, facilities were minimal and tourists were mostly middle-aged overweight Germans who shocked and appalled us by cavorting nude on the local beaches. Only later did we learn that nudity has a long tradition in this area. Few Yugoslavs spoke English. Being young, dumb and adventurous, we hitchhiked through the country, staying in the homes of locals or in empty fields and woods where we could throw down our sleeping bags. Now, more than three decades later, things are vastly different, although the country has lost none of its physical beauty. Today Croatia is tourist-friendly, clean and well run, and boasts the best marinas in the Mediterranean. Most Croatians speak excellent English and are hard working, reliable and honest. They do what they promise, from mechanics repairing our boat to the taxi driver who showed up at our boat on time at 4:30 a.m. to take Tricia, a visiting friend from Colorado, to the airport. Not that we weren't nervous about that 4:30 a.m. request. After the generally unreliable Italians, we were making back-up plans in case, as we assumed would happen, the taxi driver didn't show up. But he was there on time, actually a bit early.

Most of the best quality marinas in Croatia are ACI Marinas – Adriatic Croatia International Club – a private company that runs 21 marinas catering to boat tourists. Most marinas have a fleet of sailboats for charter, at least one restaurant, a chandlery where boat parts and accessories can be purchased, a small grocery shop and repair facilities. All the marinas are modern and well cared-for. They are secure places, fenced when appropriate, and guarded. The good marinas, natural beauty and generally mild winds, make Croatia arguably the best cruising grounds in the Mediterranean. Anyone wanting to charter a sailboat for one or two weeks would be wise to pick Croatia. This may come as a surprise, since the popular but mistaken belief is that Greece is the best place to sail. Unlike Greece, there is always a protected berth in Croatia. Except for the infrequent bora winds in the north, the winds are mild, unlike the fearsome

Greek meltemis in the Aegean. Best of all, Croatians are reliable and concerned about the comfort and well-being of their boating visitors, traits we rarely found in Greece.

Korčula

We arrived in the modern marina of the ancient walled town of Korčula after one of our longest days at sea – 70 miles across the Adriatic from Vieste. Korčula (pronounced KOR' choo la) is a small island lying about 50 miles north of Dubrovnik.

Korčula had been the site of one of our dumbest travel mistakes on our 1970 visit. On that trip, we took a bus from town to an isolated part of the island and trekked our way through thick woods to a beach suitable for sleeping bags. Suddenly we realized with horror that we had lost the bag containing our passports and money. We stumbled back to the road in the dark and hitchhiked back to town where we roused the sympathetic police who in turn roused the local bus company, all of us assuming we had left our bag on the bus. After an agonizing and fruitless search of several buses, we had to give up, forced to return to our sleeping bags to get a good night sleep and worry about our loss the next day. We hired a taxi to take us back to the bus stop where we had been dropped off earlier so we could retrace our path to our campsite. As we popped out of the taxi, to our amazement, sitting untouched on a stone wall at the side of the road, barely visible in the faint glow of the taxi's headlights, was our bag of valuables, right where we had set it earlier that evening when leaving the bus to readjust our backpacks. We were embarrassed by the turmoil we had caused. But we were giddy with relief.

Korčula is a gem of a medieval walled town, complete with moat and drawbridge. Along the narrow stone alleys inside the walled city, we visited the childhood home of Marco Polo and bought local cheese and fresh vegetables at the tiny outdoor market. We hung out at the many seaside outdoor restaurants outside the city walls, sipping the island's white wine, some of Croatia's best, and gazing over the water to the mainland across the strait or watching World Cup soccer on outdoor TVs. We had one minor crisis, although I'm sure Roka resents my referring to her anguish as minor. Poor Roka was minding her own business when a nasty, cranky cat ran across the entire length of the town square just to attack her. Roka's pathetic cries drew a small crowd of locals into the square to cluck their tongues in sympathy. Even I was scratched trying to tear the angry cat from Roka's back. Roka whimpered for a long time, confused and traumatized.

Several guide books about Korčula touted the traditional sword dancers – described as a "can't miss" show of ancient dances in the shadow of the castle. More than one guide book claimed it would be the highlight of a Korčula visit. It wasn't cheap, but how could we resist, so we and visiting friends Jan and John (who also visited us in Italy) bought the expensive tickets and headed for the show.

We hated it. The program started with an amateur brass band made up of teens and a few adults. "How sweet," we thought. But their inept playing continued for almost an hour. Then the sword dancers arrived – finally! Again disappointment. The first sword dance was interesting, but surprisingly short. When it was finished, the dancers walked in a circle for at least five minutes while the audience waited. The next sword dance was similar to the first. Then again the five-minute circle walk. Each sword dance appeared to be identical to all others. And between each sword dance, there was that tiresome circle-walking. We were relieved when the program finally ended after what seemed like days. We would have left early, but there was no way to politely leave the small amphitheater. Later we had the same reaction to the Turkish whirling dervishes. They whirl in exactly the same way for what seems like hours.

We were in Korčula again early in the spring of the next year, on our way to Greece. My cousin, Candy, and her husband, Monte, from Lopez Island in Washington, visited us and we all rented motor scooters to explore the island on a stormy day. We found the interior unaffected by tourism, filled with vineyards and farms.

Hvar

Korčula is close to the neighboring island of Hvar, a popular island with the in-crowd. The main port is also called Hvar, a stunning town with narrow medieval streets dotted with trendy bars and restaurants, all nestled beneath a 16th-century hilltop citadel. The harbor at Hvar is no more than a small city wharf. We were lucky to find a spot and it proved to be a fun place for *Avanti*, in the midst of all the hustle and bustle of water taxis, ferries, hydrofoils and trendy people at the many bars. When we returned the following spring with our friends from Newport Beach, Barbara, a former flight attendant, and Bill, a business executive, the weather was too rough to tie up on the wharf and we stayed at another modern ACI yacht marina, Marina Palmizana, on the next-door island of St Klement. It was a peaceful spot with lots of berths and a classy restaurant, but the only way to get to Hvar town was to take a water taxi – not inexpensive. It was more fun to spend the night on the busy, entertaining Hvar town wharf, but the Marina is an acceptable alternative when the weather is bad or the Hvar wharf too crowded.

Like Korčula, the island beyond the main town is wooded, interspersed with miles of vineyards, empty beaches, and quiet anchorages. Stari Grad, located on the opposite side of the island from Hvar, is less crowded and far less flashy than the main town, but proved to be a gateway to quiet biking through the vineyards to two other small towns, Vrbovska and Jelsa. It was harvest time and the vineyards were full of grape pickers. Wine-making is a family business on Hvar. Grapes are grown and harvested by grandparents, parents and children working together on postage stamp fields, then brought to in-home wineries. The smell of fermenting grapes emanates from nearly every basement and small building in each of the villages. The finished product is sold from the winemakers' homes in town or in the local outdoor market. The locals buy wine by bringing empty 1.5-liter water bottles to be filled. Most of it is pretty tasty, but Napa need not worry.

Mljet

A third nearby island, Mljet (pronounced Myet), is mostly national park. We tied up in Mljet at a dock in front of the Calypso Restaurant, one of three local eateries on a quiet bay. All three restaurant owners yelled and waved to us as we entered the bay, each hoping we'd choose his dock. There was no cost to dock overnight; as is typical in the Mediterranean, each dock owner expects payment by the visitor patronizing his restaurant. We circled, along with Candy and Monte who were visiting, closely inspecting the three offered spots. We were finally seduced by the name Calypso. According to Homer, Calypso held Odysseus captive, allegedly on Mljet, for seven years. We picked well. The family that owned Calypso fed us royally on "kid under the bell," a succulent baby goat dish baked for four hours under a ceramic bowl buried in burning charcoal. This was our most delicious meal in Croatia. Even Roka loved the place and had to be returned to the boat by the family grandmother, who was also the cook; Roka had wandered into the kitchen looking for a handout.

Dubrovnik

Less than fifty miles down the coast is Dubrovnik, a magical city. We were dismayed by the news reports in 1991 that claimed the city was being destroyed during the nine-month Serbian siege triggered by Croatia's declaration of independence from Yugoslavia. The Serbs lobbed bombs and shells from the hills above the city. We were relieved to learn that the demise of Dubrovnik was vastly overstated. When the war ended, nearly all of the bullet holes were patched and the many burned buildings re-roofed with new bright red tiles that contrast with the ancient mottled tiles. Bullet holes are still visible in the town. The Croatians seem to hold no grudges and have moved on with their lives. As our taxi driver put it, "we have a war with the Serbs about every hundred years, but then it ends and we're friends again."

The most noticeable change in Dubrovnik since our visit in 1970 was the giant gang of tourists roaming through the city, now mostly Americans instead of nude Germans. Many cruise ships stop here. But even with all those tourists, Dubrovnik remains impressive, lauded as one of the most memorable cities in Europe. The town is ringed by a high 15-foot-thick wall, designed to protect it from invaders. The top of the wall is open for public strolling. Medieval and Renaissance churches and palaces abound. The marble streets, closed to traffic, are shined to a slippery patina from centuries of use.

The marina at Dubrovnik is deservedly famous in its own right. It was destroyed in the 1991 war, then completely rebuilt. It is one of the most desirable marinas for boaters who "winter over." Although far from town, up the river that flows down the steep mountains from Bosnia, a bus travels to town regularly and taxis are always nearby. The marina features an infinity swimming pool beside a comfortable restaurant, three well-maintained clay tennis courts, a 14th-century mansion that miraculously survived the war, and an Internet site set in an outdoor arbor. Across the stream in a small village, a church spire rises from the shore. Up the stream, a local restaurant sends a boat down to the marina on a regular basis to pick up diners. Nearby small towns and hills are fertile ground for hikes and exploration. A winter here would be a treat.

Montenegro

Of course Montenegro isn't Croatia. It's a completely different country. But Montenegro is an easy drive from Dubrovnik and fits nicely into a Croatian visit. Or you can visit by boat while traveling down the coast to Greece. But that route requires a stop in Albania. Albania made us nervous. A lawyer friend of mine had been living in Albania for two years, helping her architect husband design Greek Orthodox churches and working with the authorities to modernize the

Albanian legal system. She told me that a visit to Albania would be perfectly safe, but when I asked about traveling there by sea, she was aghast. Pirates, she said. Not safe. Since it seemed to come from an authoritative source, we passed up an Albanian visit on *Avanti*.

We rented a car with Candy and Monte and drove to Kotor and Budva in Montenegro, about an hour's drive. We had been there before, as it turned out, but then it was simply part of Yugoslavia and we weren't then cognizant of the differences in the regions. Montenegro is Orthodox Christian rather than Roman Catholic. We had traversed Montenegro in 1970 on an "express" bus trip from Macedonia through Kosovo to Budva. It was a grueling trip that took 11 hours to travel not much more than 100 miles, with a vomiting woman in the seat in front of us, and the disgusting experience of "toilet" stops in fields where clearly many prior buses had stopped for the same purpose.

This time we found Montenegro to be much like Croatia, except poorer, with even more dramatic mountains and certainly fewer tourists. The James Bond movie *Casino Royale* was filmed there. We walked the walled town of Kotor and wished we could have stayed longer. We also visited Budva, one of our favorite spots in 1970. The castle that had so impressed us on that visit had since been destroyed by an earthquake. Although it was rebuilt, it now looks like a Disney phony. We were disappointed.

Split

A short distance north of Dubrovnik lies Split, the largest coastal town on the Adriatic. The Roman Emperor Diocletian retired there from the emperoring business in the 4th century AD and built a huge retirement palace covering several city blocks. It remains in pristine condition, still occupied by thousands of residents and many shops. It took an embarrassingly long time for us to realize that the large neon sign that read "305-2005" on the Emperor's tomb in the palace structure signified that the palace had been built in 305AD and was celebrating its 1700th anniversary. This lively, well-preserved palace is the same age as many of the dilapidated ruins in Rome, reinforcing the lesson we learned many times in Croatia – the best remains of Roman civilization often lie outside of Italy.

Rodolfo, our Chilean exchange student living in Barcelona, had become email friends with a Croatian architect who shared the same last name as his mother, Katunarič. They had discovered that they were in fact related and that all their ancestors had lived on the offshore island of Brač, the homeland of many emigrants to Chile. Rodolfo and his parents, Alicia and Rodolfo, arrived while we were in Split to meet the garrulous, friendly architect, now fondly known to all of us as Uncle Branko. Rodolfo was the only means of communication between Branko and his long-lost Chilean relative. Uncle Branko speaks Croatian (which of course none of us understood at all) and English but not Spanish, and Rodolfo's parents are Spanish speakers, though Alicia's English is better than she lets on. We found that the Brač/Chile connection is not uncommon. On one Croatian island, the town on everyone's lips was San Pedro, California, where many from the island had moved in the early 20th century. Since we were from California, the locals were excited to meet us since they assumed we would know their relatives. The same story is true of many places in Croatia – the townspeople from each town or island ended up emigrating to the same region, or even the same small town in another country.

Trogir

Trogir, just up the road from Split, is a 2300-year-old walled town reminiscent of Dubrovnik. It is famous for its walls and stone portals, ten romanesque-gothic churches, narrow, pedestrian-only streets and a stunning golden-doored cathedral.

We tied up *Avanti* at the city wharf in downtown Trogir, directly in front of the ancient town school, only a few feet away from the plaza where the town's school children played each day during recess, eating their brown-bag lunches and practicing their school dances. We love the town, with its perfect ancient stone streets and bustling daily market where fresh fruits and long strands of garlic are sold by gnarled old grandmothers.

Trogir is much quieter than Dubrovnik and is filled with locals, not tourists. In many ways, we found Trogir as enjoyable, if not more so, than its big sister. Of course we were tied up to the city wharf in the midst of the active town, rather than our distant marina in Dubrovnik – another example of how a town's marina or wharf colors a boater's view of an entire city.

Vis

West of Split, past the popular islands of Korčula and Hvar, half way to Italy, lies the small island of Vis, a former military reserve closed to the public until the 1990s. Marshall Tito had his headquarters during World War II in a cave on its highest mountain. This was the most isolated spot on the most isolated island in Croatia.

On our way to Tito's cave on our rented Vespa, Roka sitting between us as always, we stopped for lunch at the only restaurant in a hilltop village, where we were the only patrons. The owners, a smiling middle-aged couple who spoke no English, roasted succulent lamb for us in their outdoor wood fireplace while the grandmother of the family, dressed in black, watched us suspiciously from the next table. The owners then plopped down beside us at our table to eat their own lunches and shoved their Croatian glamour magazine at us, giggling with pride when we reached the article with photos of Princess Carolyn of Monaco dining at this very restaurant. We concluded that no place is truly isolated anymore. We also learned that James Joyce, who lived in Croatia for several years in his youth, favored a Plavic wine from Vis. We took a bottle home to a friend who is one of the world's James Joyce experts. Sadly for her, it wasn't very good.

Less than five kilometers from Vis is the tiny barely inhabited (population 11) island of Biševo with its little-known Blue Cave. We took *Avanti* to the mouth of the cave and I jumped into the water and swam into the luminescent, brilliant turquoise cave. I've never been to the Blue Grotto on Capri, but I can't imagine that it could be any more spectacular than the grotto on Biševo.

Kornati Islands

North of both Split and Vis are the remarkable Kornati Islands, accessible only by boat, composed of 147 islands scattered like pebbles in an area twenty miles long and five miles across. Deforested long ago by mainlanders clearing land for their sheep, the islands are now abandoned by both people and sheep. Old stone walls that divided the grazing lands still crisscross the now barren hills. Limestone outcrops swirl in dramatic patterns reflecting the forces of nature that built the islands from a former sea floor. The islands' coves are deserted except for tiny seasonal restaurants that serve visiting boaters.

Due to fishing restrictions, the snorkeling here is better than anywhere else in Europe, though it still doesn't compare well to the Great Barrier Reef. Astronauts have reported from space that the sea around the Kornatis is the clearest in the world.

We cruised here for days, rarely seeing another boat. We pulled into a quiet cove each night, tying on to a mooring or pulling up to a dilapidated dock, then dining at the cove's only restaurant (there was never more than one), often on octopus caught while we watched. The dramatic, barren land contrasted with the clear blue sea, and the sunsets filled the entire sky with brilliance. Chartering a sailboat in the Kornatis for a week would be heaven.

Islands North of the Kornatis

North of the Kornatis, dozens of islands dot the coast, each containing a single small medieval town.

We especially enjoyed Rab, with its stone walls enclosing many tall-spired cathedrals.

One of our other favorites is Mali Lošinj, where we twice pulled in to escape the bora winds. The town is horse-shoe shaped, colorful and fun, with many boats selling fruits, vegetables, olive oils and olives, and many paths around the island perfect for biking.

Each Croatian island has its own personality, but all share the charm of being tiny, ancient seaports filled with friendly Croatians. You can't go wrong.

Istrian Peninsula

Traveling north of Mali Lošinj, we fought the waves generated by the infamous bora winds, finally reaching the elegant town of Opatija on the mainland. As a resort town on the "Croatian Riviera," Opatija was much favored by the Austro-Hungarian emperors in the 19th century and still radiates a turn-of-the-century decadence. The town remains packed with Austrian tourists who, locals claim, believe this part of the coast still belongs to Austria. It was a fine place to wait out the winds.

Opatija marks the southeastern edge of the Istrian Peninsula, an area ruled by Italy for centuries, and still heavily influenced by its Italian past. The most impressive sight on the Istrian Peninsula is the well-preserved Roman coliseum at Pula, located on a scenic bay. Its exterior is nearly intact, unlike the Coliseum in Rome. The interior has not fared so well – the old stone seats were removed in the Middle Ages for use in constructing the town. Like many coastal Croatian towns, Pula has a delightful town center with a mix of

Roman portals, temples, medieval churches, and towers, and in addition, a restaurant dedicated to James Joyce, who once taught English here.

Back to nudity. Our first encounter with nude Germans in 1970 was not out of character with Croatia. It is the European country with the longest nudist-beach tradition; it is reported that half of all European "naturists" spend their holidays here, mostly in Istria, but also on several of the islands. An estimated fifteen percent of all tourists to Croatia, over one million people, visit the nudist beaches. The most famous of the nudist resorts is the gigantic Conversada on the Istrian Peninsula, with a daily capacity of 18,500 visitors. Imagine that many nude people in one place. As we cruised through Croatia, we found that a large number of our fellow cruisers had taken up the practice while on the sea. We don't know whether this display of bodies stemmed from long-standing Croatian tradition or whether the real cause was the level of inebriation achieved by visiting Czechs, Slovaks and Poles on chartered sailboats who persistently drank far too much of the Croatian Karlovachko beer. I discovered that it was quite pleasant to cruise in the nude. Bruce, not so much.

CHAPTER 6
SLOVENIA: WHAT A SURPRISE!

The crowd cheers our arrival into the marina at Izola

No, the local celebrants make it clear: cheering is for Slovenian Olympic sailing medalist

Surreal view from trail over Lake Bled, with its tiny island church and 12th-century Bled Castle on the hill beyond

Who could have guessed? What could one expect from a country with the odd name of Slovenia? And could a resort named Lake Bled be anything but a hideout for bloodthirsty Count Dracula?

We thought Slovenia might be that miserable, mythical country created by Al Capp in his cartoon, *L'il Abner*. But Bruce was pretty sure that Capps' country was actually Slobbovia. The confusion was understandable. George W. was baffled by the name too; he called the country Slovakia, which is somewhere else entirely.

We almost skipped Slovenia. But *The Lonely Planet* guide, one of only two guidebooks we could locate on Slovenia, made the country sound fabulous. Alpine mountains in the north; quiet harbors on the Adriatic Sea in the south; an ancient unspoiled capital city, Ljubljana, that survived World War II undamaged; massive underground caves full of intricate webs of stalagmites and stalactites; a friendly, English-speaking population; little of the petty theft that now plagues much of Western Europe; and reasonable prices. What's not to like? So we headed to Slovenia. It was a brilliant decision.

Slovenia was formerly part of Yugoslavia, placed there in 1918 at the end of World War I after the Austro-Hungarian Empire collapsed. It is a Roman Catholic country, like Croatia and most of Europe, but only a small percentage of its people consider themselves religious. Slovenia declared its independence from Yugoslavia in 1991, then successfully repelled a brief but ill-advised armed attempt by the Serbs to retain control. It is one of those Eastern European countries that became a part of the European Union in 2004. It adopted the euro in 2007, after our visit. Perhaps the country now regrets that change. When we visited, the currency was the tolar – one dollar bought about 185 tolar.

The north of Slovenia is reminiscent of Austria, with some major mountains (the Julian Alps) but not quite so much over-the-top gemütlichkeit. Actually, embarrassingly, we did dance the polka one evening, but only because we were at a festival. The coastal towns are a bit like a well-behaved Italy (Trieste is only a few miles away), but the beaches consist of large pebbles or concrete, even worse than the typical pebbled beaches found in most of Europe. It's also a bit like Croatia, with most everyone helpful and fluent in English, as well as German and Italian. We understand the eastern part of the country is influenced by Hungary, but going there was a bit beyond our reach.

There are only a few ports in Slovenia, all on the Adriatic Sea just south of Trieste. We headed *Avanti* to Izola, the town with the biggest marina, thinking it would be the safest. *Avanti* would have to fend for herself while we explored the country. It turned out to be a modern marina with good facilities.

As we pulled into port, we were greeted by music and hundreds of cheering Slovenes. We were impressed and flattered by such amazing hospitality until we learned that the cheering was actually for the Slovenian Olympic bronze medal winner in sailing, an Izola native, returning home victorious from Athens. We joined the party, drank the tasty local beer, danced our Slovene polka, and photographed the handsome conquering hero, bedecked with his Olympic medal and colorful garlands. At a neighboring seaside town the next day, we were greeted by two town drunks who paraded around with their own banner honoring the same Olympic hero. We'd never before seen anyone drinking alcohol straight from a 5-liter jug. Needless to say, they were impressed by our digital photo of their hero, taken just the night before at the party in the marina.

Izola is a small village with no local car rental outlets. When we learned that Budget would deliver a car from a neighboring town directly to the port, we phoned them up and were soon motoring across the country, headed toward Ljubljana and Lake Bled.

Slovenia is tiny – half the size of Switzerland. The entire country can be driven from north to south in less than three hours. The capital city of Ljubljana lies on a new toll road that spans the entire country from Austria in the north to Croatia in the south.

It took under two hours to reach Ljubljana, where we stopped for the night. We had no hotel reservations, as usual, but located the elegant 1905 four-star Grand Hotel Union, located just a block from the historic main square. Luckily for Roka, it welcomes dogs.

Ljubljana is laid-back and lovely, full of cafes lining the river that meanders through town, musicians playing on street corners and piazzas and crowds of locals strolling the riverbank in the evening. Farmers peddle flowers and vegetables in the town's large open-air market just across the river from the main town square. The town enchants visitors with a well-preserved medieval section and a large castle on the hill behind the town, open to the public, which is an easy 15-minute hike from the main square. Ljubljana is a bit like a small, non-touristy Prague, just a bit harder to spell.

In Ljubljana's main square is a statue of the national hero, France Prešeren – not a warrior, not a politician, but a poet who published only one slim volume of poetry. He had a sad and disappointing life, spurned by the only woman he ever loved. What's not to like about a country with a hero like that?

We ate dinner outdoors by the river's edge while the evening walkers paraded by. A soulful jazz singer performed at an outdoor café while we discussed America with an interested Ljubljanan carpenter who recognized our American accents, which are rarely heard in Slovenia. Like most Europeans, he was most interested in our opinion of our president – then George W. Bush – and his foreign policy, both almost universally disliked in Europe.

Then it was on to Bled, pronounced just the way it's spelled, located about an hour away. The name still made us nervous – that Dracula thing – but we persisted.

Frankly, Lake Bled looks phony. It's too perfect, a setting out of a magical fairy tale. The small lake is perhaps a mile across, and deep blue. Forested, deep green hills rise on all sides of the lake. Dozens of wooden rowboats ply its waters. Sea gulls collect on the shore. In the center of the lake, Bled Island sits quietly, graced by a small church with a high spire from which a massive bell peals. Completing the fairy-tale picture, 12th-century Bled Castle, perfect in every way with ramparts, a tower, moats and a tiny chapel, looms over the lake on the far shore, clinging to a high cliff. Sleeping Beauty would be a fitting resident. Lake Bled is pure magic.

We decided to try out the Hotel Vila Bled, part of the exclusive Relais & Chateaux chain, located halfway around the lake from the town. The hotel is entered through massive gates opening onto a stately, four-story mansion set on the lake. We're not normally Relais & Chateaux types – too pricey and usually impossible without reservations, but we decided to give it a shot since the prices seemed reasonable and it was reputed to be dog-friendly. Ten minutes after we drove through the gates, we were admiring the view from our cavernous two-room suite with wall-to-wall windows opening onto the lake, the church and the castle.

Vila Bled was built during the time of the Austro-Hungarian Empire by an Austrian prince and then later rebuilt for Tito, for his use in entertaining foreign guests. The influence of the Soviet era still showed. In the fancy reception hall on the second floor, curtains had been drawn back to reveal a huge Soviet-realism fresco – strong muscled workers in heroic poses with factories in the background. It could be hidden by curtains, presumably for guests with anti-Soviet sensitivities. The hotel grounds seemed endless, scattered with lounge chairs for sunning, sleeping and reading. From the hotel, it was a short walk to the lake.

Vila Bled keeps a small fleet of rowboats for hotel guests. The three of us hopped in one and rowed to Bled Island where we pulled the huge rope that rings the bell in the church steeple. We rowed to town to sample Bled's famous cream cake, an overly-sweet vanilla and whipped cream concoction. Despite a few downpours, we hiked for hours in the mountains, reaching the highest peak with the grandest view over the lake. We swam in the lake, warm enough for swimming because of the hot springs that are its source.

The area around Bled is mostly pastureland with hay racks, cows, alpine houses decked with flower boxes bursting with red geraniums and snowcapped Mt. Teglev, the highest peak in Slovenia, rising in the distance.

English is spoken nearly everywhere in Slovenia, not just by those who deal with tourists, and normally with a perfect American accent – a result of watching American television. Most Slovenes are also fluent in German, Italian and Croatian. They don't expect their visitors to speak Slovenian, for good reason. The language is difficult – it is Slavic and packed with too many consonants and not enough vowels, decorated with various types of accent marks. We learned to count in Slovenian, and the morning greeting was a simple "dobro jutro" or, as in Croatia, "dober dan." The Slovenes are kind and friendly people, so a heart-felt "thank you" in Slovenian (same as Croatian), "hvala," became second nature for us. The Slovenes seemed thrilled at our bumbling attempts to speak their language, which of course only encouraged us to try more. Their own language appeared to us to be essentially identical to Croatian. Of course our Croatian didn't extend much beyond "dober dan" and "hvala," so subtle differences between the two languages passed us right by.

Slovenia is an unexplored gem with an old Europe graciousness, yet modern and comfortable. The food is reasonably good, not great (don't even think about France). The scenery varies from quiet seashores to wooded, alpine mountains, the cities and towns historically preserved. The people are warm and friendly, all happy to welcome you to their country and eager for you to like them. Who would have guessed?

CHAPTER 7
GREECE: WHITE-WASHED, WINDY, GLORIOUSLY DISFUNCTIONAL

The Temple of Poseidon in Sounion; the most stunning sight in Greece, where Aegis jumped off the cliff to his death, giving Aegean Sea its name

Quiet Sounion gets wild: I had to swim to our runaway dinghy to rescue it from dangerous seas

Like goats? They are everywhere in Greece, Turkey too

Sunset with wine and cheese at the Santo Winery, Santorini

Brothers Makis and Giannis
dance at Telesilla in Corfu

Delicious roasted corn for sale
on dock in Paxos

American ex-pat Pan lives on
Hydra where he helps boaters
navigate the treacherous harbor

Roka suns herself on ruins
of Roman amphitheater on
the island of Milos

Watch that wreck! Zea Marina is
Athens "finest" marina

Petros of Mykonos has
the run of the town

Dramatic temple on Aegina

Yum! It's dinner

No motorized vehicles on
Hydra, only donkeys

If you look carefully, you can
see this donkey is biting me

Cats are everywhere in
Greece, frightening poor Roka

Goat warning sign on a
monastery in Ithaka

Religious pilgrims crawl to
hilltop cathedral from harbor on
the island of Tinos

"I felt once more how simple and frugal a thing is happiness: a glass of wine, a roast chestnut, a wretched little brazier, the sound of the sea. Nothing else."
— Nikos Kazantzakis, *Zorba the Greek*

Things are just different in Greece. It's unlike any other country in Europe, mostly in unpleasant ways, but in some nice ways as well. Most but not all of our problems resulted because we were visiting by boat. Land-based visitors would never know.

First, there are almost no real marinas. There's one in Corfu, one in Athens, one to the southeast of Athens on the Aegean, and one on Samos. Most towns have only a town wharf for visiting boats. This can be great fun since town wharves are normally in the heart of the town, with lots of action and interest. But town wharves rarely provide water or electricity, and almost never toilets or showers. For a country that would appear on the surface to be a paradise for boating, its boating facilities are surprisingly undeveloped. This wasn't a disaster for us since we had large boat batteries so we could run *Avanti* for several days without outside electricity, although we had to use the generator from time to time to charge them up. The fans we bought to keep *Avanti* cool worked only on 220 volts, so we had some hot nights in Greece. Eventually we realized an inverter would allow us to run a fan on the 12-volt system safely, but it took a few years of sweltering to figure that out. Sometimes we're not the smartest boaters on the sea. And even where there are electric outlets on Greek wharves, half the time they don't work. There are many half-finished marinas. Someone sinks lots of money into a marina to build the docks and basic infrastructure, and then just stops, leaving a half-finished hulk. Houses in Greece are like that also – many half completed – but we understand there is a tax benefit to not completing a house. It's hard to see any benefit from an unfinished marina since, along with no amenities, there's no one collecting overnight fees. There is no cost to stay in these unfinished marinas, but frankly we'd rather pay and have a nice place to stay. We expect that a good Greek marina would be quite profitable. We surmised that Greeks are not successful entrepreneurs. Perhaps they are just naively optimistic when they start a project and then surprised when they run out of funds to complete it.

Second, and a bit hard to get used to, no toilet paper is permitted in toilets. The public sewage system cannot handle toilet paper. Apparently fancy Greek hotels have some sort of plumbing system that overcomes this problem, but we wouldn't know about that. In all Greek toilet stalls, there's a waste can for used toilet paper. It gets tiresome, but we got used to it. In fact, when we arrived back home from Greece, it was hard to stop putting toilet paper into the waste basket at home – sort of gross. Try to avoid having guests in your home who have just returned from Greece. We eventually adopted the Greek model on *Avanti*, especially after we had to have all our clogged toilet pipes reamed out in Croatia, a disgusting task.

Third, Greek bureaucracy and irrational fees and taxes are almost enough to keep any sane person from going to Greece. We met boaters who went from Italy to Turkey as quickly as possible to avoid the random inanity. Greece requires boaters to register and get a "log book" when entering the country. This can be a long process involving interminable lines and hostile bureaucrats, and it is often done incorrectly. We had big problems after arriving in Lesbos from Turkey in 2008 because Greek officials on the subsequent island of Thassos insisted we had been given the wrong log book by officials on Lesbos. Fortunately, they allowed us to proceed, but with much clucking and heavy scowling, as if we had deliberately asked for the wrong log book. Boaters are required to check in with the local port police at every stop, again a long, tedious process with lots of paperwork (multiple carbon copies, lots of energetic stamping). Forcing EU citizens to register with the port police is a violation of EU policies, but that didn't stop the Greeks from applying their registration requirement to everyone. We tried to ignore the rule most of the time, as did most Europeans, but we didn't want our log book to remain completely empty. So we made sure to visit a local port police office every few weeks. The fee charged by the port police for registering boaters is a pittance, often less than one euro, a sum clearly inadequate to cover the cost of this "service." Greece is overloaded with truly useless government bureaucracy. On top of the waste and inefficiency, Greek citizens don't believe in paying taxes and it appears that most wealthy Greeks cheat on their taxes big time. We totally understand why the Greek economy is in terrible shape. The other cute trick of the Greeks is requiring that written evidence of boat insurance be in Greek. No other country requires this. So included with our insurance renewal each year, we received evidence of coverage in Greek as well as English. We once witnessed boaters without the Greek translation at a port police office. Their papers had been confiscated and they were not permitted to leave until the proper Greek translation was produced. They had to phone their British insurance company to request that the proper translation be faxed, but were still at the mercy of the Greek fax machine being inoperable or the fax being lost upon receipt. We felt great pity for them.

On the other hand, you must take meticulous care in following the rules, or at least be cagey when violating them. When we returned one spring after leaving *Avanti* in the marina southeast of Athens for the winter, we stupidly decided to visit the port police for our first stamp of the season. We should have just left and ignored the rules – remember that when you travel in Greece. Our log book was confiscated and we were told we had violated the law by not turning our log book into the customs office before we left *Avanti* for the winter. Talk about obscure and rarely enforced rules! Even the staff at our enormous marina had never heard of it. After several days of visits to multiple offices, and payments of close to $1500, we were allowed to leave. When we left Greece in 2009 on our way back to Italy, we took the criminal path rather than subject ourselves to more of the bizarre Greek bureaucracy. We just left. No checking out of the country, as required. No turning in our log book. We heard later that checking out of the country in Corfu is a nightmare so I'm sure we made the right decision. As we left Greece behind, we worried that the Greek authorities would chase us down, but then decided not to worry after mulling over their general incompetence. I have read there is now a cruising tax in Greece that can be high, but its enforcement is spotty. Having a boat in Greece is financially risky.

Fourth, the food is actually good and less expensive, and the wine certainly no worse, than in Croatia, and often lots better. Croatian food is actually not all that great. Once we reached Greece, we could eat tender, delicious Greek lamb and lots of eggplant dishes. But Greece is no France or Italy – the food is pretty much the same everywhere – souvlaki, eggplant, extremely expensive fish.

Fifth, we often got to dance Greek dances at night in local tavernas. And throw dishes. That was good, especially given all of the frustrations created by traveling in Greece.

Sixth, there are cats everywhere. That was bad news for Roka. For details, see Chapter 7, Traveling with Your Pet.

Seventh, we had to deal with not only a new language, but also a new alphabet. "They" say it's impossible to learn a new language if you're over the age of 50 (which, sadly, we are, by quite a lot). We tried to prove "them" wrong. We got pretty good with our upsilons, epsilons and omegas. And kalispera to you, too.

Eighth, we were in the land of the Greek Orthodox Church, a bit like the big Catholic churches in western Europe, but with many more candles, married priests in impressive black robes and hats, and interesting hammered votive plaques hanging everywhere in the churches, representing various objects of prayer – a heart could represent a prayer for love or a prayer that a heart ailment would be cured.

And finally, there are few German tourists in Greece, although they were everywhere in Croatia. They've been replaced in Greece by the British, who for some reason are scarce in Croatia. There are few

Americans in either place, other than the hot tourist spots – Dubrovnik, Athens, Fira on Santorini, and Mykonos – and the Americans who do visit are mostly just passing through on a gigantic cruise ship.

The Ionian Islands: Corfu, Paxos, Kefalonia, Ithaka, Lefkada

Traveling from Croatia to Greece, we decided to avoid Albania, so we took the longer route back through southeastern Italy, then directly south to Corfu, the most northerly of the Ionian Islands, to the west of the Greek mainland.

My favorite Greek Islands are the Ionians: Corfu, Paxos, Kefalonia, Ithaca and Lefkada, similar in many ways but each with a different personality. Unlike the generally brown and barren eastern and southern Greek islands, the Ionians are nearly all green, many heavily forested. The food is interesting, consisting of many local dishes not found in any other parts of Greece, some found only on a single island. Wines are so local that wines from Kefalonia are not available in the shops on Ithaca, only a few miles away. Tentura, our favorite Greek liqueur, tasting of cloves, cinnamon, nutmeg and citrus, is made in Patras on the mainland just east of the Ionians. Other than on Kefalonia and in Patras, it's almost impossible to find. We located a bottle in one shop in Athens. Most wine shops hadn't even heard of it.

Corfu

Corfu is the most famous Ionian island and hosts the most tourists. We had been here in 1970 and we were shocked by how much it has been developed – mostly badly. But it is still an appealing place. *Avanti* had lots of repair work done in the marina there, including fixing yet another malfunctioning toilet. Gouvia Marina is one of the few big, modern marinas in Greece, but it is not near the customs office where each boat must check into and out of Greece when arriving from or leaving for another county. The Greeks seem unconcerned about imposing burdens on visitors. The customs office was a few miles away in a building almost impossible to locate. Fortunately we had our bikes – other boaters had to take taxis to get there.

A block from the marina, we ate at our favorite restaurant in Greece, Telesilla, family owned and run. Two brothers, Makis and Giannis, dance traditional Greek dances there nightly in the summer, sometimes convincing their dad to join in, and they throw dishes.

On the way back through Corfu in 2008, we stayed in a pint-sized marina in the middle of town, nestled under the old Venetian fortress from which the Venetians controlled the Adriatic for 400 years. The town was a short walk away, through the fortress and over the moat to town. It had fewer amenities than Gouvia, but we loved its ambiance.

Paxos

Paxos is my favorite Ionian island, perhaps because it was cut off from the mainland by a blow from Poseidon's trident when he wanted to create a perfect place to hang out with one of his lovers. He did a good job. Paxos is only six miles long, crisscrossed by narrow roads that pass ancient olive trees and isolated beaches. Dramatic white cliffs line the remote west coast. Unlike Corfu, there are no busloads of tourists – in fact there are few visitors at all. It's a perfect place to rent a motorscooter. Gaios is the tiny capital with only a few spaces for visiting boats on the wharf. If you can score a spot, you'll be living in the middle of a small, friendly Greek community. It takes less than five minutes to walk from one end of the town to the other. Diners are served by imported Eastern European waiters since there aren't enough permanent residents in Paxos to fill all the summer jobs required to serve the few vacationers who do arrive. Local beaches are empty and pristine. The small town of Lakka sits on a peaceful bay at the northern tip of the island where many boats anchor. We visited Lakka by motorscooter one windy day and were grateful that we were in the more-protected waters of Gaios.

Kefalonia

The big deal here is Captain Corelli. This is where the story set out in *Corelli's Mandolin* takes place and where the movie was filmed. The use of the name Corelli on restaurants and shops is a bit overdone, but don't let it put you off – this is one fabulous island. Kefalonia is a large island, dramatic, mountainous and undeveloped, with the magnificent 13th-century Castle of Agios Georgios and a sophisticated winery with a taste testing technique unheard of in Napa Valley – bottles and glasses are set out on tables for visitors to simply pour their own with no supervision. We went to the Monastery of St. Gerasimo, location of the remains of the patron saint of Kefalonia, conveniently located adjacent to the winery. The patron saint is so important to the Kefalonians that, so we were told, half of the males on Kefalonia are named Gerasimo.

The waters around Kefalonia are the most spectacularly blue in Greece. They are best viewed from the road from Fiskardo past the picturesque village of Assos to the capital city of Argostoli, where narrow curves open on to breathtaking views. We stopped along the way for a swim in the rough waters at famous Myrtos Beach, where the neon blue sea laps onto a crescent-shaped soft-sand beach at the base of rugged white cliffs. In Kefalonia, we stayed in the pricey fishing village of Fiskardo, located on the northeast tip of the island, where we were visited by Polly, my dear friend from college, and her husband, Eric, a professor at UC Irvine. It's a popular spot with no marina – just a crowded wharf where boats prowl like sharks waiting for someone to abandon a spot. We were lucky both times we visited, although on our first visit we had to spend two days on the outskirts of the wharf where we felt insecure and the sea was rough. After waiting and watching, we spied a space opening and powered *Avanti* to the wharf to nab it. The second time, a spot opened magically just as we pulled in. On a hill on the outskirts of town is another favorite restaurant, Nicolas' Taverna, where the charismatic owner is able to convince even the shyest of patrons to join him in Greek dancing. Not so much plate throwing though.

Ithaca

Ithaca is located only a few miles from Kefalonia. This island was the home of Odysseus, where Penelope sat patiently weaving while she waited for him to return. We visited the site of Odysseus' palace and the field he was plowing when he was grabbed and forced to go to Troy to fight. Throughout the Ionians, we heard multiple tales of Odysseus, each island making conflicting claims about the location of important events in the *Iliad* or *Odyssey*, but we thought Ithaca had the best claim to being Odysseus' true home. The main city in Ithaca, Vathy, isn't as attractive as the towns on the north end of the island, but it had more wharf space. In Vathy, Eric slipped off *Avanti* when trying to leap aboard and ended up in the water. It was exciting fun for all of us except Eric, who didn't find it all that amusing.

There are two small town wharves at the north end of Ithaca, Frikes and Kioni. Each has several restaurants and tourists shops, but not much more. But the scenery is glorious with ruined Genoan windmills on the surrounding hills. On the top of the highest mountain overlooking Vathy is the run-down Monastery of Panaglia Katharon, surrounded by goats. On the door is a sign asking visitors to keep the door closed so goats can't come in. We complied.

Lefkada

Lefkada is a large island, and, for us, the least interesting of the Ionians. Huge Vlyho Bay is adjacent to bustling Nydri, a town sporting a large statue of Aristotle Onassis. It has quiet water and easy anchoring. Just east of Lefkada is Skorpios, the island owed by Onassis where Jackie Kennedy spent so much time. We anchored there for lunch and a swim but didn't go ashore. No one is allowed to set foot on this private island. We watched the few isolated houses hidden among the trees on the island, thinking about Jackie Kennedy sunning herself and swimming there so many years ago.

Each of the Ionians is wonderful, each different. We understood why Odysseus wanted to go home, even though it did take him a while.

Delphi

From the Ionians, a boat can head south to navigate around the Peloponnese – a long journey. We passed that up and instead headed directly for Athens, a few days away through the Gulf of Patras and the Gulf of Corinth. This route passes by the famous Oracle of Delphi. We'd been there in 1970, hitchhiking after riding the ferry from Corfu to the west coast of Greece. This time we berthed at one of the nearby harbors, Galaxadhi, where worried travelers from all over the world have dropped anchor for millennia to trek up the mountain to the Oracle for advice. Delphi is stunning and the ruins are impressive. The ancient Oracle was actually a young woman who sat in a chamber beneath the Temple of Apollo breathing toxic gases that arose from the depths along two active earthquake faults. When she was sufficiently drugged, she would proclaim a cryptic message to the local priests, who would then translate it for the weary traveler. A bit like Timothy Leary, we thought. We begged the Oracle for advice, but she apparently wasn't drugged enough to speak to us.

Athens and Sounion

With some trepidation (since we learned nothing from the Oracle), we continued to Athens, passing through the two-mile-long Corinth Canal into the Saronic Sea. We headed directly to Athens where we found a safe harbor in a new marina, now called Flisvos, adjacent to the Olympic stadium built for basketball and volleyball in 2004, and bearing the '60s-sounding name of "Peace and Freedom Stadium." The stadium stands empty, rarely used, like much of the decaying Greek Olympic infrastructure. Beware of this marina. It is designed for huge boats with crews, so has few amenities for little boats like ours. We seemed to be the only transients in the marina. I think we were allowed to stay because we planned to leave the boat there for almost three weeks. The two people running the marina, although well meaning and kind, seemed inflexible and somewhat confused. They didn't know how to deal with a little boat like ours. A port police office is housed at the marina, important since we were required to register, but there were no actual port police there – not just on lunch break, but never. The marina people insisted that we take a taxi to the next harbor to register, a trip of about 15 minutes. We didn't of course, but the experience made us realize once more why so many Greeks ignore laws in their country.

Athens was a furnace during our first visit. At over 100 degrees, we were living through the hottest day of the year. We made our way into town by metro from our little harbor. Walking out of the metro, we were stunned by the view of the Acropolis directly before us. We had forgotten how magnificent it is, surreal in its beauty, perched high above the city. There are several Athenian restaurants with commanding views of the Acropolis. Our favorite is Pil-Poul, an expensive rooftop restaurant, we now recommend only for summer dining. Friends went there off-season at our recommendation and had to eat in a dreary, non-view interior room, but still had to pay the high prices. The Plaka district, below the Acropolis, is the tourist area. It's a fun place to hang out.

When taking a vacation from *Avanti*, our favorite hotel in Athens was St. George Lycabettus in the quiet Kolonaki area. Some rooms have great Acropolis views. Near the Acropolis, we also liked the less expensive Herodion and Hera. The Hera has underground parking that we used when we had Roka, who was not allowed in the hotel. She could stay in the car when we went out to dinner, but then we would sneak her into the hotel in her airplane bag in the evening. Since Roka is always quiet (unless someone knocks on the door, always a risk), we have never been concerned with bringing her into our hotel rooms at night to sleep.

To us, Athens is a bit dreary, though we ended up spending a couple of weeks there as a result of our various departures and arrivals at the Athens airport. Most visitors are thrilled with the Archeological Museum, but we disliked it. It houses some memorable art and sculptures, but also room after room of indistinguishable displays of shards and other nondescript archeological finds. We thought most of the collection should be removed and catalogued in a back room so that the public portion of the museum would be considerably smaller and display only the best of its collection. After a single exhausting visit, we had no interest in returning.

We spent much of our time in Athens in Piraeus, the location of Zea Marina. Zea is the most desirable marina in the Athens area for transients, likely because it's also the only marina in Athens open to transients. It is difficult to find a berth there. Athens needs more marinas. Zea's access to restaurants and shopping (especially the four-story Carrefours department store just across the street) is a benefit to visitors, but the half-sunk boats near the entrance to the marina were disturbing, especially since they were still there when we returned to Athens several years after our first visit.

The Acropolis makes visiting Athens worthwhile, but frankly, we found Greek ruins in other parts of Greece and other countries just as impressive.

The one sight near Athens that should not be missed – one of our favorite spots in the Mediterranean - is Cape Sounion, 50 miles southeast of the city, home of the Temple of Poseidon, a graceful shrine perched on a windblown hilltop, surrounded on three sides by the sea. We challenge anyone to name a Greek anchorage more magnificent than the bay that sits directly below the Temple. We anchored here several times, spending hours each evening absorbing the beauty of the lit Temple, gloriously glowing through the night. For dinner each evening, we chose between two lively tavernas on shore, where we rowed from *Avanti* on our dinghy. Across the bay, opposite the Temple, is the chic Cape Sounio Resort, a long walk but a short dinghy ride from *Avanti*. The resort's elegant main building is surrounded by guest bungalows and an Olympic-size pool. An upstairs, always-empty outdoor dining room overlooks the Temple. We had no trouble being seated at each visit at the best table with an unobstructed view of the illuminated Temple. Most hotel guests are on a full-board plan so they eat at a different hotel restaurant, one with crowds and a limited view, leaving the best dining area to us.

Avanti lived in a nearby marina during two winters and the Cape Sounio Resort kept us sane. Once we were forced to live on board in the marina's parking lot for over a week, awaiting *Avanti's* transfer from the land to the sea. This period was so grim I don't even want to talk about it. We couldn't use our boat's head, meaning if we needed the toilet in the middle of the night, we could either use a make-shift chamber pot or climb down the wobbly ladder required to get off the boat and bike to the bathrooms, about ¼ mile away. The marina was hot, dry and windy, with no trees, only roses covered with dead pink blooms. There was no restaurant in the marina. Bike-accessible restaurants in town were sad. Our pathetic life on board made us yearn for a touch of luxury. Dinner at Cape Sounio Resort was a perfect cure for our blues, although it was far away and required hiring a rental car. The only nearby car-rental company specialized in dilapidated wrecks rented at new car prices, but we were desperate. We spent one night in a Resort bungalow, luxuriating in the shower and thrilling that the toilet could be reached in three seconds rather than a half-hour. That night was bliss, so much finer than our chamber-pot life on *Avanti*. At the Resort, we stood out as Americans. After only one phone call to make a dinner reservation, I never again had to give my name – upon hearing my voice, the maitre d' would say "Good Morning Mrs. Clark." When I let him know we were celebrating my husband's birthday one evening, we were presented with an oversized birthday cake – the entire cake. Even more surprising, they didn't charge us for it. Sometimes the Greeks can be so disarming.

We never felt secure anchored at Sounion – the anchor often dragged in the gusty winds. We came close to catastrophe there. I had taken our dinghy – then motorless due to our fickle dinghy outboard – to shore with Roka for a walk. I was shoeless. Upon our return to the shore, the dinghy was gone, washed out into the bay. I could see it floating into the distance, bouncing along the rocky shore. At the end of the rocky shore, it would clearly take one final bounce around the end of the point and disappear into the vast sea. Roka and I tried walking along the shore, hoping to get close enough to the dinghy to grab it. But the rocks were sharp and the dirt full of knife-like stickers, all focusing their venom at my unprotected feet. We had to give up and return to where we started. The man renting paddleboards on shore refused to rent one to me due to the rough seas. I gave him no choice with Roka, even though he said no, no, no. I handed him Roka's leash and walked into the water to swim out to *Avanti* to talk things over with Bruce. We agreed that he would stay on *Avanti* to mind the home front while I returned to the water in snorkel and fins to try to chase down the dinghy. It was windy and the sea rough, but I was swimming in the direction of the wind and waves and we got lucky when the dinghy got caught up in the rocks just as it was about to head out to sea. I managed to reach the dinghy, but actually pulling myself up over its rounded, slippery side to get aboard was a task I could barely perform. I finally struggled aboard, located the oars, and started rowing, now struggling against both wind and waves. Ever so slowly I gained ground until reaching calmer waters where I was finally able to rescue frantic Roka from her disgruntled keeper. I slept all afternoon

The Saronic Islands: Aegina, Hydra

Aegina

Speaking of impressive ruins, try Aegina (pronounced EGG-ee-na), the most visited of all Greek Islands, just south of Athens. Aegina was the commercial hub of the Mediterranean until attacked and subjugated by Athens in the 5th century BC. Athenians now come by the boatload to Aegina to escape the heat of the city. The Temple of Aphaea, constructed atop a pine-covered hill when Athens and Aegina were major rivals, is the best-preserved ancient temple on any Greek island. The temple can be reached by car or taxi from the marina after passing miles of pistachio trees. Aegina is Greece's largest source of pistachios. You're likely to be the only visitors to the temple.

By mid-afternoon in the summer, the island's small harbor is full and latecomers must anchor in the quiet bay to the south of the rock-enclosed harbor. The town of Aegina, the eponymously named capital, is a beehive of activity. We spent many enjoyable hours watching the scene unfold from our deck. The high-speed ferries pull in and out. The large, slow ferries have their own dock just north of the harbor. Horses bedecked with ribbons and flowers trot by pulling tourist carriages. Carts selling fruits and vegetables line the port. Elderly Greeks observe the world from their second-floor balconies across the street from the boat-lined wharf. Crowds of Athenians pour from the ferries into the street abutting the wharf. Numerous bars and restaurants directly across from the boats in the marina entice tourist, many emitting a fine mist of water over their outdoor patios in an attempt to keep their customers cool. A block from the wharf, the fish and meat market serves up tables of gorgeous fresh fish and cows' heads.

We spent far too long in Aegina for several reasons, some happy, some not so much. The happy reasons were that we had many visitors who flew into Athens and a trip through the Saronics was a perfect cruise for many of them. Anyone with only a few days to spend in Greece would be well advised to take the ferries to Aegina and Hydra, two of the most attractive and accessible Greek islands. We visited Aegina with three different groups of visitors.

The not so happy reason was our diesel fuel disaster. One morning we filled *Avanti's* tanks with diesel fuel, as we had done dozens of times before, from the local Elin "minitanker," a truck that drives up and down the wharf with a little fuel tank on its back. This time the fuel was polluted with water, apparently the result of a massive thunderstorm the evening before. When we pulled out of the harbor with our new fuel, we traveled no more than 100 yards before both engines stopped dead. We and our guests – the same Jean and Bruce who visited us in Portofino, Italy – panicked as we started to drift toward the rocks. Ferryboats bore down on us. Bruce radioed the harbor for help and out came a "rescue" vessel full of incompetents. We yelled for them to throw us a line so they could pull us in. They threw us the entire line, both ends. After some frantic words, they seemed to understand that they should hang on to one end of the line and they managed to pull us the 100 yards back to port. For their half hour of incompetent work, they insisted we pay them 500 euros. We negotiated it down a bit, but not much. One week and at least $1000 later, not counting the water that had to be extracted from *Avanti* for which we'd paid $8 a gallon, we were ready to go again. Not surprisingly, the diesel purveyor was never seen again after he insisted that his fuel couldn't have possibly caused our problem. The only silver lining is that we met our "Sean Connery" mechanic, a clone of the actor except for the hair (he had some). He radiated the same air of mystery as Connery. He described how he had been granted American citizenship as a reward for services fighting as a mercenary in Southern Rhodesia. We were impressed but also angry that our government would grant U.S. citizenship to a foreign mercenary as a reward for fighting an undeclared war. For the next month, we checked the diesel filters every hour or two and continue to drain excess water. But that wasn't the end of this disaster. Somehow we managed to get to Crete and back, but as we neared Aegina a month later, one engine stopped working again. We had to have our Sean back to remove still more water. It took several months before the engines operated properly.

Hydra

Next we stopped at the island of Poros, not a bad place, but tainted by the rip-off harbor "official" who demanded that we pay 30 euros for the use of electricity on the wharf for one night (we declined) and by the failure of our engine as we were trying to leave in the morning, caused by our water-laden engines. The engine failure resulted in our anchor tangling with another boat's anchor, the first but not the last time this happened to us. We had no clue what to do. Lots of yelling and cursing by other boat owners ensued and a crowd gathered. While Bruce maneuvered with one engine trying to avoid hitting other boats, I hung off of the bow ladder struggling to get the two anchor chains untangled, trying to glean some understanding of what to do from the many on-lookers shouting contradictory instructions in incomprehensible languages. We emerged exhausted but victorious, the chains untangled, limping off toward the horizon on one operating engine. We don't talk much about Poros.

Hydra (pronounced EE-drah) is a different story. Of course we got our anchor tangled there as well. It's part of the Hydra experience. One dilapidated old sailboat that lives in the harbor, likely unseaworthy, is owned by a spritely bearded American from Chicago named Pan. He takes charge of helping boats get settled into the harbor and helps the big boats tie up on the outer side of the town jetty. We have no idea if he gets paid, and if so, by whom. He's a crusty old guy, but warmed up when we gave him an Obama bumper sticker. He wanted to send a photo of himself posing with it to his Chicago buddies.

The harbor in Hydra is so small that boats anchor in front of each other. The first boat throws out its anchor and backs its stern to the wharf to tie up. The second boat throws out its anchor and backs its stern to the bow of the first boat, tying itself to the bow of the boat behind. That means boaters are scrambling over other boats to get to the land and back. What a mess. Since every boat has to lay an anchor before backing into its spot, it's inevitable that anchors get completely and hopelessly tangled. If you're not in a hurry to leave, it's terrific entertainment each morning watching other boats struggling to pull up their tangled anchors as they try to leave.

Hydra is one of our favorite places. Both of our children visited us there: Andrea with her then-fiancé Jason, and Adam with his soon-to-be-fiancée Meagan. Hydra town is set in a steep-sided inlet, where grey and white mansions built by privateers and blockade runners in the 18th century climb up the hills that surround the harbor. Hydra is famous as an artists' town, but most artists have left, likely discouraged by all the tourists. Still, the town retains an artistic flair. No vehicles, not even bicycles, are allowed in the town. All hauling is done by donkeys and they are everywhere, along with their piles of manure. I was sure they were loving and adorable until one bit me while I was trying to make friends. The main wharf is lined with restaurants serving coffee or ouzo. One can sit there sipping ouzo and watching the donkeys parade by, weighted down by all sorts of odd items, including lumber and mattresses. Cats abound, keeping close watch on fishermen cleaning their catches. Swimming off the rocks just out of town is popular. Masochists can take the long, steep hike in the hot sun to Moni Profiti Ilias, an active monastery. After a difficult uphill hour or two, the final ascent is strait up 1000 stone steps. Our favorite eating spot was Xeri Elia, inland a bit, under big graceful trees where live bouzouki music is performed most nights. We visited Hydra three times and would go back in a flash.

Monemvasia and Kythera

Talk about being off the beaten path. These two spots are about as remote as anywhere we were in the Mediterranean. Both were on our path to Crete.

The surrealistic town of Monemvasia is perched on an island off the barren eastern Peloponnesian coast, tied to the mainland by a narrow bridge. Its Venetian walls are still well-preserved. Its sister town, 1000 feet up the hill, lies abandoned and ruined. The town reminded us of Taormina in Sicily without the crush of tourists. It may be the most picturesque town that no one has ever heard of. The marina there, of course, was unfinished, so we tied up at a barren concrete dock with no water or power.

At the bottom of the Peloponnesian coast lies the island of Kythera, seemingly at the end of the world, touristed only by Australians returning to visit relatives. The locals call Australia "Big Kythera," a testament to the many Greeks from Kythera who emigrated to Australia. Kythera boasts a sparkling blue harbor nestled under an imposing mountain topped by yet another Venetian castle and the requisite white church. At the castle, we found the purple flowers allegedly used by the Phoenicians to make their famous purple dyes. Kythera, by the way, is the home of Venus.

Crete

It's a long day's cruise from Kythera to Crete, our longest leg since arriving in Corfu from Italy. In both directions we were blessed with mild winds and flat seas.

Crete is about as far away from the mainland as one can get and still be in Greece, sitting at the most southerly point of Europe, surprisingly close to North Africa. Crete is famous for the Minoan civilization, people who developed a fascinating culture from 2000 to 1000 BC. The Minoans overlapped in time with the Egyptians and Mesopotamians, but seem to have developed independently. Little is known about their culture, which appears to have been a vibrant, goddess-worshipping, non-militant society in which men and women had equal rights. The cities were filled with happy, colorful frescoes.

The Minoan civilization spread throughout much of Greece, the result of trade and commerce rather than war. The Minoans were famous for their bull dancers, those young men and women who performed flips and twirls on the backs of bulls. Also famous is the legendary Minotaur, half man, half bull, slain according to Greek mythology in the labyrinth at Knossos by Theseus of Athens. After slaying the Minotaur, Theseus left Crete to return home to Athens with Ariadne, the daughter of the Minoan King Minos. She had helped Theseus escape from the labyrinth. Theseus is greatly honored in Greece even today, but I have little respect for him. On his way home, he abandoned Minos' daughter on an island. Then he forgot to hoist the white sails on his ship as he neared Athens, a pre-planned signal to his father that he was returning alive. Instead, the black sails were flying. His father, Aegis, was waiting for his son's return at the Temple of Poseidon in Cape Sounion. When Aegis saw the black sails, he assumed his son was dead. In sorrow, he threw himself off the steep cliff into the sea. The sea was forever after named the Aegean after Aegis' tragic death.

The Minoan civilization lived for centuries side-by-side with the Mycenaean civilization, located to the north on the Peloponnesus, then simply disappeared for unclear reasons. But Crete remains full of ruins from that period. The most famous, Knossos, was to us the least satisfying. The British archeologist who "restored" Knossos in the early 1900s, Sir Arthur Evans, reconstructed the city according to his own theories, many of which have now been discredited. Because of his approach to restoration, it is no longer possible to discern what parts of the restoration are true to the original and what parts are merely products of Evans' imagination. Much more satisfying is unreconstructed Phaestos, located on a hilltop on the southern side of the island.

We arrived at the bustling old Minoan city of Chania, spelled Xania in Greek, and in English either Chania or Hania. In Greek, the X sound is a sort of guttural, back of the throat "ch." The town is popular with Scandinavians so blonds were everywhere. We docked on a busy wharf beside carts selling fruits and candies.

Lindell, a lawyer, and Sheila, an accountant, met us in Chania. We rented a car to visit the nearby Akrotiri peninsula, the location of both decrepit old monasteries and the filming of the last scenes of *Zorba the Greek*. We took our rental car over the high mountains to Phaestos, stopping for ice cream at Matala, where hippies lived in the '70s in caves by the sea while they smoked dope. When we learned that our friend Lindell had in fact hung out in Matala in those days, we were of course shocked, but filled with new respect. But he swore that he didn't inhale.

We traveled on *Avanti* to Rethymnon over choppy seas. Not being boating people, Lindell and Sheila spent most of the trip in panicky silence. Rethymnon is home to an old Venetian port and a quaint pottery shop where we all bought inexpensive, high quality fish-design pottery directly from the potter.

Crete is a huge island and we touched only the western half. In 1970 we visited only the eastern end of the island and loved it, although we were almost trampled on a deserted beach in our sleeping bags one morning by a herd of sheep. But since that time, the eastern half has been developed with fancy resorts. We decided to pass it by, choosing to remember it the way it was.

On our way back to Athens from Crete, one of our engines died – a reappearance of the fuel tank water problem, and we had to head directly back to Sean in Aegina. We finally got the engine healthy and took off to the east and to the most famous of the Greek Island groups, the Cyclades.

The Cyclades: Santorini, Milos, Mykonos, Tinos

The islands of the Cyclades are what people envision when thinking of the Greek islands – white-washed villages perched on parched brown hills overlooking the blue Aegean Sea. Many of the Cyclades islands look like that, but many don't.

There are 21 major Cycladean islands. We visited 16 of them. They are located to the south and east of Athens and the Saronic Islands. Many seemed a bit interchangeable, frankly, and I often mix them up. Their names are similar too. There are the "S" islands: Syros, Sifnos, Sikinos, and Serifos. And that's just in the Cyclades (don't forget the non-Cycladean islands of Skiathos, Skopolos, Skyros and Symi). There is an equivalent confusing set of "K" islands.

Some islands were true highlights, or in some cases, lowlights, and I'll generally ignore the others. The winners were Santorini, Milos, Delos and Tinos. The loser was Mykonos, but that may be partly the fault of the weather rather than the island. Each of the others has its good points and if you have time, visit as many as possible. Many of these islands are only a few hours apart.

Once in the Aegean, where the Cyclades, Sporades, Dodecanese and Northern Aegean Islands are located, the biggest fear for cruisers is the meltemi, the incessant Greek wind that blows down from the Alps and plagues the entire area in the summer. The Cyclades are hit the hardest. The winds can blow for days, sometimes longer than a week, and normally no boats move during a major meltemi. We believe that anyone setting out to sea during a meltemi is insane. In the Aegean, we became hooked on the Greek government's excellent website for local marine conditions, showing calm wind and sea conditions as a deep blue, with rougher conditions shown in lighter blue, then green, yellow, orange and finally, the worst in red. When the meltemis are blowing hard, the maps are pretty scary – huge swaths of bright red sweep down the length of the Aegean through the islands all the way to Crete.

Santorini

There is no way to confuse Santorini with any other island. It is the most breathtaking island on earth. Photos of the island seem unreal, but in reality they don't do it justice. Arriving by boat is magical; we cruised into the old collapsed volcanic caldera and looked straight up at the whitewashed houses draped along the top of the crater cliffs like newly fallen snow.

The only small boat marina on Santorini is on the back side of the crater – not so dramatic, but still picturesque next to the black sand beaches. The marina provided us a special evening when we danced with dozens of Greeks at a local festival, the only time we saw dancing performed solely for Greeks, not for tourists. Otherwise it was a problematic marina since we needed a car to get anywhere and the few restaurants located at the marina were best avoided.

But the rest of Santorini – what an island! The main town, Fira, is a hotbed of tourism. The cruise ships lie offshore, at the bottom of the caldera, spewing tourists out at the base of the cliff where they either ride a mule up the steep path or take a cable car. The few blocks in Fira near the tourist entryways are bleak. Rows of tacky, over-priced jewelry shops line the streets. But the natural beauty of the island overcomes even the most tacky tourist junk. And like most cruise ship locales, the passengers don't walk far and they, and the overpriced tourist shops, disappear a block or two from the top of the cable car landing.

There are two gems located in the tourist area. One is the Museum of Prehistoric Thira, full of high quality Minoan art from the local archeological site, Akrotiri. Minoans came from Crete to live on Santorini and built a large city, known as Old Thira, located on the eastern side of the crater. It is out of the way and has few visitors. We hiked there and appreciated its views and quiet serenity. The second mid-town gem is the art gallery Mati, home of the creative artist Yorgos Kypris, and full of his interesting sculptures and art. We bought a shimmering metal school of fish that now adorns the space above our family room fireplace. Our friends Winston and Susan, visiting yet again, bought an interesting glass boat. Not cheap, but striking and unique.

We visited the ancient Minoan archeological site of Akrotiri with Newport Beach friends Sue and Lois and we were not impressed. All the art had been removed to the museum in Fira and the remaining excavation was dark, dank and covered by an ugly modern roof. When Susan and Winston arrived a few days later, they asked about visiting Akrotiri and we talked them out of it. Lucky thing. The day we would have visited was the very day in 2005 that the excavation collapsed, killing one tourist and injuring others. It remained closed for seven years.

We had two favorite pastimes in Santorini. One was walking along the crater-edge path from Fira to the picture-perfect but otherwise uninteresting town of Oia, a several mile stroll. Along the way, white-washed villages and quiet restaurants overlook the crater and the sea. When our son visited Santorini several years later, where he proposed to Meagan, now his wife, we directed him to one of these little villages, Imerovigli, where they stayed in a small, white hotel, full of bright flowers, overlooking the sea – the perfect place for a proposal. Our second pastime was visiting the Santo Winery, perched on the edge of the crater two miles south of Fira. We sipped on flights of tasty Santorini white wine (four small glasses) and a plate of local cheese as the sun slipped down behind the crater.

Another fun adventure is walking down the steep path to the sea at Fira and riding the mules back up. After riding rental horses at home – those nags that will barely trot – the mules were a kick, literally. They are competitive animals, each wanting to get to the front of the mule pack, even kicking their colleagues in an attempt to get ahead. So rather than plodding up the steep trail, as I had expected, we found ourselves in a genuine mule race.

We stayed and stayed on Santorini, watching one set of guests leave and another arrive. We never grew tired of sitting at a local café or taverna, gazing across the crater and the little white towns climbing down the cliffs toward the sea.

It was hard to leave.

Milos

How does an island maintain its self-respect when it's compared to Santorini? That was poor Milos' problem, but it still squeezed into our favorites category. We actually spent a buffer night in Folegandros after leaving Santorini and heading to Milos, which gave us some perspective. Milos greeted us with a dramatic panorama of gnarled geologic landforms, exposing the colorful innards of an ancient volcano eroded to its core by the sea. Milos is famous for more than its physical beauty. The Venus de Milo was found on Milos by a peasant plowing his field in 1820. Like many Greek antiquities, it was acquired by the French under suspicious circumstances, hustled quickly off the island bound for the Louvre. We visited Milos' ancient Cycladean capital, perched on a hill and criss-crossed by narrow whitewashed streets. We were the only visitors at a small, well-preserved Roman theater a short hike from town. We ate at a quiet restaurant that served delicious food, run by an exuberant owner/chef who instantly bonded with Roka and fed her plates full of Greek food. Susan and Winston jumped onto the ferry in Milos and bade us farewell, leaving us alone again after three weeks of non-stop visitors.

Mykonos

Sadly, Mykonos ended up in the lowlight category. Mykonos was the only Cycladean island we visited in 1970. It was undeveloped and unsophisticated and we loved it. Upon our arrival on the ferry, a flock of grandmothers overran the docks offering to rent us rooms in their homes. We took up one offer and stayed in a primitive home where we flushed the toilet by pouring water down it from a bucket left in our room. Our second night in Mykonos was spent sleeping in our sleeping bags on the beach beneath the famous Mykonos windmills. The only human who wandered by was an elderly woman riding her donkey.

This time we didn't love it so much. Our initial reaction was "Yuck! So touristy!" The town was packed with tourists as giant cruise ships constantly arrived and departed. If a cruise ship stops anywhere in the Greek Islands, it's likely Mykonos. It didn't help that our so-called yacht marina was located where the cruise ships landed, a couple of kilometers from town, a barren set of concrete docks with no services, no food, nothing. In the middle of the night, we'd be awakened by the arrival or departure of another giant cruise ship or two.

On our first day in Mykonos we were forced to walk to town, a difficult and long walk on a busy road, because, after seeing Roka, the motor scooter rental shop near our boat refused to rent us a Vespa. In town, Bruce went by himself to rent a scooter, with Roka nowhere in sight. The scooter allowed us to get to town and back from the marina.

Poor Roka. She was once again attacked by a cat, this time in the middle of town. She received no sympathy from the locals. They screamed at her, angrily accusing her of being a bad dog for disturbing the cat, which neither we nor she had even seen until it was on Roka's back. Somehow an unprovoked attack by a cat is viewed by cat-loving Greeks as always the fault of the dog.

We eventually rediscovered some of the charms of the town. It was October and most tourists had left. The confusing labyrinth of white-washed narrow streets was fun to explore. We adored Petros, the friendly pelican who walks boldly everywhere – up to visitors, into restaurants. The same woman who sold me a shawl in 1970 was still weaving shawls by the church on the hill. I bought two more. Popular towns tend to have better restaurants than off-the-track towns and Mykonos was no exception. We ate well. We even visited the famous nude beaches, almost empty in October, unlike mid-summer when sultry nude bodies are packed together and the alcohol flows freely. We had visited in 1970 before the beach was famous.

Close to Mykonos and well worth a one-day visit is the island of Delos, the holy island of the Cycladean culture, later the center of the Cycladean shipping trade, the birthplace of Artemis and Apollo, and still packed with dramatic ruins of ancient temples and the old town. No humans are allowed to live on the island.

We were ready to leave Mykonos after three days. We still had ten days remaining before we had to be at our marina near Athens to catch our plane home, plenty of time. But sometimes boat travel is painfully unpredictable.

The weather turned terrible. We traded our motor scooter for a car after the scooter was almost blown off the road. The dreaded meltemi winds are usually gone by October, but not this year. The winds were high with no relief in sight. We spent hours poring over the Greek weather maps, looking for a possible break. We grew optimistic when hearing that winds were predicted to slow, but none of the optimistic predictions proved correct. Days dragged by and we started to worry that we'd miss our plane.

Finally we could wait no longer. There was a small weather window predicted for the next day, with winds a bit reduced, but still higher than we thought safe. After that, even higher winds were predicted. We arose at the crack of dawn and headed to sea for the ten-mile trip to Tinos, across the notorious Mykonos Strait, a dangerous passage even in good weather. It was worse than I could have imagined. Wind drove spray across the bow into our faces on the exposed upper helm. The sea was angry and the swells appeared to tower over us. Bruce managed to find a course through the swells that made the passage marginally bearable. I was close to tears the entire time, with a stomach that wouldn't stop churning. I closed my eyes and counted slowly, marking the passage of a quarter-mile, a half-mile, trying to divert my attention from the wild sea. Roka cowered and skidded from one side of the boat to the other, shocked that we would treat her so badly. I swore I would never return to Mykonos. Days later – actually probably only an hour – we pulled into Tinos, wet and shaken. Three tense days later we were at the Olympic Marina near Athens, our goal. Ironically, just as we pulled into the marina, the wind died and the seas calmed. If we had just waited a few more days in Mykonos, we could have traveled all the way to Athens in one extremely long day on a quiet sea. But that wait was not a risk we were willing to take.

Tinos

The closest island to Mykonos is Tinos, where we arrived, shaken, after our horrible morning at sea and where we spent only one night.

Even on such a short visit, we found the island intriguing. Tinos is a place of pilgrimage. The cathedral is holy and Orthodox Greeks trek there for worship, in hopes of a miracle. When pilgrims disembark at the port, they crawl on their hands and knees up the carpeted crawling path along the side of the street the entire distance from the harbor to the cathedral on the top of a hill. As we waited in line to enter the cathedral, pilgrims would suddenly appear underfoot, crawling past. Crawling pilgrims appear to have the right-of-way. Four-foot candles are sold outside the church for pilgrims to take inside to light. Bottles of holy water are sold in the kitschy shops lining the street to the church. The odd combination of the profound and the profane left a huge impression on us.

The Dodecanese: Patmos, Kos, Symi

The Dodecanese Islands hug Turkey and, other than Rhodes, aren't much visited. In addition to Rhodes, we visited Leros, Symi, Kos and Patmos. Leros came and went so quickly that we have little memory of it, but the others rank among our favorite Greek islands. Problems between Turkey and Greece often start in the Dodecanese, where old enemies live so close together. We often saw Greek and Turkish war ships lurking around these islands, warily watching each other.

Patmos

Patmos is one of the most important holy places of the Greek Orthodox Church and of Christianity as a whole. It was here about 100 AD in a large cave that St. John the Divine wrote the book of Revelation, including the Apocalypse, after being exiled from Ephesus. Nine hundred years later, a monastery was built in his name on the highest peak of the island. It is a huge, looming fortress, built to prevent invasion by vandals and pirates. Many religious tourists now come to this island to visit the monastery and the cave where John heard the voice of God and saw the visions of fire and brimstone he describes in his writings.

Patmos is a typical, white-washed Greek island, without the overt tourism found on some islands, but with an unusual veneer of sophistication. In the island's seaside town is a classy Greek ceramics and handicrafts shop, Selene, run by a Greek man and his Australian wife. A gourmet restaurant, Benetos, sits nearby on a small bay, separated from the sea by the organic garden where the Greek chef (whose American wife runs the restaurant) grows his vegetables. In a country of mediocre to abysmal bathrooms, most rated by us as four to five points out of ten, we found a bathroom here we rated a ten – our top possible score and the only ten we awarded in all of Greece.

Kos

Kos is where Hippocrates, creator of the Hippocratic Oath, was born and died, allegedly at age 104. After Hippocrates' death, a healing center, the Asklipieon, was built on a hill a short biking distance from town. It combined the rational medicine advocated by Hippocrates, based on the belief that illnesses often have a real physical cause, with beliefs that offerings to the gods were necessary for healing and that patients should sacrifice a chicken if cured. It remained one of the major healing centers in Greece for the next 1000 years, drawing patients from throughout the Mediterranean. The plane tree in one of the town's squares is allegedly the one under which Hippocrates taught his followers. This claim may be overblown since plane trees rarely live more than 700 years and Hippocrates lived 2500 years ago, but the current tree may be the grandchild or great-grandchild of Hippocrates' original tree. The restaurant Platanos sits on the square as well and was one of our favorite Greek restaurants. It serves a most wonderful appetizer made with chicken, dates and bacon, with a sauce of paprika, nutmeg, cinnamon and brandy.

Kos is awash with tacky tourism – shills hawking their restaurants, rows of t-shirt shops and techno-music. But underneath the shabby veneer is an interesting town, strewn with so many Greek and Roman ruins that it's hard to get around due to the many roads that dead-end at excavation sites. Most of the ruins are neither closed off nor kept up, making exploring them a genuine adventure. One of best features of Kos is its high quality marina with clean toilets and showers – one of the few in Greece. It's also near Turkey – Bodrum lies directly east across a narrow strait.

The day we were planning to leave Kos for Symi, the winds were predicted to reach 35 knots. We never go out in such ridiculously high winds. We stayed at the marina and hung out at a nearby beach where we rented two soft recliners and an umbrella for the day for a mere five euros. Our extra time in Kos did bring some benefit – we found a new sturdy table to replace the wobbly one on *Avanti*'s back deck. We had been searching for this replacement for three years, so this ill wind did blow us some good.

Symi

Symi is located across from one of the windiest corners of the Mediterranean, the Datça peninsula of Turkey. By the time we reached Symi from Kos, the wind was howling again, but this time it was coming from behind us; the boats going the opposite direction were the ones struggling.

The port in Symi is one of the most colorful in the Greek Islands. Multi-colored houses, not the typical Greek whitewashed houses, march up the steep hills beside the long, narrow harbor. *Avanti*'s stern backed onto the local market where we bought dozens of starfish for our daughter's upcoming wedding; her wedding theme just happened to be starfish and seashells. A slow fifteen-minute stroll is sufficient to see the entire town. Day-trippers from Rhodes swarm the town during the day, but in the evening it's just another quiet Greek port town, full of cats and fishermen. When we left Symi, our anchor was part of a three-anchor tangle that took time and patience to unravel. Since we were first to leave, I had the honor of untangling the mess.

We checked out of Greece on Symi to go to Turkey, a surprisingly easy process considering the pain we had in Athens. We weren't required to pay fees or fines – only the standard 88 cents to process our papers. We had to visit only two offices, although one of them did require two visits.

The Sporades: Skiathos, Skopelos

The Sporades include Skiathos, Skopelos, and Skyros and are located to the north of Athens in the Aegean. We visited Skiathos and Skopelos, but the sea was too rough to go to Skyros, a bit more south and east than the others. These islands are popular with Greeks, in part because they can be reached in a few hours' drive from Athens. In addition there are hordes of British who come by ferry to Skiathos. Otherwise, these islands are pretty much off the tourist track.

We were a bit put off by the gangs of Brits in Skiathos, so we were soon off to nearby Skopelos, a few miles to the east, reputedly the greenest island in the Aegean. It was indeed tree-covered and quiet. A small ferry harbor welcomed us on the west side of the island, a short bus ride away from Glossa, one of those perfect white-washed towns on the hill above the harbor. At elegant Agnani, the finest restaurant in Glossa, we sat for hours drinking ouzo and talking with the owner, whose grandfather had started the restaurant in the mid '50s. We sampled some of the most interesting and creatively prepared food we found in Greece. Our favorite was a salad of sea fennel and caper greens, both picked wild by the owner's son at the base of the nearby cliffs that drop precipitously into the sea.

A second harbor on the northeastern side of the island is also named Skopelos. The small town rings a white-washed church on the hill. On a bike ride, we found abandoned apricot trees weighted down with ripe and falling apricots. I filled my bicycle basket and we ate them for days. Skopelos was the filming location of *Mama Mia* so everyone in town had a movie star story. The most beloved person in Skopelos was undoubtedly Meryl Streep. Every restaurant and shop owner had a heartwarming Streep story, and her photo, usually posing with the locals, adorned almost every shop. It was reassuring to us that the kind-seeming Ms. Streep is actually like that in real life.

Northern Aegean and Macedonia

The Northern Aegean Islands are scattered to the east, southeast and north of the Sporades. They include Chios, Ikaria, Lesbos, Samos and Thassos. We missed Chios and Samos but visited the others.

Ikaria

We were in Ikaria for only one night. It was nondescript except for its name – named after Ikaris, that vain man who ignored his father's warnings and died as a result. His father had made them both wax and feather wings so they could escape from the labyrinth in Knossos – the same place our old friend Theseus had killed the Minotaur – and warned him to stay far from the sun lest his wings melt. Ikaris, young and foolish, flew close to the sun anyway; the sun melted his waxen wings and he plunged to his death. His body washed ashore on an unnamed island which was then named Ikaria in his honor. In the harbor is a large statue of Ikaris. The Greeks take their myths seriously. Recent studies show that inhabitants of Ikaria have some of the longest life expectancies in the world, likely due to the slow pace of their lives. That seems right to us. Life is slow on Ikaria.

Lesbos

We arrived in Lesbos after visiting Turkey, which meant visiting four offices, gaining many new stamps, and standing in several long, excruciatingly slow lines. After receiving two completely opposite sets of instructions about checking in at other Greek harbors, we were officially checked into Greece and headed to the northern port on Lesbos, the picturesque harbor of Molivos. After having to move *Avanti* several times to accommodate the local fishermen, we settled in for a couple of days under the town's castle. We rented motor scooters to explore the island. I immediately ran my motor scooter into a ditch and still, several years later, bear a large scar on my knee as a result. The scar is so straight that even orthopedists have asked about my "knee operation." I managed to recover quickly and was out on the scooter again the next day, bandaged of course. Lesbos with its green mountains and empty roads is perfect for a scooter ride. This is the famous home of the poet Sappho, a gay icon, and the island attracts many gay visitors.

Limnos

The forlornly isolated island of Limnos lies directly in the path of the Dardenelles. As far as we could tell, we were the only visitors there. We heard rumors that sometimes Northern Greeks come to Limnos on holiday in July and August.

As with Lesbos, a huge castle looms above the harbor at Limnos. Below the castle are the cliffs where the women of Limnos threw the bodies of their husbands into the sea after slitting their throats. The men had rejected their wives and started hanging out with Thracian slave women. This betrayal occurred because a curse from Aphrodite had caused the wives' breath and armpits to stink. Fickle men! With their husbands gone, the Limnian women lived happily by themselves until Jason and the Argonauts arrived. Jason and his crew looked pretty good after all those years without men, so the women invited them to stay and the island was soon repopulated. Understandably, Bruce became concerned that his various complaints about me over the years might lead to my emulating the Limnian women's revenge, resulting in his ugly demise. He hung back from every cliff edge. He survived.

Thassos

Another wooded island, Thassos, hugs the shore of Northern Greece and is not far from Bulgaria. Apparently it has become a popular vacation spots for Bulgarians. We looked for signs of visiting

Bulgarians, to no avail. On Thassos we were joined by our Congresswoman friend, Loretta and her lawyer boyfriend (now husband) Jack, and we all motor scootered around the island looking for the perfect beach, waiting for the winds to die and trying to find fresh arugula. There's not much to do on Thassos.

Macedonia

The northern region of Greece is known as Macedonia. An area in the former Yugoslavia is known as the Republic of Macedonia. This has created an international confrontation. The Greeks have refused to allow the Republic of Macedonia to use that name. Greeks are angry that the Slavic Macedonians have tried to appropriate such "Greek" heroes as Alexander the Great. The Greeks refer to the Republic of Macedonia as the "Former Yugoslav Republic of Macedonia" (abbreviated as FYROM). The UN has been trying to mediate this dispute for years. Half of the world, including the U.S., uses the name Republic of Macedonia. The other half, including the UN, most of Europe, Mexico and Australia, uses FYROM. It's a mess.

In Greek Macedonia, three peninsulas hang down from the north into the Aegean like cow's teats, the most famous containing Mt. Athos, home to many Greek Orthodox monks. Women are forbidden to set foot on the Athos peninsula. Even female animals are prohibited, with a few exceptions such as hens for laying eggs. Surrealistic monasteries dot the rugged mountains and coast, giving the peninsula the appearance of a sea-bound Tibet. Since we had three women on board (Loretta, Roka and me) we couldn't even anchor near the Athos Peninsula.

We headed instead to a quiet bay on the next peninsula, where there were no tavernas, forcing me to prepare a barely edible dinner on board, after which Loretta insisted she would do all future cooking. After a quiet night, we traveled around the bottom of the Sithonia Peninsula to the fancy resort marina of Porto Carras. "Fancy resort" is a phrase that must be used with caution in Greece. While Porto Carras looked good, it had issues: the toilets were a long slog from the boat and not appealing, the touted wi-fi network didn't work, and the local dock hand was surly at best. Still it was a comparatively classy place. The hotel sold the International Herald Tribune, the restaurant had good food and, best of all, there was a live band, allowing us to sing along to "Besa Me Mucho" over and over with Loretta and Jack. The beach was close and there was a working washer and dryer, although the dryer cooked wrinkles into our clothes.

After Loretta and Jack departed, we rented a car and visited Thessaloniki, Meteora and the Zagora area. Northern Greece is obsessed with Alexander the Great and his father Phillip, and the various palaces and ruins from that time shouldn't be missed. Meteora and Zagora are each unique and stunningly beautiful, but since they are a side-trip for any boater, I won't discuss them. We later rented another car to visit the Peloponnese, including Olympia, the ancestral home of the Olympic Games. The wooded mountains to the east of Olympia, often snow-covered in the winter, are also highly recommended.

CHAPTER 8
TURKEY: EXOTIC, DIVERSE, OUR FAVORITE

This sweet boy sold us lousy gum for 80 cents – a huge profit

Most tourists miss the unusual museum in Seljuk, near Ephesus

Wall tombs in Dalyan carved by the ancient Lycians, 400 BC

| The family of this girl in Kalkan creates these ceramic dishes based on historic Ottoman designs | Early morning: time to fry up Turkish pancakes for visiting boaters in Kapi Creek |

Nervous orphans in white at their circumcision ceremony in Fethiye

Tomb Bay is the place for a haircut and ear singe in a beachside shed

Bruce tries a Lycian tomb for size in Termessos

Our blow-up kayak is perfect for Bruce to explore this half-sunken Lycian tomb near Üçağız

At this remote crusader castle in Anamur, the ticket seller
was sound asleep

Peaceful Kekova Roads viewed from the top of the castle in
Kaleköy; *Avanti* is the big power boat on the dock

Many friends are shocked when we tell them that Turkey is our favorite Mediterranean country. They have the sense that Turkey is a difficult and perhaps dangerous "third-world" country. They've likely suffered through "Midnight Express" too many times. This attitude is changing, but it still exists.

Western Europeans tend to have similar negative ideas about Turkey, which we believe stems from the large number of Turkish immigrants in Western Europe. Bruce and I have often thought that the Turks in Western Europe are a bit like Mexicans in some parts of the U.S. In both countries, usually the poorest immigrants, often from small rural towns, fill the menial but highly visible jobs in their host countries, in restaurants, hotels and hospitals. The wealthy and better educated immigrants from both Mexico and Turkey, more likely from larger, more sophisticated towns and cities, are far less likely to work at visible but menial jobs. So many Western Europeans, much like many Americans, have distorted views of the countries from which these vast numbers of poor immigrants arrive. My Swiss cousin was stunned to learn that we found Turks so likeable.

The Turks we met and learned to love are much like Americans, except that most speak at least two languages. They are friendly, hard-working, reliable and responsible. Need to have your boat fixed in Italy? Greece? Turkey? Always pick Turkey. Looking for locals willing to help you out? Easy. For example, unlike the dysfunctional procedures in Greece for entering and leaving the country, entering and leaving Turkey was simple – we hired the local "customs agent" who had an office in our marina to handle our entry – for $35 he went to all the required offices to obtain the required visa, stamps and boat permit. Such a civilized idea. Of course, toilet paper still goes into the bin, not the toilet; some things must just be accepted.

Turks are eager to please and almost always friendly. They would occasionally stop us on the street just to make sure we knew where we were going, and maybe for the chance to practice a little English. One man on a motor scooter knocked on our rental car window to make sure we weren't lost. A taxi driver outside the small airplane terminal near Marmaris, where we arrived late on a flight from Istanbul, asked if we needed help. We told him we didn't need a taxi, but were trying to locate our rental car. He then spent fifteen minutes tracking down someone from our car rental company. We offered him a tip for his help, but he refused, saying he was pleased to help us out. He had nothing to gain from helping us, but Turks are like that. Our rental car agent, once found, handed us the keys to the car he had just driven from his office in Marmaris, then walked away. We have no idea how he got back to Marmaris, over an hour away. We would have given him a ride but we didn't think of it in time. And being a helpful Turk, he didn't ask.

Turkey is a Muslim country; we soon became accustomed to the five-times-a-day call to prayer from the minarets located nearly everywhere. Istanbul, the largest city in Turkey, has been a secular city for almost 100 years; these days, however, there are signs of change. More women are covered, some so thoroughly that they must peer out of tiny slits in their burkas. The interior of Turkey is religiously conservative. The coast is a secular place with few covered women. We analogize Turkey to the U.S., with our blue coastal states and red interior states. The Islamic political party now in power would like to impose more religious laws on the country and give Islamic fundamentalism more sway. That would undermine the basis of modern Turkey established by the passionately secular Atatürk in the early 20th century. At this point, it's not clear how it will all turn out. When Turkey seemed destined to join the European Union, care was taken by the Islamic government to reign in its religious leanings. Now that joining the EU seems unlikely, religious fundamentalism is on the rise and becoming a divisive issue.

The Turkish language is difficult. We never got much beyond hello and thank you. Pronunciation can be an issue, but it helps to know the following rules: i) the letter "ç" is pronounced "ch"; ii) the letter "ş" is pronounced "sh"; iii) the letter "c" is pronounced "j"; iv) the letter "ğ" is not pronounced at all, but makes the preceding vowel longer, and v) the letter "ö" is pronounced the same as in German, a bit like 'ur'. There are two different "i"s, one with a dot and one without, pronounced differently, but it took us a long time to even notice the difference and we never mastered that rule. Many proper Turkish names in this book are spelled incorrectly since they are spelled with dotted "i"s – in reality, many of those "i"s should be the undotted variety. Other than those basic rules, you're on your own.

It was a relief to arrive in Turkey after spending so many months in Greece. Unlike Greece, Turkey has many excellent marinas where we could berth with a Med-mooring without dropping our anchor, thus avoiding the constant anchor tangling problems. Nearly everywhere we found nice bathrooms and showers and even some washers and dryers. Most marinas had their own restaurants, sometimes excellent ones, and often a chandlery where reasonably priced boat parts could be found.

The physical appearance of Turkey surprised us after we had spent so much time in the barren Greek islands. Most of the coastline is wooded, radiating aromas of pine and fresh herbs. The forests extend to the water's edge.

Our path around Turkey was confusing. We first arrived in the bay of Marmaris, then cruised east along the Mediterranean almost to Antalya before returning to Marmaris where *Avanti* wintered over. The following year we again traveled east, this time all the way to Alanya and Northern Cyprus. Our return trip west took us from the Mediterranean back into the Aegean, then north to Ayvalik, the most northerly port we visited, near the entrance to the Dardenelles. There we left Turkey and returned to Greece via the Greek island of Lesbos. We never took *Avanti* to Istanbul – it was too far, and we could find no marina that would work. Since every flight to or within Turkey went through Istanbul, we spent lots of time there and it remains one of our favorite world cities.

Since our journeys through Turkey were so convoluted, this chapter will simply start with the most northerly port of Ayvalik and proceed south and then east.

Ayvalik

There are no Americans in Ayvalik. Actually, that's not surprising. We were there for almost a week due to needed boat repairs and soon realized that Ayvalik is not an exciting city. To put it into perspective, our biggest excitement in Ayvalik was witnessing the mid-town collision between a sheep and a motorcycle.

The best part of Ayvalik is nearby Pergamon, a sprawling archeological site, perched high on a hill, strewn with Greek and Roman buildings, a large amphitheater and thousands of red poppies. There are also four rug stores in the adjacent "modern" town of Bergama. We were leaving Turkey soon for Greece and I became overcome by a desperate longing for just one more Turkish rug. However, rug buying is a difficult and time-consuming business in Turkey. Walking into a rug store represents a major commitment. Often the shop-keeper's whole family stands by watching as the young beefy sons and other helpers grab rugs from the many piles around the store to throw at your feet for examination. Tea is a requirement and pleasantries must be exchanged. The young men start to sweat under the strain of hurtling piles of rugs. The owner's forehead beads up at the thought of a sale, and he launches a hard-sell as soon as he notes the faintest whiff of interest in a particular rug. "This rug is of especially wonderful quality." "The old woman in the small village near Van who wove this rug spent many, many months on it – look at the quality! Look at how fine the weave is." "Here, let me tell you the meaning of each of the symbols in the rug. And the colors, of course, are made only from organic vegetable dyes." And finally, the coup de grace: "I have a very special price only for you." Children watch intently from the dark corners of the shop. The wife insists, "And please, you must have more tea." Then there's the ultimate haggling over price, with lots of sighing, wringing of hands and occasional moves for the door. After three stores and several hours, we emerged with one medium size rug and two small ones – and my internal rug monster was satisfied.

Foça

South of Ayvalik, Foça's miniature harbor is a magnet for visitors from the closest big city, Izmir (formerly Smyrna), about 50 miles to the south. A major metropolis in 600 BC, Foça was one of our favorites in 1997. This time, the town was packed with a weekend throng, including a singer belting out '70s Motown songs and the provincial governor, apparently campaigning. The place was rocking.

We figured everyone would be gone the next day, a Monday. But we were wrong – it was a national holiday, Youth and Sports Day, a day that also commemorates Atatürk, the founder of modern Turkey. A ceremony with a military band and straight lines of extremely young sailors and soldiers each toting a frightening looking Uzi, took place right beside *Avanti*'s berth.

Alaçati

Alaçati lies south of Foça, on the south side of the Çeşme Peninsula directly west of Izmir. Not long ago, Alaçati was a town in decline. An old Greek Ottoman town, most of its population was forced to leave the country in the early 20th century as part of the population exchange between Greece and Turkey. But in the last few years, the town has been transformed into an upscale retreat for a growing class of wealthy Turks who come for its beaches as well as the renovated old stone Ottoman houses on its narrow streets, now transformed into boutique hotels with sidewalk cafés and upmarket restaurants run by famous chefs.

We spent a week here after *Avanti* was hauled out for the winter in the marina just outside of town. The big, calm but windy bay by the town has become a world-famous windsurfing venue. The town is about an hour west of Izmir and 15 minutes east of the actual large tourist town of Çeşme, with a classy new marina, a small Genovese castle and a Seljuk caravansary.

South of Alaçati, we pulled into a primitive harbor in the obscure walled town of Siğaçik (even knowing the rules of pronunciation doesn't make this one easy, but it sounds a bit like suh-AH-chek). The small harbor looked calm, although it proved to be less protected than it initially appeared. We walked through the entire town in about ten minutes, admiring trucks full of watermelons. As we wandered through the town square, we heard someone speaking English. We looked around, but saw only Turks. We kept listening and finally tracked the voices to four Turkish-Americans eating lunch in the square. They would normally have been conversing in Turkish, but for some serendipitous reason had lapsed into English. They invited us to join them and we soon discovered the many life threads we had in common with two of our new friends, who live in Long Beach, near our home: University of Michigan, Yale and Yale's crew team, for starters. They own a summer home in this quiet little town. This was one of the greatest gifts we received from our travels. They have become some of our closest friends.

Kuşadasi and Ephesus

Kuşadasi is the port closest to the ancient ruins of Ephesus and the hub of the Turkish cruise industry. Upon breathing a whiff of Turkish air, cruise ships descend on Kuşadasi like ants swarming a pungent picnic basket. The marina is large and well-protected. Kuşadasi is a pleasant but unremarkable town, but Ephesus is a marvel. We had visited in 1997. The most noticeable change from our first visit was the vast increase in tourists. Near the famous library of Ephesus, it was hard to turn around without running into an American, Japanese or French tourist toting a pointed camera. The ruins are world-renowned. The small Ephesus museum located in Selçuk (SEL-chuk), a nearby town, is often overlooked by tourists, to their loss. The museum features several unusual, perfectly preserved statues of

Artemis, the Greek fertility goddess to whom Ephesus was dedicated. On all her statues, beautiful Artemis is adorned with a series of rounded gonads and groups of bats decorate her ears. We also appreciated the outdoor market in Selçuk. It was one of the few places in Turkey we found to buy spacious, comfortable cotton Turkish pantaloons – the same ones worn over the centuries by Turkish women and still worn in most provincial Turkish towns.

Bodrum

It was in Bodrum in 1997 that we were hit with the lightning-bolt idea of traveling the Mediterranean in our own boat. It was here, where the hotels looked so sad, that we opted for a night on a Turkish gulet. This time we had *Avanti* and didn't need a hotel, or so we thought. The Milta Bodrum Marina is pleasant but expensive. There is an attractive mooring field south of the castle that would be nice in cooler weather. But we were faced with the hottest weather we had experienced in our entire eight years in the Mediterranean – 108 degrees! Usually we can survive with all our fans on high. But this weather far exceeded our fans' capacities, so we were driven to seek a hotel to wait out the worst of the heat. Right beside the marina we found a modern air-conditioned hotel with a pool. We were trapped in the hotel for four days. Except for early morning and late evening, it was even too hot to swim in the hotel pool. We were relieved when it cooled enough for us to return to *Avanti*.

The ancient fort in Bodrum was still impressive and the old town was fun to explore on foot. Bruce enjoyed the Museum of Underwater Archaeology located in the fort. However, just as in 1997, we weren't enthralled by Bodrum and it remains on the bottom of our "favorite places in Turkey" list.

Bodrum to Marmaris

This stretch of coast is a famous yachting area, alleged to host the greatest number of touring yachts anywhere in Turkey. Despite the hype, we were often alone when we stopped for lunch in a quiet bay, and there were rarely more than a half dozen other yachts in the bays where we anchored for the night.

We cruised for several days east of Bodrum, enjoying the quiet coves and warm blue water. We swam at the beach where Mark Antony brought in barges filled with soft pink calcareous sand from North Africa (unlike the local gravelly beach sands) so that his beloved Cleopatra could bathe in appropriate luxury. Other than the chickens sitting beside us on the beach, it was perfect.

We anchored at the mouth of Amazon Creek – short, tranquil and heavily wooded – and kayaked up the river. Then the winds came up and *Avanti* was pummeled. We worried about our anchor dragging and *Avanti* drifting away. In those conditions, we normally not only drop an anchor, but also tie the stern of *Avanti* to a tree or rock, usually by my swimming a line from *Avanti* to the nearest shore. This time, after I reached shore and was poking around for a good tree for tying the line, my leg hit some spiny sea urchins, leaving sharp barbs that remained painfully embedded near my knee for many years. The winds were so high that we decided to tie lines onto two different trees, a first for us. This took pressure off the anchor and made drifting less likely.

We visited Çokertme, where the only visible structures were four seaside restaurants standing side by side. We picked Rosemary's Pirate Restaurant – named after the owner's daughter (her name was Rosemary, but we don't think she was actually a pirate). Our table sat on a rickety dock suspended over the water. The restaurant featured a blazing bonfire on a platform in the sea beside our table. We spent the night anchored in a silent bay nearby. The restaurant sent a dinghy to fetch us for dinner and take us back after we finished.

Soon we reached the Datça Peninsula, which juts out from the Turkish mainland toward the west. Once around its end, we passed from the Aegean into the Mediterranean. This protruding spit of

Turkish land bumps against two Greek islands. We spent four days slowly cruising this rugged coast, with its pine-covered mountains, tiny villages, ruins from several civilizations and a multitude of quiet bays. At the tip of the Datça Peninsula are the ruins of the ancient Greek town of Knidos, a main seaport in the 4th century BC. There we met six couples from Colorado while hiking through the ruins. They graciously invited us for drinks and dinner on their elegant chartered gulet in exchange for a couple of trays of ice. Turks don't seem to understand the American need for ice when the drink of the hour is gin and tonic. We thought this was an exceptionally good deal for us. The leader of the group explained that he owns an oil company that had made him rich, so he was treating all of his friends to this trip. What a pal.

We visited Marmaris several times and *Avanti* spent two winters there. Our marina was the huge Marmaris Marina, located a few miles from town. There is a communal van called a dolmus that trundles back and forth to town from the marina over a narrow, winding road. That was okay, but slow, so we eventually rented a motor scooter or car on each visit. Marmaris Marina is one of Turkey's finest, with a large swimming pool and a well-stocked market. Does your boat need work? This is the place. We hear that West Marine has now moved into town. Best of all is the delicious food at the marina restaurant, which in our view is the best marina restaurant in the Mediterranean, serving thick, tender steaks – a rarity anywhere in the Mediterranean – that were both delicious and inexpensive. But even this modern restaurant geared toward European tourists did not serve pork. Pork is impossible to buy in Turkey, even in specialty groceries designed to serve British tourists. Turkey is a Muslim country, but we were still surprised that pork was unavailable given the country's secular history. We flew to a wedding in Romania during our stay in Turkey and bolted down as much of our favorite pork salami as we could find – plus we arrived back in Turkey with several pounds of pork salami bulging in our suitcases.

The town of Marmaris itself is a bit disappointing. Our favorite place there was the large Migros grocery store, where we stocked up several times. Marmaris has an extremely long wharf where dozens of gulets are sandwiched together waiting for paying guests. It's hard to believe that there are enough tourists to fill them all. Restaurants line the wharf, each with a shill trying to lure passers-by in for lunch or dinner. The shills are usually friendly and fun, but they grow tiresome quickly. It was here we tasted one of our favorite Turkish dishes: lamb and vegetables presented in a burning ceramic vase. The flaming vase arrives at the table where it is smashed with a hammer to release the wonderful tender lamb stew.

Marmaris to Fethiye; Dalyan

The sea from Marmaris east to Antalya is the best cruising area in the entire Mediterranean, encompassing the towns and villages of Marmaris, Dalyan, Fethiye, Kalkan, Kas, Kekova Roads and Antalya. This is our favorite part of our favorite country.

The history in this part of Turkey is overwhelming and readily accessible. Steep mountain faces are covered with elaborate ancient tombs, carved into the rock by the Lycians, who ruled this part of the world almost 3000 years ago. The shore is dotted with ruins of castles from the same period and others built more recently, some during the Crusades. Hundreds of Lycian sarcophagi dot the landscape, often lying on their sides or at odd angles after being upended and rolled downhill by the earthquakes that have hit Turkey over the past three millennia.

The area is dotted with several villages with small marinas or docks for visiting boats, where women in traditional Turkish pantaloons and head covers sell their wares – scarves, shawls, simple beaded jewelry – from baskets or cramped stalls. The call to prayer, that eerie atonal chant, floats from nearby minarets five times daily, reminding us constantly that we are not only in a different country, but also a very different culture. Secluded bays abound. Life here is simple – fishing, raising goats and chickens, and, fortunately for us, serving food to the boaters who anchor in the warm, turquoise waters at the base of the pine-covered slopes. The locals are eager, even anxious, to make sure we are happy. They go out of their way to help, seemingly expecting nothing but a "tesekkur ederim" (thank you) in return.

We anchored in quiet coves near tavernas accessible by dinghy, or tied up on rickety docks, watching the millions of stars overhead and listening to the roosters crow and goats bleat. One cove, near the town of Dalyan, abutted a beach where endangered loggerhead sea turtles nest, so walking on the beach at night is prohibited. We saw only turtle tracks.

Dalyan was so enjoyable that we visited it three times, one day trip on a chartered boat and two overnights at the comfortable Dalyan Resort, which sits right on the river. The day trip was on a chartered Turkish boat from nearby Ekinçik. *Avanti* was unable to navigate over the shallow sandbar blocking the Dalyan River from the sea whereas the Turkish boat was long and wide with the shallow draft required to cross the sandbar. The decks were covered in cozy Turkish rugs. We had the boat to ourselves, along with our Australian friends Jan and Malcolm, who had stubbornly returned for another visit despite spending time with us on *Avanti* in France.

Dalyan is one of the highlights of Turkey. The ruins of the ancient town of Caunos, a Carian and Lycian city at least 4000 years old, stand where the river meets the sea, among the endangered turtles. The Carians sided with the Trojans in the Trojan War. The Lycians dominated the area until around 100 BC. Up the river are Lycian tombs carved into the ochre and yellow granitic mountainside. The shore is dotted with small restaurants where patrons can admire the wall tombs, watch the boats floating by, and select their own meals by traipsing into the kitchen to pick out mezes, those delicious Turkish appetizers. Trees and telephone poles are festooned with storks' nests full of baby storks peering down at the humans below.

Fethiye and Fethiye Bay

To the east of Dalyan looms huge Fethiye Bay. Fethiye Bay has everything a boater could want – the interesting town of Fethiye, picturesque coves dotting the bay for anchoring or tying to a dock, and quiet, clear waters. There is actually a second town in the bay, Göcek, but we disliked it because of the miserable experience we had with its uber-fancy marina with incompetent dockhands, eventually resulting in a high speed chase and our payment of a large sum that we didn't owe, extorted from us as the price of being allowed to leave. It wasn't much of a town either.

The town of Fethiye also has a classy marina that is part of the adjacent elegant hotel, the Ece Saray Marina & Resort. The hotel's large pool is available to visiting boaters. While it's not cheap, we thought it was worth the price. However, we did manage to foul a line there, requiring the expense of a professional diver to rescue us.

Fethiye is a small but busy Turkish town. We were surprised to find a nearby town that is totally British – it could have been dropped by helicopter from England – filled with pubs and fish and chips shops. In downtown Fethiye we sat with a contingent of Brits to watch the British soccer team lose to Portugal in the 2004 World Cup. The visiting Brits were so lubed with alcohol by the end of the game that they didn't seem to care much that their team had lost. We surmised that they weren't true soccer hooligans.

On another day in downtown Fethiye, we found ourselves in the middle of a large parade of costumed dancers, marching bands, and clumps of small boys ages four to nine, all dressed in white. We were aghast to learn that this was a circumcision ceremony for orphaned boys and that, when the parade ended, each of these little guys would be going under the knife. A Turkish tradition.

Fethiye has many rug shops and is one of the best places in Turkey to buy a kilim or rug. It also prides itself on its recently excavated 2nd -

century Roman amphitheater that serves as the site for various plays and musical programs.

Just outside of Fethiye is the eerie deserted Greek village of Kayaköy. After World War I, Greek Christians living in Turkey were expelled and forced to return to Greece, even though their families had lived in Turkey for hundreds of years and didn't speak Greek. Greek-speaking Turks whose families had lived in Greece for centuries were forcibly returned to Turkey in exchange. Ethnic cleansing. Kayaköy is one of the towns where the Greeks lived and were forced to leave. No one has lived there since 1920 when the Greeks left. It is empty – silent and unsettling. Louis de Bernieres, author of *Corelli's Mandolin*, wrote a spell-binding, tragic novel about these Turks, *Birds Without Wings*.

We spent over a week cruising in Fethiye Bay, mostly anchoring in some of the isolated coves, where there was always one taverna for visiting boaters, and almost always a tell-tale satellite dish, meaning we could watch that evening's World Cup game. Even the most modest bayside taverna has TV satellite coverage and the crowds watching the soccer games were boisterous. Fethiye Bay is heavily populated with vacationers from Germany, England, France and Italy.

Kapi Creek is the most popular cove in Fethiye Bay, located just inside the entrance to the Bay from the sea. The small marina is constantly packed to its full capacity of about twenty boats. Best to come early. A taverna borders the shore, its tables set just feet from the water. Goats roam the hills, wandering among the ruins. Every morning a Turkish woman and her son make traditional Turkish pancakes on her small boat in the marina, selling them to the visiting boaters – your choice of filling: jam, goat cheese and herbs, or chopped olives. An ice cream boat also comes by regularly, the first we'd seen since France. Sometimes life is perfect.

At our favorite cove, named Tomb Cove after the Lycian rock tombs carved into the mountainside above the water, a small hut on the beach displayed a sign advertising massages, haircuts and shaves. Bruce took advantage of the opportunity to clean up with a haircut and a stropped straight-razor shave. He was surprised when the barber lit up an alcohol-soaked wad of cotton on the end of some long tweezers, to burn out his ear hairs. When it was over, he looked remarkably handsome. Our favorite part of Tomb Bay was the makeshift rope swing near our anchorage where we could climb a small hill, grab the swing, then hurl ourselves out over the water, letting go at just the right spot so we'd be flung high in the air before crashing back into the warm water.

Wall Bay, another favorite anchorage, is close to ruins known as Cleopatra's Bath, claimed to have been used by Cleopatra herself. There at an open-air taverna we ate the goat that we had watched all afternoon as it turned slowly on a spit over a fire pit.

Fethiye to Kekova Roads

Kalkan and Kaş are two mid-sized harbor towns between Fethiye and Kekova Roads. Our first trip to Kalkan was one of our worst days on the Mediterranean, full of multiple crises. A few hours after we pulled out of Fethiye with Australian friends Jan and Malcolm, danger arose suddenly. A Turkish Coast Guard ship sped toward us, blocking our path. We stopped in a state of confusion, as *Avanti* churned and bounced wildly in the Coast Guard boat's wake and the growing wind-driven swells. Over their loud-speaker the officers told us to go to channel 08 on our VHF. We were, they officially informed us, about to enter into a live firing range. We must turn back. This part of the coast was closed until six o'clock.

This was not what we had in mind. We didn't want to go back to Fethiye Bay. The only nearby anchorage, Olu Deniz, was not recommended for an overnight stay. So we decided to hide out in Olu Deniz until six, then make a mad dash for Kalkan. It was nervous time. If things didn't go perfectly, we would be left at sea after dark – definitely not a good idea, especially since our depth finder wasn't working and we could easily run aground.

The sun sets late in the Mediterranean during the summer, so it was still daylight during our trip to Kalkan, but the sea was rough since we were broadside to the swells. We reached Kalkan as dusk fell, only to find the small harbor completely filled. We were left to find an anchorage outside the harbor where we were subject to unpleasant swells and the possibility of smashing into the jetty during the night if our anchor dragged. We anchored and tied a stern line to the jetty to keep us stable. Our fears proved far too real. We awoke in a panic at two in the morning to *Avanti* bouncing wildly and the sound of our anchor dragging on the sea floor. It was too dark to see much of anything. We waited nervously until the swells subsided a bit and *Avanti* seemed to stabilize, then slept fitfully. In the morning, we saw that she had turned 90 degrees during the night, but otherwise she was fine. It was one of our worst nights.

We were greatly relieved to find a spot in the harbor the next morning. Kalkan is a pleasant enough town. By some strange coincidence we ended up here on Bruce's birthday two years in a row. Naturally we bought a birthday cake and some fireworks. The fireworks were probably not a good idea. We almost burned down the marina – they were not the "safe and sound" variety sold in the U.S. On top of that, Turks don't bake birthday cakes quite like we do, so the cake wasn't a huge success. On the other hand, it wasn't so terrible that it prevented us from ordering exactly the same cake for the next birthday. We bought the dangerous fireworks again too.

Many potters work in shops that line the main street of Kalkan, throwing and painting their pots. Their work is exquisite, painted in traditional Turkish designs, some exact copies of ancient Ottoman patterns from Iznik, the famous city that produced the Ottoman-era tiles that decorate the most ornate of Istanbul's mosques. The prices were reasonable and we took home several platters and bowls.

Kaş is much like Kalkan. We watched a World Cup game with dozens of others in the town square, including some obnoxious Australians. Our find there was an impressive pottery shop located on the waterfront that creates pieces with unusual, simple fish designs. We bought a few as gifts. My son's favorite coffee cups are from that shop in Kaş.

Kekova Roads: The Best of the Best

Kekova Roads is perfect, our favorite place on our favorite coast in our favorite country. The two tiny towns, Üçağız (OO-cha-eez – clearly one of the most difficult names for Americans to master) and Kaleköy, have beckoning restaurant docks that offer the luxuries of electricity, water and fresh bread. Boats can also anchor anywhere in the shallow protected waters of Üçağız Bay. The deeper, more active waters of Kekova strait are rimmed by shallow inlets inviting a swim or overnight stay. The strait is created by the elongate Kekova barrier island that lies parallel to the coastline a half-mile away from the mainland, fully protecting the coast and the inner Üçağız Bay from all weather.

The town of Üçağız is accessible from the highway by a poorly paved, twisty 15-mile road, so few cars visit. Three rickety wooden docks in the town beckon entering boaters. When a boat appears, each dock owner runs to the end of his dock, waving the flags of the one or two countries he thinks may be the boat's home country, competing with the other docks to lure the new boat to come in and spend the night. Once a lucky dock owner is selected, the other two owners shrug and await the next boat. The lucky winner is eager to be of service. "Can I help you tie up?" "Do you have any trash I can take?" "Tomorrow morning I'll bring you some fresh bread – no charge of course." "Let me hook you up to water and electricity." What a surprise! Of course, the electricity came from a long extension cord from shore and the water from a hose strung along the dock. Still, any electricity is surprising on these dilapidated docks.

And the cost for all this? Nothing. The only expectation is that the visitors will eat a meal at the dock owner's taverna.

We stayed first at Onur's dock, where handsome Turgay smartly waved his American flag to lure us in. By the time we left and he'd learned there were Australians on board, he bade us goodbye waving both American and Australian flags. On a second visit we stayed at Ibrahim's dock and, of course, ate at Ibrahim's restaurant, where a local dog climbed onto the sofa beside me and rested her head on my lap during dinner. I missed Roka, who had been left home with our daughter after all her hardships in Greece. We never did make it to Hassan's dock, although we did eat at his restaurant one night after he begged us to try it. One other night we anchored in the quiet bay, but that didn't stop both Turgay and Hassan from motoring out in the morning, each in his sputtering motorboat, to bring us a loaf of freshly baked warm bread. How could we not love this place?

Nothing much goes on in Üçağız – it's only a short block long and features one or two rug stalls, lots of hungry cats, many Lycian tombs from about 400 BC, fishing boats being painted and sanded in preparation for the new season, a squadron of old wooden Turkish gulets awaiting the expected tourists, and a gaggle of old, wrinkled women in baggy pantaloons and scarves, selling cheap bead jewelry from rickety tables.

In the Kekova strait lies an old Roman-era sunken city, much of which is now beneath the sea after subsiding during an earthquake in the 2nd-century AD. The ruins are the target of glass-bottom gulets full of visiting tourists. Swimming is not permitted since this is a federally protected site, but I did kayak over the ruins on our blow-up kayak. In addition, along with Jan and Malcolm, we hired our own gulet tour with Bariş, an eager young Turk who spoke a bit of English. He brought along his wife who spoke no English at all. He said it was their first outing for hire in their new gulet. We glided slowly over the ruins, then headed off to a small bay where we swam in the clear waters and were served the ubiquitous Turkish tea. We had found Bariş and his family in a small house outside of town on our way to investigate the many sarcophagi that cover the local hills. It was not possible to reach his boat from his dock because half the dock had collapsed into the sea. He had to maneuver the boat to a neighbor's dock so we could embark.

Kaleköy, the other town in Kekova, is a ten-minute jaunt on *Avanti* from Üçağız and accessible overland from Üçağız by a small dirt road. Again we found three dock owners vying for *Avanti* to visit. On Baris' recommendation, we picked the Hasan Roma dock – not to be confused with the Hassan Deniz dock immediately adjacent. It provided the requisite water and electricity, but not the level of service we'd expected after staying with the most helpful and friendly Turgay on Onur's dock in Üçağız.

Kaleköy is the former Lycian town of Simena; the sunken ruins we had visited on the other side of the strait were formerly Simena residences. Present-day Kaleköy consists of three docks with restaurants, a couple of pensions, one small "supermarket" (a broom closet with three bags of crackers is called a supermarket in this part of Turkey) and a few houses. It is built on the ruins of the ancient town, so tombs, sarcophagi and crumbling walls are scattered about town and sometimes incorporated into buildings. Kaleköy means Castle Bay – the town is named after the famous crusader castle that sits on the top of the hill, a steep ten minute walk up through the town. The trail passes dozens of open stalls where pantalooned women sell hand-goods, and tag along behind visitors climbing the hill to the castle, continuing all the while to peddle their scarves, shawls, and tablecloths from the baskets they carry. The women are relentless. When a new boatload of day-trippers arrived, we were nearly bowled over by the flying pantaloons and scarves as the women rushed down the hill to the dock to try to score a sale. One woman, our "new best friend," climbed the rocks to the top of the castle with us hoping for a sale – no easy task even for a goat.

166

Kaleköy is famous on tourist brochures for its sunken sarcophagus beside the harbor. We explored it, and the other partially sunken island ruins, in our favorite *Avanti* toy, our inflatable kayak. Sarcophagi also dot many of the hillsides throughout Kekova, abandoned except for a random tourist and the ubiquitous flocks of goats.

We visited Kekova Roads three times. On our first visit, we were with our Australian friends, Jan and Malcolm. One time we were by ourselves. On our third trip, we were accompanied by my college roommate Marg and her husband, Fred, a former U.S. Senator who also ran for President in the Democratic primaries (Carter won). Bruce was a bit intimidated by the thought of hosting Fred "the Senator" on our humble boat, but fortunately Fred was such a low-key yet entertaining guest that Bruce was soon completely at ease.

Antalya

Two major towns lie between Kekova and Antalya: Finike and Kemer. They are complete opposites. Finike is a traditional Turkish town with few outsiders, likely because there are no real attractions. On one visit, Finike was celebrating its annual festival, which included a lackluster beach volleyball tournament (we thought we could beat many of the contestants) and the city park packed with itinerant vendors, all sleeping each night in their booths. The other town, Kemer, is upscale, modern and full of foreigners and flashy shops. Kemer is one of the famous and popular marinas for "wintering over." Winter guests are regaled with evening movies, trips to Antalya for the symphony, ski trips in the local mountains, tennis tournaments in the adjacent park and Turkish language lessons. There are also interesting ruins in this area, especially Myra. Myra was the home of the 4th-century AD bishop who became known as St. Nicholas. It was jarring to see a giant picture of an American Santa Claus welcoming us to the city. Myra was where St. Nick's bones were stolen by the Italians, who moved them to their church at Bari. From then on, St. Nick was known as St. Nicholas of

167

Bari, clearly unfair to his true hometown. Myra also has a Roman theater and the most well-preserved and dramatic Lycian cliff tombs in all of Turkey.

Antalya is a big non-descript city except for its ancient town and seaport, a small area of tiny streets, barely wide enough for one car. Antalya also has a modern symphony hall and an active cultural life of symphonies and operas.

Outside of Antalya are several ruins worth seeing, including the beautifully preserved amphitheater of Aspendos. The best in our opinion was the ancient city of Termessos, a city built on a mountain top so protected that even Alexander the Great gave up trying to conquer it and just passed it by. A long, hot, difficult hike takes visitors to the top of the mountain. This grim trek keeps down the number of visitors. The reward at the top is a theater high on a wooded hill, looking up to the jagged cliffs of the mountain rising above it and below into the steep valley to the sea. Hundreds of sarcophagi, jumbled and overturned by earthquakes, are scattered over another nearby hill in the city's necropolis. They are fun to play in.

Alanya

Seventy-five miles east of Antalya is Alanya, home of a 12th-century crusader castle that covers the entire promontory jutting from the city into the sea. We decided to spend a night at a renovated 13th-century inn that overlooks the castle, the town, and a 12th-century mosque. The town was formerly used by caravans of traders who traveled from Asia to buy and sell at the medieval bazaar. *Avanti* stayed in the comfortable marina in the heart of town. The town has some ragged edges; it is the center of a tacky tourist industry appealing mainly to Brits looking for a place for alcohol and sex.

Anamur

Anamur was the farthest east we ventured in Turkey. Most tourists stop at Antalya, failing to reach Alanya and certainly not Anamur. The marina closest to Anamur is Bozyazi, a small place guarded by a harbor master who sat directly beside our boat watching over us intently, perhaps because a foreign boat this far east is a rarity. The area is picturesque – craggy mountains rising from the sea, rich with ancient ruins, covered with fields of bananas. The bananas struck us as odd; the dry climate is unlike the famous banana growing regions in Central America and Hawaii. But there they were. Banana stands dot the highway between Anamur and Alanya. Sitting on the narrow beach in Anamur, jutting into the sea, is a sleepy Disney-perfect medieval castle, the kind every child dreams of exploring, with turrets, dark staircases and crenellated walls. The ticket-seller was sound asleep so we just walked in. On the other side of town, amid wildflowers on a hill by the sea, the ancient Roman city of Anamurium lies in ruins, with dozens of two-chambered tombs (one chamber for the deceased, the second for the family to give offerings), several large public baths, theaters and basilicas, a hilltop castle and city walls creeping up the mountain. We were accompanied by a few cows chewing contentedly. In Anamur we spent an hour drinking beer and talking with a 70-something Kurdish man, a former circus strongman we met on the colorful exercise equipment installed by the city in a seaside park. He told us he lived part of the year in Anamur and the remainder in Basel, Switzerland. He claimed he had lived by himself since his wife died, but then admitted to having a 26-year-old blond Moldavian bombshell "friend" whose photo he proudly produced. Our only common language was German, so the conversation consisted mostly of his talking and our listening and madly trying to remember our German vocabulary.

We'll definitely return to Turkey. We have visions of a gulet trip along the south coast. We plan to visit our friends from Siğaçik at their home there. Turkey remains close to our hearts.

CHAPTER 9
NORTHERN CYPRUS: BRIEF, TRAUMATIC

The big Eastern Med Rally party in the old fortress in Girne, the
Northern Cyprus capital

Yes, we did humiliate ourselves by parading through town
in pirate garb. Note my cool severed hand.

We joined up with the Eastern Mediterranean Yacht Rally (EMYR) in 2007, meeting the fleet in Kemer, near Antalya. This 80-plus boat rally starts in Istanbul each year and travels along the coast of Turkey to Alanya, then heads to Northern Cyprus, Syria, Lebanon, Israel and Egypt.

This sounded exciting to us, although we were concerned because the fleet consists mainly of sailboats that travel much slower than *Avanti*. We decided to give it a try. We had fun in Kemer and Alanya and made new friends from England, France and Sweden. The rally is a big deal to the cities it visits. The participants are feted, fed and entertained by each town, and the parties often include the mayor and other local VIPs. The locals move their fishing boats out of the harbor to make room for the gang of traveling EMYR boats.

As it turned out, there were only two other powerboats on the Rally, both slow, lumbering boats that happily travel at five knots. *Avanti* hates to go that slow and it's not good for her diesel engines to travel under about eight knots for hours at a time. Since all boats are required to arrive at the next scheduled port at essentially the same time, our speed required that we start later on each day's leg than the rest of the fleet. This became a serious problem on the leg from Alanya to Northern Cyprus, a 100-mile overnight trip. The fleet took off late in the afternoon, leaving us alone in the marina with the returning fishermen and a Turkish security contingent provided by the city to guard the EMYR boats. Two policemen sat for hours in their car watching over *Avanti*. We finally told them we felt perfectly safe and they could leave, which they did, much to their relief.

That night we pulled out in the dark at 3 a.m. *Avanti* had never been out at night so we were extremely nervous. There was no moon. Our newly purchased, inexpensive radar didn't work at first, but then started to work sporadically. Our new night binoculars were fun and allowed us to locate the lights on the fishing boats at sea, but I still kept envisioning running into some unlit flotsam or fishing boat. But the sea was calm and the night was cloudless, and soon the sky began to lighten. We started to relax.

In the middle of the passage between the landmass of Turkey and the island of Cyprus, with many hours and many miles to go, the wind started to strengthen and the sea began to churn. Our stress levels rose dramatically. The sea worsened. *Avanti* started to bang and lurch. Bruce set her direction to quarter into the rising waves, but there are only a few degrees of direction that allow the boat to move forward into the waves without smashing into the troughs if pointed too high, or rolling around wildly if pointed too low. Even then, in big seas there is a lot of spray coming over the bow and lots of rolling between waves.

In the high winds, the spray blew sideways across the boat and the upper helm became unbearable. These were the conditions in which we would never voluntarily leave port. But we were stuck. We could hear dishes and glassware crashing in the galley.

I could no longer stand the strain and abandoned the top helm for the first time ever. I crept below and huddled under a blanket in the fetal position, refusing to look outside or acknowledge the banging going on around me. I worked on a crossword puzzle to distract myself from our certain doom. Finally even Bruce abandoned the upper helm; it was too windy and streams of sea spray constantly drenched him. He came downstairs to run the boat from the lower helm, something he had never done. Not expecting this, we had failed to remove the front window cover, so we couldn't see out the front of the boat. Bruce had to peer out the side windows. We need not have worried about running into anyone – there was no one on the sea but us. We still had hours to go. That was when I started to work on Plan B, an alternative to continuing with EMYR. It's remarkable how seldom things actually go according to Plan A. I swore that if we actually made it alive to Cyprus, I would not go through this hellish experience again.

Of course we did arrive in Cyprus and weren't permanently scarred by our experience at sea, although we were a few hours late since the high seas had required us to run the boat slowly. Other Rally members had started to worry about us. But soon the trauma was forgotten. The cold beers at the dock helped.

We found Northern Cyprus historically fascinating. We studied up on the inane dispute between the Northern Cyprus Turks and the Southern Cyprus Greeks that has kept this island divided and hostile since 1974. We visited a site where we could see dozens of big tourist hotels at the east end of the island – 10,000 beds worth of expensive high-rise hotels on the beach. The entire area is now a ghost town, utterly abandoned and fenced off because it is now incorporated into the UN buffer zone, a casualty of the Greek-Turkish hostilities.

The comfortable port town of Girne threw a huge reception for the EMYR cruisers at the ancient castle in town, attended by the President of Northern Cyprus. That was followed by a fun pirate dinner where everyone on the Rally dressed in their pirate best and marched through the town, much to the amusement of the locals. My fake severed hand was a big hit.

We knew that for us, the Rally was over. The next leg was another 100-mile passage, partly at night, followed by a night passage along the coast of Syria to Lebanon. On *Avanti*, we would be alone on these trips. The final nail in the coffin of our EMYR adventure was the report we got from other Rally members about the logs floating on the sea on the passage from Alanya to Northern Cyprus. The logs had been seen at night by a Rally boater who warned everyone else. Of course we knew nothing about them since we had no radio contact with the fleet. That was it for us. Although we had not hit any of the logs, their unknown existence along our path brought home to us the danger we faced by traveling apart from the rest of the fleet. Yet we simply couldn't travel slowly enough to stay with the sailboats.

When the fleet pulled out on its next leg, an overnight passage back to the Turkish mainland port of Mersin, we bade a fond farewell to our new friends, planning to meet them all again in Lebanon, where we thought we would fly to join up with them when the fleet arrived. Then we sat, relieved, sipping our white wine at a quiet restaurant overlooking the marina and the sea, watching the many sails on the EMYR boats disappear over the darkening horizon. Northern Cyprus proved to be the farthest east *Avanti* would travel

The next morning we embarked on the much simpler 50-mile trek back to the closest Turkish port, Bozyazi. We considered trying to visit the southern, Greek side of Cyprus, but the difficulties caused by the hostilities between the two countries were too much to overcome. We loved Northern Cyprus and felt loyal to it. So it was easy to think that we'd seen the best part of Cyprus and we didn't much care about the Greek side.

Eventually, despite our plans, we didn't make it to Lebanon because hostilities broke out there between the various often-contentious adversaries. As a result, most of the tours planned for the EMYR Rally in Lebanon and Syria were cancelled. We did manage to visit both Lebanon and Syria the next year, flying from Rome before picking up *Avanti* for the season. I even met Syrian president Bashar al-Assad. But that's another story.

Instead of visiting Lebanon, we filled the time we would have spent with the Rally by flying to Egypt and Jordan. It's that Plan B again, often far more interesting than Plan A.

.

CHAPTER 10
OUR JOURNEY IS DONE

Our visit to Northern Cyprus was as far east as *Avanti* took us. We idly thought about returning west along Northern Africa, but only Tunisia and Morocco seemed sufficiently friendly and to get there, we would have to traverse Algeria. We decided that was not a great idea.

After we left Northern Cyprus, we headed west, taking several years to retrace our steps through Turkey, Greece, Italy, France and Spain. We ended where we started, in Palma, Mallorca. We were sad that our wonderful eight years was ending, but also eager to get on with new adventures.

As it turned out, it took almost 18 months to sell *Avanti*. Our former boat broker had moved to Denia. This was sad for us since we thought him both competent and trustworthy. He recommended another broker in Palma whom we found to be neither. After a few months, we switched brokers.

We left *Avanti* in a berth in downtown Palma, hoping she would draw attention. If we had to do it again, we would have hauled her out. We learned that buyers who are genuinely interested will do a great deal of due diligence before they come to see a boat they might buy. If we had hauled her out, we would likely have been required to put her back in the water for inspection and viewing two or maybe three times, but that would have been much less costly than leaving her in the water the entire 18 months. But we didn't know and there were no impartial advisors available.

Avanti was purchased in December, 2011, by a Scottish couple. She now lives on the south coast of England. The Scots seem quite fond of her. We were pleased to learn that they did not change her name so she is still our dear *Avanti*. We wish her well.

PART II: A PRACTICAL GUIDE TO CRUISING ON A SMALL BOAT IN THE MEDITERRANEAN

CHAPTER 1
DREAMS MEET REALITY: WHERE DO WE START?

Decisions, decisions. It can get overwhelming. The issues keep coming and few are easy to resolve.

The initial decisions are personal. The answers cannot be found in a book. You have to peer into your soul, your expectations for the future and your psyche for the answers. These are the first decisions we faced, but you may have different issues or additional concerns:

1. Were we mentally and financially ready to change our schedule and retire or cut back substantially on our work?
2. Were we willing to be away from home for months at a time?
3. Would we enjoy life together on a small boat?

After we answered "yes" to all of those, or at least didn't answer with a firm "no," more decisions loomed, these a bit more susceptible to research and analysis:

1. Should we buy or lease a boat?
2. Where should we go?
3. Should we get a powerboat or a sailboat?
4. What size boat should we get?
5. What features did we want or need in a boat?

The Personal Decisions

Ready to Retire?

It is difficult to give up your life's work. Humans gain much of their personal identities from work. They are comfortable with their working life and a job provides money. While it is possible to start a major boating adventure without retiring, either a major shift in your work schedule or dropping out of the work force temporarily is almost a necessity. Neither may be conducive to a successful future career.

We concluded that full or semi-retirement seems especially hard for men whose wives don't work outside the home, as well as for their wives who have become accustomed to having the house to themselves. These men sense that home is their wives' territory, and their wives can't imagine having their husbands at home all day. Couples who both work outside the home seem to have an easier time. Neither has had control of the house and they expect an equal playing field on the home front when they retire.

Some fear the loss of their source of personal identity when they retire. There's no simple answer to this dilemma. I saw a therapist. Bruce didn't, but never seemed to have a problem. Some are so sick of working that the psychological issue is less of a problem. Others can't stand this loss and end up going back to work.

It seems to us that many who retire make major mistakes. Some simply leave work one day without a plan for what will be in store for the next day, year or decade. Many of these retirees become adrift and often end up frustrated or bored, longing to return to work. Others make big changes immediately upon retiring, such as selling their homes and moving elsewhere. These retirees sometimes return within a year or so, finding that the greener pastures weren't actually so green and that they missed their friends and familiar surroundings.

Ready to Leave Home for Long Periods?

Some people are just homebodies. The idea of being away from home, family and friends for months at a time is not palatable. Others find the logistics of leaving home for extended periods too daunting to attempt. Still others determine that maintaining a house plus having addition boat costs is prohibitive financially. For these people, life on a boat in the Mediterranean or anywhere else is probably not the right decision.

Is the Boating Life Appealing?

Boaters who have traveled extensively on small boats know the answer to this question. For the rest, even those like us who have owned small boats, the answer is not obvious. Living on a boat may sound irresistible, but the dream and the reality can differ dramatically.

Our advice is to try it out before making any rash decisions. Try chartering a sailboat or powerboat in the Caribbean, on the Intracoastal Waterway or in the San Juan Islands. Go for a week. That should give you an idea of what cruising is like and whether you can get along with your partner in such a small space. For couples, both partners need to think cruising would be a fun life. Otherwise, somebody is going to be disappointed at best and resentful at worst.

One essential characteristic for enjoying this type of life is the ability to change plans on a dime. More often than not, plans don't work out; a carefully planned itinerary is impossible to follow. There are unexpected events that shred the best of plans – bad weather, emergency repairs (often requiring needed parts to be shipped across the country) or no space in the marina where you hoped to stay. If you can't handle sudden changes and disappointments, you'll have trouble. Then there are those minor mechanical boat problems that seem to crop up constantly. You'll likely be miserable if no one on the boat has any diagnostic or repair abilities,

Where to Go?

The seas are vast and varied. Ports and harbors abound. Some areas are more logical, practical and attractive than others, but there's almost nowhere around the edges of any sea on the planet where you can't have an adventure on a boat. Some places don't work so well for powerboats because there are insufficient harbor facilities or fuel docks. Other places aren't so good for sailboats because the winds are too light or inconsistent. Some places aren't safe because of sea conditions or local bad guys – think Somalia. And some places are simply easier to get to and move about in than others. But it's a big world. There are boats designed for every location. Do you want to push away from the dock in San Francisco and head west for Honolulu? Do you think you would prefer the idyllic 3-knot pace of the canals of France? How about some raging gales off the coast of Newfoundland? There have been boats designed and built for each of these nautical treats, and they don't look or behave much like each other.

North America. For many people, travel by boat within United States waters is ideal. There are no new languages to learn, basic necessities, boat parts and fuel are always available, shops, people and places feel familiar and comfortable, and the cost to travel to and from the cruising grounds is usually manageable. The entire east coast is accessible when the weather cooperates, and cruisers regularly take off from Florida to the Caribbean or from Maine or New York's Hudson River into the Great Lakes. There is the "great loop", up the east coast from Florida, into the Great Lakes through the rivers, down the Mississippi to the Gulf of Mexico and back to Florida. From Florida and the Caribbean, truly adventurous boaters can reach the Pacific through the Panama Canal and then travel north through Central America, Mexico, California, the Pacific Northwest and Alaska. The options are plentiful.

South Pacific and Round the World. There are just as many options on other continents and seas. The Pacific waters of Fiji and the Tahitian Islands are exotic and popular though hard to reach. From there, you might as well keep on going and circle the world.

We have met many intrepid sailors who have done just that, voyaging through the sometimes pirate-infested waters of Java and Borneo, past India, the Seychelles and Madagascar, then into the Red Sea and through the Suez Canal to the Mediterranean. Our personal view is that this route is followed only by the extremely brave or the seriously deranged. We have heard tales of pirates and bandits attacking cruisers, among other disasters. We're just not as adventurous as some and prefer to remain in calmer waters.

We have met these apparently deranged sailors in the Mediterranean, many of them Americans or Australians, who have circled the world, ending up in the Mediterranean, the quietest and most "civilized" leg of their journey, before taking on an Atlantic crossing. They did not appear to be insane, but we knew they were. We met one round-the-world traveler from San Francisco in the bathroom in the marina in Barcelona where she was calmly dying her own hair, lamenting the loss of the fancy San Francisco beauty salon she left behind. In San Francisco, she had owned a chain of high-end women's clothing boutiques, but closed them down to travel with her husband on an around-the-world adventure on their 60-foot sailboat. They planned to spend only a couple of years at sea, but when we met them, they had been traveling for over ten years. She was funny and gracious, and provided me with a much-needed hot tip: a woman on a boat down the dock from us gave great haircuts for only $12. I found her.

Another American sailor in Barcelona hailed originally from our hometown of Newport Beach. He pulled into the harbor in Barcelona ten years earlier and hadn't left.

We met a young couple in Turkey who had left California on a 32-foot sailboat in the mid-90s, stopping in Australia long enough for the birth of their daughter, then heading around India, through the Red Sea and Suez Canal. The husband told me that they planned to sell their boat since they were expecting their second child. That seemed to be a rational course of action. "Okay," I thought, "they've come to their senses. They'll go home and settle down." I was wrong. They had decided to buy a larger boat that would accommodate two kids.

We met sailors who were off the coast of Thailand when the huge tsunami hit in 2004. They didn't initially notice the huge waves since they were at sea, but their tales of bodies, shoes and children's toys floating by them over the following days were chilling.

The South Pacific and round-the-world sailors are a distinct breed, willing to be on "blue water" out of sight of land for days or weeks on end, valuing the adventure and danger over the luxuries of a hot shower and a good meal with a bottle of wine at a local tavern. We are of the more slothful, luxury-loving breed. We need a shower every day, a cozy restaurant, tasty food, and the sense that we are safe. Yet those crazy round-the-worlders who refused to go home were present in every marina and harbor we visited. The cruising experience can be so enthralling and heady that people just keep going.

The Mediterranean. This was our choice. To us the benefits were obvious. Many people in this area speak English, yet the culture of each country is unique and fascinating. Most harbors were built in ancient times and are still surrounded by ancient city centers. The old harbors are too small for modern commercial and military ships, so they have been turned over to fishing fleets and yachties like us. These harbors are a treasure for boaters. Beyond the docks stand ancient city walls, forts, cathedrals and palaces, many of them illuminated at night. The docks are frequently lined with local outdoor markets, tavernas and cafes only a few feet away, and the view from the aft deck of our boat in most harbors far surpasses the views from even the most expensive hotel in town. We could usually sit on our deck at any time of day or night, watching the busy local scene unfolding before us. The best example was Venice, where we pulled into a private marina on San Giorgio Island, directly across from St. Mark's Square. For a marina fee of about $30 per day, we enjoyed electricity, water and the most impressive view of Venice imaginable, which we enjoyed on board over drinks in the evening and breakfast in the morning.

In the Mediterranean, the distance between ports is ideal. Towns built in ancient and medieval times had to be close enough to each other to be reachable in one day by foot, horse or rowed boat. Our longest days were always less than 100 miles, and 40 to 60 miles was more typical. At our cruising speed of 12 knots, that meant our travel days at sea were usually not more than five hours.

For us, the Mediterranean was perfect.

What Type of Boat?

Sailboat or Powerboat?

There is no right or wrong answer to this question. Don't listen to the fanatics espousing either sail or power. There are many variables to consider.

Where Do You Want to Travel? If you decide to go around the world, your only practical choice is a sailboat, if only because of the distinct lack of fuel stations in the middle of the ocean. However, you can cross the ocean by powerboat on a breed of trawler, usually more than 50 feet long, designed specifically to cruise oceans and to carry the fuel it needs along with it. It relies on a relatively small single engine to maintain a speed of seven or eight knots. You won't have any trouble recognizing these boats because the builders advertise their long-range capability on every page of their magazine ads. Most other powerboats are intended for coastal cruising and are too fuel-needy for ocean voyaging. Coastal cruisers also need frequent engine maintenance and repairs, and perhaps more importantly, a safe berth in a storm.

Most cruisers agree that places such as Tahiti or the Caribbean are perfect for sailboats. The attraction is the open water sailing itself rather than land-based visiting and sightseeing. Cruisers in these locations sail with the trade winds for days, and anchor in protected bays when near land. Onshore facilities are generally limited or absent. Distances between islands are often great, requiring that most time on board be spent en route from one destination to the next, so the ability of a good cruising sailboat to stay out for days or weeks with no land-based help is important. Boats built for that kind of cruising, and their crews, need to be extremely self-reliant and capable of managing all kinds of seas and repairs.

The Pacific Northwest and Alaska are best for powerboats. Although the weather can be cold and rainy for much of the year, many of the best cruising grounds in these areas are protected from violent seas. Being in bad weather for extended periods is more pleasant on a powerboat than a sailboat, not only for the roomier, more comfortable indoor living space, but also the better visibility and better protection when piloting the boat. When the winds are quirky, and often non-existent, as they are in the Pacific Northwest, powerboats make sense since sailboats must spend so much time motoring anyway.

In the Mediterranean, either a sailboat or powerboat is just fine. If your planned cruising grounds are as benign as the Mediterranean, your decision depends on your personal tastes and desires. Most boaters in the Mediterranean travel by sailboat, but there is a large contingent of powerboats. We were swayed by the benefits of a powerboat in the Mediterranean. First, the winds are inconsistent. During the spring-to-fall season, a week can pass with no wind at all, when all travel must be by power, followed by another week with winds so high that sails cannot be hoisted. So there is little opportunity for actual sailing during much of the Mediterranean summer. On the other hand, fuel is far more costly in Europe than the United States, making sailboats more economical. The second benefit of power is that passages between ports are often 50 miles, sometimes farther, and this distance often takes a sailboat ten hours or more, requiring an early start, when the sun is rising, or an evening arrival, when the sun is setting. Given the higher speeds of powerboats, a day starting at ten in the morning and ending by three or four in the afternoon is usually feasible.

Try Chartering First. To help answer the question of which type of boat to choose, try a bareboat charter for a week on the one you are least familiar with, or maybe a week on each. Chartering companies can be found on the Internet. Two of the oldest and largest charter companies are The Moorings and Sunsail, but there are dozens of others. At both The Moorings and Sunsail even power catamarans are now available for charter. You need to be experienced on the water, or take a few lessons, but most places will provide lessons or even provide an instructor to go along with you if you prefer (of course at a higher cost). The cost is not cheap but not outlandish either – often $2000 and $4000 per week – sometimes a little less expensive for a sailboat. If you remember that the boat is also your accommodation for the week, and may have enough space for a few friends to go along and help pay, it's not so bad. And it is worth the cost if it helps you make some important decisions.

Basic Differences Between Sail and Power. It helps to consider the basic advantages and disadvantages of sailboats and powerboats in deciding which is right for you.

Sailboats. Sailboats have some real advantages.

- Cost. First, and most important for many, sailboats are generally less expensive. The initial cost of the boat is substantially less than for a powerboat of the same length. A sailboat from 36 to 50 feet long, about the right size for cruising, can be acquired new for less than $250,000, and used sailboats in good shape can be found for under $100,000. In addition, the cost to own and maintain a sailboat is substantially less, partly because sailboats, even under power, use so much less fuel than powerboats, and also because the mechanical parts are not so large, sophisticated, breakable or expensive.

- <u>Range</u>. Since sailboats use substantially less fuel, they have the ability to travel a greater distance between mandatory fuel stops. This provides traveling flexibility. Powerboats appropriate for the Mediterranean need not have a range of more than 200 miles. In many parts of the world, finding dependable sources of clean fuel en route is a major problem, so a powerboat with such a short range is highly risky. A powerboat that has run out of fuel is a disaster – sailboats without fuel can at least put up their sails to get back to port.

- <u>Stability</u>. Sailboats are more stable in rough seas and high winds since much of their weight is in their keels below the water line, and their hulls are designed to ride with the water rather than try to force it out of the way. When storms hit us and winds came up unexpectedly, with choppy waves of four feet or more, our boat performed badly with its shallow hull. A sailboat would be more comfortable in those conditions.

Powerboats. Of course powerboats have their own advantages. Many powerboat travelers began as sailors. We fit that category. In our eyes, powerboats were always "stinkpots." We ended up overcoming our pro-sailboat bias and started appreciating the advantages of powerboats.

- <u>Speed</u>. Powerboats get you to your destination faster than sailboats. Even under power, a sailboat rarely moves as fast as its maximum hull speed, which for a 40-foot boat is about seven or eight knots (one knot, or one nautical mile per hour is about ten percent faster than one regular mile per hour, so we usually think of them as roughly the same). Its hull speed is limited by the so-called bow wave that the boat creates in front of it as it moves through the water. The same is theoretically true for a full-displacement powerboat, such as many of the older Grand Banks trawlers, but with sufficiently big engines and enough horsepower, even the newer full-displacement boats can reach or exceed their theoretical maximum hull speed by a few knots. Although it's not pretty at the fuel pump the next day, those extra knots can make a big difference on a long day's cruise. We found the Grand Banks trawlers too slow for our taste, but others adore them. A semi-displacement boat can get its hull up and "plane" across the water, traveling over the top of the bow wave it creates. This allows it to go faster, but also uses more fuel. Our boat could go as fast as 20 knots in a pinch, and travel comfortably all day at 12 to 15 knots. For us, the little bit of extra speed was important for two reasons. First, we could quickly get away from a dangerous or uncomfortable situation, like an approaching storm. And second, we could spend more time in port and less on the water, important to someone like me who loves being in an interesting European port more than spending hours on the water. A powerboat can leave a port later than the sailboats and still beat the sailors to the next port. This is an enormous benefit both for enjoying the towns along the way and also because available berths in most Mediterranean marinas are not unlimited. Since they are allocated on a first-come first-serve basis, early arrivers have the advantage in snagging a berth. A grueling twelve-hour trip in a sailboat took us only a comfortable four to five hour.

- Comfort. Powerboats are more comfortable. This was crucial for us since we planned to live on the boat for months at a time. We appreciate comfort. Most of the living area in a powerboat is above rather than below the water line. In cold weather this means the cabin stays warmer because it is not surrounded by the heat-robbing effect of a cold sea outside a thin layer of fiberglass. More important for us was being able to sit inside on a cold evening or during foul weather, surveying our surroundings through the large windows in the main saloon, something not possible in most sailboats. Our boat also had an upper deck, allowing us a high perch for watching the world when the weather was good.

Size

By the time we were ready to get serious about buying, we had chartered three boats, ranging from 32 to 42 feet. The 32 and 36 foot boats seemed too small. They might be fine for the two of us, but we wanted room for friends and family to visit. We decided that a boat length of 40 to 45 feet would be big enough for the two of us plus a couple of guests, but small enough to manage without a crew, and would fit our budget. For those picking a sailboat, a larger size might be fine. Larger sailboats can be easier to handle than equivalent sized powerboats. We have seen two novices handle sailboats up to 60 feet by themselves. Since sailboats are less costly, a larger one might still fit your budget. If you're not planning on having guests – and we met several people who couldn't imagine wanting guests aboard – a smaller boat should work fine. And although we think they are mentally deficient, we met people who happily sailed their 30 to 40 foot sailboats across the oceans without a problem.

One thing we did not consider, because we didn't know we should, is that some of the loveliest harbors in the Mediterranean are too small for boats much larger than about 40 feet. We also learned that the overnight prices for marina berths are based on boat length, so the cost of berthing fees for a larger boat can add significantly to your operating costs.

Other Important Features

Visit an in-the-water boat show to check out the many types of boats on the market. There are differences in bedroom layouts, decks, air conditioning, speed, age, number of heads and showers, types of toilets, types of fuel used (diesel versus gasoline), and on and on.

- Boat Layout

This is a matter of personal taste. We prefer the master stateroom at the stern of the boat (called an "aft cabin") with a smaller guest stateroom in front. Aft cabin bedrooms are usually large with a head and shower. Having the guest bedroom at the other end of the boat, with its own head and sink (but often no shower), provides both the owners and their guests some privacy.

We also like having a flying bridge (also known as an upper helm) where we could pilot the boat with great visibility, sit outside in good weather and enjoy the view of the passing scenery. We had the ability to pilot the boat from inside the main cabin (the lower helm) on *Avanti*, but we seldom used it. In bad weather, it's useful to be able to run the boat from inside, but our philosophy has always been that if the weather is that bad, we shouldn't be on the water.

Finally, a large deck area to sit outside for drinks and meals is a must. For us, living outside on our boat is an important part of the cruising experience. When spending the warm summer season on a boat, it makes sense to look for a boat that lets you enjoy the sun and the view. But an area of shade on the deck is important since the sun is out almost all day every day, and no one wants to make constant trips to the dermatologist to remove those irritating pre-cancerous skin growths.

- Engines.

Gas vs. Diesel: Bruce is convinced that diesel is safer and more dependable. Gasoline fumes are explosive; diesel fumes are not. Since we had a fuel leak in each of our engines at two different times, both resulting in a puddle of raw fuel in the bilge compartment under the engine, we are adamant about the safety issues associated with fuel. There is not much difference in price between the two fuels. It also seems to Bruce that diesel engines are more dependable than gasoline engines. Diesel engines are heavier, but weight and fuel efficiency continue to get better in the newer models.

Engine Size: The size of the engine you select is important. Buying too small an engine means you give up the ability to pick up speed at a time that going fast may be helpful or even necessary. But buying an engine larger than you need isn't a good idea. Diesel engines are supposed to run in the range of 60 to 90 percent of their maximum power. Constantly cruising at a speed below the boat's optimal speed can produce maintenance problems. When the engine runs too slowly, the carbon in the diesel fuel fails to properly vaporize and the engine will eventually clog with unoxidized carbon. Look for a boat with a cruising speed (not top speed) that correlates with the speed you most enjoy. For us, that meant we should not buy one of those fast Italian gas-guzzlers, which cruise at a blistering speed we find uncomfortable, nor would we like a full displacement trawler that tops out at under ten knots.

Single vs. Twin Engines: There are differing opinions as to whether a single engine is "just as good" as two engines. The major argument in favor of a single engine is that it uses less fuel. Since many of the problems with diesel engines come from dirty fuel and most twin engines run off the same fuel tank, if a single engine has a problem, there's a good chance that both will. We had a number of problems with engines over the many thousands of nautical miles we cruised. The load of dirty fuel we took on in Greece did indeed wipe out both engines in a heartbeat. But we had a number of problems that affected only a single engine, and the second engine made a huge difference. When we had a fuel leak in one engine, we just shut that engine down and kept cruising until we could get the faulty engine repaired. We're convinced that two engines are better than one.

- Holding Tank

One problem with our boat was its undersized holding tank – the tank that holds toilet wastes until they can be discharged into the sea at least three miles offshore or pumped out at an on-shore pump-out station. The holding tank size is not a characteristic that drives many boat decisions, but it is something to ask about. Our holding tank filled up in a couple of days, more quickly if we had visitors. We tried to use marina toilets as much as possible. Our small holding tank was a big nuisance.

Most U.S. marinas are equipped with pump-out stations where the holding tank can be emptied. We were appalled to learn that pump-out stations are almost non-existent in the Mediterranean. We saw only one or two in eight years of cruising. In actuality, many boaters in the Mediterranean never seem to use a holding tank anyway, even in the marina. This is sometimes obvious from the foul aroma wafting from a local boat. Turkey takes the hardest line on holding tank usage and there were rumors of huge fines levied there on boaters who had emptied their holding tanks inside the 3-mile limit. But even in Turkey, there are few pump-out stations. In our experience, holding tanks are rarely used in Spain, France and Italy. Gross. Remember that before you dive into your marina for a swim.

CHAPTER 2
BUYING THAT BOAT

You've made the decision to go. You've decided where to go and whether to buy a sailboat or a powerboat. You've made a list of the most important features you want in your boat.

Now it's time to start looking.

Where to Buy

The first step is obvious: the Internet. An amazing amount of information is available at your fingertips on the Internet. There are websites loaded with boats for sale, with multiple photos of each boat, so it's fairly easy to figure out how the boat is laid out, its condition, its amenities, and of course its price. The number of boats for sale may give you pause – why are all those people selling their boats if owning one is so much fun? Whatever the reason, it's just your luck that there are so many boats to choose from, and they are located all over the world. Two of the largest boat-selling sites, www.yachtworld.com and www.boats.com, each post well over 150,000 boats for sale. There are many other sites. Most boats for sale are listed on multiple sites, but the numbers alone tell you that you have plenty of boats to choose from.

Bruce does not believe in buying a new boat, mostly because they arrive from the factory with few accessories, so in addition to paying the big bucks (or euros or yen) for the boat itself, you must spend another fortune on needed equipment. Those missing items include a dinghy with outboard motor, a life raft, much of the desirable electronic navigation equipment, interior furnishings, lines, anchors and power winches. When somebody else has owned the boat, most of those accessories are already aboard and outfitting the boat to your needs is much simpler and less expensive.

We decided to buy our boat in Europe. Some people ship their powerboats from the U.S. on various transport ships such as DYT or SevenStar, but at a hefty price. Many U.S. sailboat owners sail their boats across the Atlantic. We've noticed that those decisions to brave the crossing are often made late at night at a local watering hole somewhere on the Chesapeake or in coastal Florida, but most of the sailors who try it actually do arrive safely in Gibraltar after a few weeks. One problem with bringing a boat from the U.S. is the difference in the electrical set-up for shore power: the 110-volt system on U.S. boats is not compatible with the 220-volt European power sources.

We learned from the Internet sites that most of the available boats were of no interest to us. There were lots of sailboats, but we had already ruled them out. There were many sleek, racy Italian powerboats. But those ostentatious Italian ones are designed to go fast in protected waters; they are not designed for living aboard, nor are they fuel-efficient in the least. We were able to locate about a dozen boats with the basics we were seeking – a semi-displacement motor yacht capable of cruising at 12 to 15 knots, with twin diesel engines, a small guest cabin in the bow and an aft cabin for us.

The available powerboats in the Mediterranean that fit our needs were clustered in a few locations, mostly where many British and Germans congregate for the winter. The most interesting were in Mallorca and Barcelona. We emailed inquiries. Some boat brokers were responsive. Some were not.

The Search and Sale

If you choose to buy your boat in the Mediterranean, you'll likely need at least one and maybe two trips to Europe to find it.

We found a British broker we thought was trustworthy and competent in Palma, Mallorca, the location of most boats of interest to us. Much like a real estate broker, a boat broker works primarily to get the deal done, but is paid by the seller (usually about ten percent of the sale price), so is not technically representing the buyer. At the same time, many boats, including *Avanti*, are not sold like houses through an exclusive broker, so you can pick the broker you like and he (or rarely she) will work with both you and the seller.

Our new broker took us to see *Avanti* and we decided to pursue her, but we took our time once we learned that she had been for sale for over a year. After a month or so, we reached an oral agreement with the seller through our broker.

Like most agreements, in order to be binding, the purchase agreement must be in writing and should include the price, which accessories (dinghy and outboard motor, life raft, linens, plates and cookware, etc.) will be included in the sale, an option to drop out of the deal if the marine surveyor finds serious problems, and any other conditions that seem important, such as obtaining any necessary financing. Your broker will have the standard form, but there is no substitute for carefully reading and understanding the contract yourself. Take time to think about the contract conditions that are important to you. This may be the last time you have a position of power in negotiations. Make sure there is a legal search of ownership and outstanding liens, in addition to obtaining a warranty of title from the seller. The warranty requires the seller to take responsibility for any undisclosed obligations to a third party, such as the marina, repair yard or anyone else who claims some rights against the boat. Unfortunately, a violation of this warranty may require a lawsuit to enforce, a difficult if not impossible task for an American in Europe. But most sellers will think twice before providing an untrue warranty and an honest seller who is unaware of a title problem may in fact cure a problem discovered after the sale closes without a lawsuit.

The Boat Survey and Sea Trial

Every boat sale should require a professional boat survey and sea trial. Often this is performed by the professional surveyor with neither the buyer nor seller present. Nearly all of the boat's operating systems (electrical, fresh water, waste water, fuel, engine and transmission, to name a few) seem to be either hidden behind some wall or understood only by professionals, so you are not likely to find most problems by examining the boat yourself. The marine surveyor goes through the boat in a systematic way, examining each element for its condition and performance, then prepares a long (10 to 20 pages) report that summarizes all the problems he could find with the boat's systems. Invariably, a few problems do crop up in the surveyor's report, so you have the opportunity to figure out how much extra money you might have to put into the boat to bring it to top condition, and whether the seller should help you by paying for the fixes or lowering the price, or whether the problems are so major that you should drop out of the sale. Negotiations between the buyer and seller usually resolve these issues. Part of the surveyor's job is to inspect the boat when it is out of the water – meaning a boat already in the water will need to be hauled out – to check for blisters in the fiberglass hull and problems with the propellers or the rudders, among other issues. The surveyor requires that all the boat systems be turned on to demonstrate that they operate correctly, and he takes the boat to sea to observe how it runs at full power. We hired a local marine surveyor recommended by our broker, but only after we confirmed through our insurance broker that he had the reputation as a tough boat critic. Even our highly-regarded surveyor failed to find what proved to be a big and expensive engine problem, so a survey doesn't give you a 100% assurance that all is well. Our surveyor did find a number of problems that the seller repaired before the sale was completed.

Berthing, Registration, Insurance, Repairs and Maintenance

Owning a boat in a foreign country is more complicated than owning a car at home, but there are a lot of similarities. As a foreigner, you sometimes get the benefit of the doubt from authorities when you don't follow all the rules, so it's worth trying to fake it if you make a mistake.

<u>Berthing.</u> Fortunately, no immediate action was necessary for us to find a spot for *Avanti* since we were able to keep her in place (at an additional cost). Otherwise, we would have had to find a new spot immediately. I expect our broker could have worked this out, but finding a new berth may be an important contract contingency. You can't just park a boat on the street.

<u>Registration.</u> We had to register *Avanti* someplace. Since the Iraq war was pending and it was clear that we Americans were not going to be popular in Europe, and since it seemed that the new millennium world was filled with America-hating terrorists, we were nervous about registering her as a U.S. boat. Because a boat is legally required to fly the flag of the country where it's registered, the only way to avoid the potentially confrontational, terrorist-attracting U.S. flag would be to register her in another country. We learned that it is possible to do just that, but would require us to create a corporation in that other country and have the new corporation hold title. This seemed to be far too much of a hassle for the potential risk. We decided that if we flew the U.S. "anchor" flag, any random terrorist would likely be confused and think we came from some strange Caribbean tax-shelter country. We hired an American boat registry consultant to handle the actual registration (called documentation) with the U.S. Coast Guard. Since the boat would not actually be in the U.S., we did not need to register her in any specific state and thus were not required to pay any state sales tax, although California still made an effort to get us to pay. The Coast Guard documentation process is simple and inexpensive. The documentation papers must be shown in every marina you visit. File a copy of the bill of sale with the Coast Guard as soon as you purchase a boat and keep the registration document they send you with the boat at all times.

We agonized over changing *Avanti's* name, but finally decided against it. But we did replace the bulky square version of her name on her stern with a nicer script version. We added the name of our town, Corona del Mar, as her home port, but we did not include the state or country. We figured the ever-lurking terrorist would assume we were from Spain. Of course the name *Avanti* is Italian which we figured would confuse mad bombers even further. We ordered the new vinyl script stick-on name from our local West Marine, our new favorite store, and when we returned to Mallorca, it was a simple job to scrape off the old letters and stick on the new.

Insurance. Our boat broker directed us to a local Mallorca boat insurance broker who obtained insurance for us from a British company for under $2000 a year. We never strayed from that broker. We never had a problem. In our eighth year, we had a claim for fiberglass damage that cost $10,000, of which the insurance company paid $8000. The following year our premium did not increase. That seemed odd to us, but we were pleased. The company provided the necessary papers to enter every port that asked for insurance documents, including a Greek language version required by ports and marinas in Greece. Insurance rates have gone up a bit over the years and tend to increase as one goes farther east in the Mediterranean. Our most expensive year was when we were in Turkey but the cost was still less than $2500 a year. It went back down again once we were back in Western Europe.

Repairs and Maintenance. Inevitably, the marine surveyor will find a few boat problems and there are maintenance requirements that always pop up when you take possession of your boat. For us, the immediate expenses included an oil change (15 quarts in each engine) and a new coat of anti-fouling paint to keep barnacles and other creatures from making their homes on her hull. When anti-fouling paint is needed, it's common to also change the "zincs," which are there to be sure that any random electrical circuits flowing through the boat corrode the disposable zinc anodes rather than any working metal boat parts such as props or rudders. It all seems complicated, but good boat yard mechanics know all about these things and will be able to advise you and complete the work competently. A good boat broker knows all the local mechanics. Unless you feel especially comfortable with the inner workings of a boat, it's best to rely on professionals.

The cold realization that your boat expenses did not end when you forked over the purchase price will likely hit you when you get your first bill for repairs or maintenance. We were told to budget around ten percent of the purchase price for annual repairs and maintenance. Fortunately, the amount we actually spent was substantially less, but we often made up the difference by buying new equipment. If you start off with the understanding that you need to budget those repair and maintenance dollars, the impact of a $1000 anti-fouling paint job becomes more palatable. At $200 per gallon for the anti-fouling paint, you might feel pretty good that you still have some money left over in the budget to cover that $600 oil change.

CHAPTER 3
PUTTING YOUR HOME LIFE IN ORDER:
THOSE PESKY DETAILS

We have a long checklist of "to do's" that we pulled out each year before we left home for Europe. The first year, we spent many hours preparing the list and working out all the details. After the first year, we could quickly copy the old list and make the appropriate tweaks for that year.

Here is our "bare bones" list:

1. Prepare the house
2. Store the car(s)
3. Arrange for mail delivery and cancel newspapers
4. Arrange to pay bills
5. Handle pet issues
6. Arrange communications with home
7. Notify banks and credit card companies; prepare to get money abroad from ATM machines
8. Prepare a list of what to take

Of course each of these categories has many subcategories. But it's important to make sure you have a focus on all the major matters that need to be resolved.

The House

We thought of three possibilities for our house; there may be more. Your choice will likely depend on how long you plan to be away, how comfortable you are leaving your house empty, and the health of your finances.

The first option – clearly the most drastic – is to sell your house. We met many Americans who had done just that. Most now live on their boats all year, but some traded their houses for small condos, often near their grown children. Many people plan to down-size at about the time they retire anyway, so this option may not be as dramatic as it first appears.

Those who sell their homes usually become all-year cruisers. Winter in the Mediterranean can be rough; storms and cold weather are a challenge. As a result, all-year cruisers usually pick a marina in one of the warmer parts of the Mediterranean and settle in for the winter. They may take their boats out to sea for a few days at a time, but only during calm spells. We never "wintered over," but we hear it's fun, especially in certain trendy marinas where large communities of boaters spend the winter.

Many marinas work hard to attract boaters who winter over. They offer an extensive menu of winter delights. The marina in Kemer, Turkey, just west of Antalya, is famous for its off-season program. We stayed in Kemer for a couple of weeks and saw the wonderful setup, with a convivial dining room and bar, tennis courts, well-stocked library with books in many languages, and even a sewing room handy for sailors needing to make winter sail repairs. The list of events and activities planned for the marina "residents" includes trips to nearby Antalya for the theater, symphony and ballet, Turkish language lessons, ski trips to the local mountains and frequent movies in the dining room. Other marinas don't need any special activities to attract winter visitors – they are in the middle of exciting, vibrant places. Barcelona is one. The marina in Dubrovnik is also extremely popular for wintering. Reserving a spot in the most desirable winter marinas can be difficult.

The second option is simply to close up the house while you're away or ask someone to house-sit. Relatives or friends can often be recruited to house-sit. This is the perfect job for those unemployed adult children. If you leave your house unoccupied, be sure to let the neighbors and the local police department know how to reach you, and to designate someone to be responsible for making emergency decisions. You never know when a water heater will start to leak or a storm will drop a big branch on your roof.

The third option is the one we chose – renting our house. Bruce and I argued for a few months about whether this was a good idea. We planned to be gone for five months during our first cruising year but we also planned to take a break to return home for a few weeks. A return home during mid-summer would be more complicated if we had no place to stay.

Bruce opposed renting; he thought renting would be far too much trouble. He also thought it was risky and would endanger the vulnerable or valuable possessions we own. And he wanted to be able to stay at home during our summer break. He agreed that the income from renting would be nice, but argued that it would not balance the inconvenience and risks. His vote was to leave the house vacant and ask my sister to check on it now and then.

I was in favor of renting. We live near the beach in Southern California, a magnet for summer visitors. I thought we could find a good, responsible renter. I admitted that it would be ugly preparing the house – at least the first time – but I also thought it would be good discipline for us to clean out our house. Valuable possessions? I disagreed with Bruce. We have little of real economic value – a couple of TVs maybe, but they would be hard to steal. I figured we could safely store the things with sentimental value. I argued that someone living in the house would be the safest course; an empty house could be an invitation to trouble. We could protect ourselves by making sure we had creditworthy tenants and by insisting on a big security deposit.

Bruce finally agreed to try renting, but only if the right person came along. I agreed.

Part of our rental offer included our paying for our pool service and gardener, as well as all utilities other than gas and electricity. Having the tenant pay gas and electricity made sense since these are costs they can control, and we were nervous about the cost of extensive use of our gas-greedy outdoor Jacuzzi. We wanted to make sure that the pool and garden were properly maintained so we were willing to foot those bills. We also decided to provide the cleaning services of the woman who cleans our house weekly, in part to have a friendly pair of eyes on the place, and in part because we couldn't bear to tell our loyal helper that she had no job for the next few months. We paid for the cable TV and high-speed Internet connection after finding that it was more work than it was worth to cancel them and restart them upon our return. We decided to put a block on our long distance phone service but the phone company never did get that one right. The failed block wasn't an issue since the tenant never abused the long-distance service and reimbursed us for his few long distance calls. We put clauses in our lease giving us the right to come back into the house to get our clothes when we were home, and to allow my sister to stop by the house to keep an eye on it and care for some of the plants.

Our plan was a success. A congenial businessman from Colorado with a temporary consulting job in the LA area rented the house for five months. His financial status was impeccable. We had a good lease and a big security deposit. Our listing realtor was a big help.

The amount we received in rent was enough to cover our mortgage payments, property taxes, homeowner's insurance and all the services we provided, plus a little extra. We spent a dreary month cleaning out the house and trudging to Goodwill with countless car-loads of bags and boxes filled with stuff we clearly didn't need. It was grueling, but after that ugly first-year clean-out, the process in subsequent years was relatively easy. We handled the storage problem by reserving our study and one or two hall closets for our own belongings. This made a huge difference. Instead of hauling all our possessions to some remote storage facility, we walked them down the hall and stacked them in boxes in our study. We replaced the study's doorknob with a lockable one and locked it when we left.

Since we rented the house furnished, we left all our furniture, linens and dishes in place, removing only items with sentimental value. We prepared a 20-page instruction book explaining everything about the house. Bruce actually learned a few new things once he was forced to explain in written detail why some of the electric switches on the wall seemed to be wired to nothing or how to take apart the built-in vacuum system to clean the tank.

The first year couldn't have gone better. During the summer our water heater started to leak badly. We would have had major damage had no one been in the house. Our tenant immediately identified the leak and the water heater was replaced in one day. Then our top-of-the-line (i.e., overpriced) refrigerator stopped working, and the tenant and realtor got that repaired in a couple days. The house looked great when we returned. It helped that our tenant knew to call our real estate agent when something went wrong. Our agent found just the right property maintenance person to solve all problems. We later left a list of trusted repair people for our tenant to call directly if a problem arose.

The next year, we rented the house to a different tenant, a family that regularly escapes from the hot Palm Springs desert to the beach during the summer. We worried about the risk of their children drowning in our swimming pool, but that proved unfounded. The two talented, well-behaved daughters spent their summers swimming competitively for a local club team. They were our tenants for nine years. I knew we were fine when my sister came to check on the house and told me that, frankly, it looked better than when we live there. She likes to rub that sort of thing in.

The problem of where to stay when we returned during the summer also worked out well. We took up offers to stay in friends' spare rooms when home for only a few days. When home for over two weeks, we were fortunate to have friends who offered to let us house-sit while they were away. If friends with vacant rooms or houses are not available, it's not that expensive to stay at a local hotel for a few days.

We made sure to let our homeowner's insurance company know that our house was being rented. We were always assured that it wasn't necessary, but you never know.

The Cars

Like the house decision, what to do with cars can be tricky. Selling is an option that makes sense if you plan to be gone for a year or more. But if you plan to leave home for only part of the year, you're not likely to want to go through the cost and hassle of constantly buying and selling cars.

If you leave your house vacant or have a house-sitter, your cars can be left at home in your garage. If you rent your house, you'll likely have to find someplace else to leave cars so your renters have space for their cars.

As the not-so-proud owners of three cars, we had problems. Since we have a three-car garage, we provided for only two spots for the tenant in our lease, allowing us to leave our old 1949 Dodge in the third space. That wasn't a problem for our tenants.

But we still had two other cars. If you ask around among your relatives and friends and offer nice gifts (good wine for example), someone may find an available space for a car. But two cars presented a problem.

One year we left our aging minivan on the street – not a great idea. A neighbor finally complained to the city, apparently fed up with seeing it every day. The car was tagged for towing, but by luck we arrived home and moved it just before the tow truck arrived.

Another year I rented a space in the garage at my office for one of our cars at a reasonable rate, and Bill, the kindly building night-caretaker, kept an eye on it.

Later we left one car in my sister's garage. And for several years we left one of our cars (and sometimes our dog, who didn't want to revisit Greece with us, or visit Turkey at all) with our daughter and her husband in Sacramento. They liked having our car available for trips since it was larger than theirs.

One year we rented a spot for one car in a car storage facility. The cost wasn't too bad – less than $100 per month. We bought a car cover and the car was fine when we returned, although it took a visit from AAA to get the engine started. No matter how we have stored them over the years, nearly all of our cars have suffered from dead batteries after a couple months of storage. Even having a friend start a car every few weeks may not suffice to keep the battery charged. Bruce solved this problem by buying cheap plug-in battery chargers at Sears and the batteries were fine after that. He suggests using one that stops charging when the battery is fully charged. Other types keep "trickle" charging, which can result in an overheated battery that boils off the water in the cells and ruins the battery. Make sure to get the right kind.

Mail Delivery

Mail delivery can be a problem. Relying on mail forwarding by the U.S. Postal Service is sometimes a throw of the dice. Regardless of how carefully we did our paperwork at the post office, even after discussing the forwarding with our letter carrier, we didn't receive all of our mail. It was sometimes returned to the sender with the notation that we had moved and had no forwarding address. The problem was usually caused by a substitute letter carrier on our route.

Initially we forwarded mail to my office, where my assistant could open it and email us with a list of anything important we received.

After four years of retirement, I lost my assistant at work so we started forwarding the mail to my daughter, who didn't much appreciate the responsibility of looking over our mail.

A post box could work also, but you still may need someone to check through the mail for important items. It's amazing what shows up in the mail over a few months.

And don't forget to cancel your newspaper, assuming you're one of the rare breed that still reads one.

Paying Bills

Given the problems with mail, we now opt to pay nearly all of our bills automatically. Most credit card companies, utility companies and mortgage holders offer this service. It sometimes takes several weeks to set this up, so don't leave it to the last minute. At first we worried about paying credit card bills we hadn't seen, but credit card rights include the right to challenge charges for up to 60 days after the bill is sent. Many credit card companies permit viewing your bill details on-line which can be done from your smart phone or a convenient Internet cafe.

On-line banking also allows automatic payments. We pay amounts that are the same each month in this way, such as the pool service, car payments, and the gardener.

Those few creditors who don't allow automatic bank payments are the biggest problem. Some will send email statements if requested and those can be reviewed on line and paid through on-line banking. Some send only paper bills, even if an email is requested. The stop-gap measure is to have forwarded mail reviewed by a friend or relative for bills that slip through the cracks. This is a big burden to place on someone, but if your mail helper knows what to look for – maybe just doctor and dentist bills – it can be manageable. The bill details can then be emailed to you and the bills paid through on-line banking. In eight years we had only one glitch, with a resulting late fee, but that's not much different than our similar failures at home.

Pets

What to do with beloved pets can be an emotional issue. Leaving them at a kennel doesn't work well except for short periods. Animal-loving relatives or friends are an option if they are willing. We often care for my sister's dog when she's away and she cares for ours. Most boaters we met either no longer have pets, or have children or close relatives who are willing to take them for long periods.

The other alternative, which was our choice, is to take your dog or cat along. Details on how to take a pet along with you are in this Practical Guide under a separate chapter.

Communications

Communications is one of the hottest topics among boaters and one of the biggest issues when living abroad on a boat. It's also an area that is constantly changing as new services come on line. Everyone wants to know how others are communicating with home without spending a fortune. The good news is that every year communications systems get easier, faster, and cheaper. So do your research. What we describe here is undoubtedly out of date.

Mobile Phone

Mobile phones are a good example of a constantly changing service. What we learned the first year was totally irrelevant several years later. But still there are some basic issues to consider.

The first thing we learned about phoning home from Europe was that using our American cell phone in Europe, if it was possible at all, was prohibitively expensive. So before we left, we purchased an "unlocked", "tri-band" cell phone. In the U.S., most phones provided by your service provider are "locked," meaning that they can be used only on their network. Each cell phone contains a SIM chip that connects the phone to the cellular network. In the locked phones, only your provider's SIM chip works. In the unlocked phone, a new SIM chip from a different service provider can be slipped into the slot in the phone which then connects you to that service's network.

Once in Europe, you can buy a local phone that contains a SIM chip (either locked or unlocked) or just the SIM chip alone to put in an unlocked phone you already own. It is also possible to buy the SIM chip for any country on the Internet before you leave home. That way you can give your new phone number to friends and family before you leave, and you'll be able to use you phone as soon as you arrive. But it does cost more than buying the SIM chip in Europe. When you buy a SIM chip or phone, be sure to get the phone instructions programmed into English if possible, and learn the code to enter to get messages from the local service provider in English. The instruction booklets that come with the phone are not usually written in English, so you will need some help from the shop sales staff.

The great thing about the cell-phone systems in Europe is that they offer "pre-paid time" plans. With these plans, the SIM chip initially contains a minimal amount of phone use time, calculated in euros, so you can use it immediately upon purchase. But you'll need to buy a "time card" as soon as possible, available in any kiosk. The time card contains a serial number that you dial in on your phone and the euros on the time card are automatically transferred to your phone. There is a local number to dial to find out how many euros of time remain on your phone. Local calls vary in cost, but tend to run about five cents per minute. Unlike the U.S., in Europe you are charged only for calls you make from your phone, not calls you receive from others.

The cost of a simple locked or unlocked phone with a SIM card was initially about $100 and included about $30 of time. The prices went down every year, to closer to $50 for a phone with SIM card. The

SIM card alone is inexpensive. We bought a SIM card in Greece for four euros that contained one euro of time.

The phone systems in each country we visited worked well – generally superior to the U.S. based cell phone systems. There are two or more competing systems in each country so it's important to look at the differences to determine what works best for you.

Using your local mobile phone to communicate with the U.S. can be tricky. The cost per minute is high – often $1 per minute or more, depending on the country. The trick is to have your friends and family call you; since there is no charge for incoming calls, you will pay nothing. Our children bought discount phone cards over the Internet at a low cost. Sometime these discount phone cards charge a higher rate when the call is to a mobile phone, but even so it was far less than the price to call them from Europe on our mobile phones.

By the time we reached Greece, we had two phones, so we started to buy two SIM chips. That meant that Bruce and I could call each other easily. This was helpful if one of us had left the boat for shopping or some bureaucratic duty and we needed to report that we were delayed or ask about needed groceries. When we arrived in a new country, our first stop was always at the mobile phone shop. These shops are common in Europe and there is always someone in the shop who speaks English, at least at some level.

Land Line Phones

Discount phone cards are also available in Europe. The problem is that most of them do not work for mobile phones and those that do are about as expensive as using your own local mobile phone. However, when you do need to call the U.S. and you are in a port, the discount phone cards work on public phones. Public phones are far more common in Europe than in the U.S., but that may not last much longer.

Smart Phones

Initially, our most important means of communication with home was my Blackberry. We started with just mine, but later Bruce got one as well. Their popularity has plummeted, but they had advantages for us in Europe. We used them primarily as email devices and Blackberries excel at that. Blackberries had much better pricing for various overseas options than other services. Some services charged by kilobyte usage and were outrageously expensive.

Computers

We always took along a laptop as well as Blackberries and smart phones. The computer is terrific when wi-fi is available. Some marinas charge for wi-fi service, often up to five euros per hour. Others offer free wi-fi as part of the marina package. Wi-fi allowed us to connect to the Internet and browse to our heart's content, either on a computer or on a smart phone. It also allowed us to connect to Skype for free video calls to our family from anywhere we traveled, although now that's possible on smart phones and tablets as well. Some cafes and restaurants provide free wi-fi. They are often American based, Starbucks and McDonalds in particular. We expect this service will continue to grow.

Internet Cafe

When all else fails, there's always the Internet cafe. Every port town has several and costs are reasonable. Many but not all have printers available and some have cameras to use for Skype. Because of smart phones, the number of Internet cafes is decreasing.

Getting Money Abroad

Getting money abroad has become easy and nearly foolproof with credit cards and ATM cards. There is no need to carry travelers' checks. You should let your bank and credit card issuers know when and where you're going. If you don't, they are likely to panic and cut you off.

Credit Cards

Most but not all shops, fuel docks, marinas, boat supply houses and large grocery stores accept credit cards. But always be prepared to pay in cash. The credit card devices are sometimes broken, especially at fuel docks. Or your card may be rejected because credit card companies, paranoid about their cards being stolen, often disapprove a large transaction, even if you have given them advance warning. That happened to us frequently when buying diesel fuel – the $500 or more charge triggered all sorts of alarms. We carried several credit cards – American Express, Visa and MasterCard – because we knew there would be times when one or more would be rejected for unexplained reasons. American Express is rarely accepted. Some places will reject a credit card because it does not have the implanted chip that all European credit cards now have.

The downside of credit cards is that some of the companies and banks charge extra when you use your credit card abroad – they add on a surcharge for currency exchange. Capital One is one with no currency exchange charge. Look around for one without these fees because they add up. We find that the actual exchange rate used by the credit card companies is extremely fair, but keep a close eye on your bills and try to understand exactly what you'll be charged before you start out.

ATM Card

We got most of our money through our ATM cards. Credit cards are not accepted everywhere in Europe, so cash is necessary. There are ATM machines everywhere. There may still be charges levied – sometimes surprisingly high – but generally it's not much different from using a credit card. Each European bank charges a different amount, so try various banks to see how high a fee they charge. Cash is easy to use, and sometimes will bring you a discount (if you ask for it) since the merchant does not have to pay his side of the credit card charge, which can be surprisingly high. We carry three ATM cards issued by three different banks. Each card has its own limit, so having several cards allows us to get more cash than is permitted on a single card. That came in handy several times when we had a major boat repair and owed money to a mechanic who had no ability to accept a credit card. Once we had to use all three cards for several days running to gather up enough money to pay a big boat bill. You can arrange a high per-day ATM limit with your own bank – just ask. I have a $2000 per day limit on each of my two bank accounts. But don't count on getting that amount from any one ATM machine. The local machines impose their own limits – sometimes as low as $100, with the highest we've encountered being around $900. Usually you can use your card a second or even a third time in another bank's ATM, until you reach you own bank's limit.

We carry more than one ATM bank card for another reason. Sometimes bad things happen to ATM cards. One time my bank decided to simply cancel my ATM card because of its own internal error. In Turkey, an ATM machine ate my card, although a friendly Turk, seeing my visible distress, went into the bank and asked the bankers to return it to me, which they did. After that experience, I tried to use ATM machines only at banks that were open, where a banker could retrieve a randomly eaten card from the back of the machine, but the disappearance of my ATM card never occurred again. Due to the withdrawal limits and possible disasters, it's smart to carry two or more ATM cards. Consider opening a second or third checking account at a different bank at home, put a couple thousand dollars in it, and get an ATM card. Tell your banks that you will be in Europe for a few months too, so they don't panic when the ATM charges start rolling in. Try to maximize your withdrawals at any one time, since ATM's usually charge a flat transaction fee, in addition to their cut for converting dollars to euros. But there is no more convenient way to get cash when you travel and the exchange rates are usually fair.

What to Take

Deciding what to take is hard. There's so much you'll need. The important thing to know is that almost everything can be bought in Europe, although sometimes at a higher price. The things you should try to take (since they cost much more in Europe) include all boat equipment that is not big or bulky, such as a portable GPS, anything electronic and mag flashlights. Bring one or two voltage reduction transformers so you can use your 110 volt U.S. electrical appliances on the 220-volt European system. And of course you will need plugs that convert the two-prong plugs we normally use into the European three-prong plugs – they are difficult to find in Europe.

We found that on board we don't use lots of items that are necessities at home. Consider making a list of the items you use each day at home, then think about whether you might want to wean yourself away from them when cruising. For example, we gave away the television that came with the boat, in part because we don't cruise in places where there are local stations in English and in part because we simply weren't interested – too much other excitement. But we listened to music, usually from CDs we took along with us. We took hundreds of still pictures with our three digital cameras and downloaded them to our on-board laptop computer. We made CDs of the downloaded pictures so all our picture files were backed up. But we didn't take blank CDs with us because they are for sale everywhere in Europe and they are cheap.

By spending two weeks on board shortly after we bought *Avanti*, we started to learn what the boat was missing. Our used boat already contained most of the items we needed to survive, including dishes, tableware, and pots and pans. But the last owner lived a different life style than ours so we took many trips to the local discount stores to stock up. When we figured out what was available and the price differential between Europe and home, we were able to decide what we should buy at home and carry along.

We have never been hassled by customs in any European country when we brought in parts for the boat or household utensils, even when we brought a couple of inflatable kayaks as checked luggage. We concluded that there is no problem bringing personal items to Europe to outfit your boat, as long as they fit within your airline luggage limits. We never have been asked to report items to customs.

Shipping items over from your local West Marine store is a different story. Those items must go through customs, and that can be a huge hassle and big expense. Each shipment will likely be subject to a large customs charge.

There is at least one boat chandlery in nearly every major marina for purchasing boat parts and accessories. None is as large as West Marine. However, even if a local chandlery does not have what you need, they can often find the item elsewhere and have it shipped. Sometimes these shipments can occur overnight or within a couple of days, sometimes not. If shipped within the European Union, there will be no customs charge.

Buying new or replacement equipment for your boat in Europe rather than at home has the advantage that repair parts are then easily available, whereas parts might not be for boat equipment that is not sold in Europe. Equipment sold in the local chandleries was usually found on a shelf right beside its replacement or repair parts.

We bought bulky but needed replacement pumps, filters, and engine parts in Europe. These parts are generally reasonably priced and are available in most marinas. Some bulky items such as on-board barbeques and kayaks are substantially more expensive in Europe so it may be worth the hassle of bringing them over as luggage on the airplane.

And don't forget your passport. Make sure its expiration date is at least six months after you plan to return home. If you happen to have some free time and decide to visit a non-EU country near Europe that requires a visa, you'll learn that many countries will not issue a visa on a passport that expires within six months.

CHAPTER 4
PUTTING YOUR NAUTICAL LIFE IN ORDER

Now the mail is being handled, the packing is done, and everything at home is prepared for your absence. It's time to get going.

Our boat purchase was completed in February 2003 and in April we flew to Mallorca for a week to learn how to operate our new boat and to determine what repairs or upgrades it needed. This trip proved necessary to make sure the boat would be ready to start our journey in May.

During our April visit, we made decisions about interior refurbishing, including replacing the uncomfortable mattress in the master suite and reupholstering the tired-looking built-in seats in the main saloon. The existing interior fabrics were over ten years old and the busy brown, orange and gold pattern was no longer appealing or fashionable. We wondered if it ever had been. We also arranged to have the off-white drapes professionally cleaned in hopes that some of the water stains might come out. They didn't. We later found they came out with plain old hand washing. Our boat broker hired a service to clean the boat before we arrived. We inspected the existing cookware, bedding, towels and other items, keeping some and tossing lots. We made certain that the refrigerator, oven, stove, microwave and toilets were working. We checked out the navigation equipment and ordered some new navigation devices to replace the most outdated items we had inherited.

Necessary Nautical Equipment

Avanti had not actively cruised for several years. Its previous German owner, Dieter, used it as a weekend retreat, flying down from his home in Wiesbaden. He took it out only in local waters and only in good weather. As a result, the navigation system hadn't been updated and we thought it couldn't be trusted.

Bruce determined that our boat would need to have at least these basic pieces of equipment for safe cruising:

- good GPS receiver and electronic chart plotter, along with memory chips containing charts for areas we would visit;
- backup set of paper charts;
- working radar unit good for at least a 12-mile range;
- reliable autopilot system to keep the boat on track under any sea condition;
- compass that would allow us to triangulate our position from landmarks on shore;
- depth-sounder to read depths to 100 meters;
- knotmeter measuring our boat speed in the water (a useful addition to the GPS unit that shows the boat's speed and direction over ground);
- Navtex unit for weather forecasts;
- good binoculars.

The boat already had a passable collection of navigational equipment. The original autopilot system worked well and the boat was equipped with a functional knotmeter and depth sounder, a good manual compass, and an older, but still acceptable, radar unit. There were already paper charts on board that would take us at least to the eastern side of Italy where we could buy more.

The big problem was that the GPS unit and the chart plotter were from another era. Not only were there no longer any memory chips of charts available for this plotter, but the black-and-white screen was so faint it was useless during daylight hours. And we needed a good set of binoculars.

GPS and Chart Plotter. Bruce is not a fan of integrated navigation instruments because if one part breaks, the whole system can become useless. So we opted to replace the old GPS unit and chart plotter with one that displayed the latest electronic charts clearly even in the bright sun, but was not integrated with the autopilot system. We then created trip plans using waypoints on the chart plotter, but the chart plotter did not automatically send the waypoints on to the autopilot. When we arrived at a waypoint, a buzzer went off in the chart plotter and we had to manually change the boat's direction ourselves. For a few thousand dollars extra, we could have created an integrated system so the boat would turn automatically at the waypoint, but we thought that wasn't a good investment. Anyway, we weren't comfortable with relying on equipment to change the boat's direction – it seemed far too "hands-off" to be safe.

The fairly expensive Raymarine chart plotter we bought was probably our most useful piece of electronic equipment. The system used a GPS receiver to show the precise location of our boat on an accurate nautical chart displayed on a ten inch screen. It showed in great detail the coastline, local rocks, shallow spots, and even buoys and markers. Sometimes it would read a few feet off course due to vagaries of the early ocean surveys, so when we were near shallow water or rocks, we couldn't rely on it exclusively. It could also be zoomed out to show hundreds of miles of the surrounding land and sea to give us the big picture of our location. It calculated the number of miles to our next port or to any other landmark, and provided us the needed bearing to set on our autopilot so we could get to where we want to go. As we traveled, it told us how far off our course we were and how to correct our course. The basic unit cost over $1000 without the electronic charts. Charts to cover the entire Mediterranean cost up to another $1000.

We also carried a second independently powered hand-held GPS unit at the helm as a back-up to our chart plotter. GPS is the easiest and quickest way to locate yourself at sea. Our GPS unit could locate us anywhere on the earth's surface to within less than 15 feet of our true location. The U.S. military has the power to turn off the system if there is an emergency somewhere in the world. Sometimes we suspect they do turn it off locally when U.S. warships are nearby or we're near a local country's naval base. But since so many people are now dependent on GPS, turning it off for more than a short period would create unbelievable chaos, so we think it won't happen.

Bruce also insisted on having paper charts as a backup to the chart-plotter. He had learned how to determine the location of our boat using a compass and a paper chart, together with some landmarks visible from the boat, and we practiced these procedures in our captain's license class as well. We never actually needed these skills, but they are good skills to have in an emergency.

Radar. We had an old radar system and some of the controls no longer worked. Since there is rarely fog in the Mediterranean during the summer and we didn't plan to cruise at night, we decided not to upgrade. Finally, in our fifth year of cruising, we needed a better radar system to travel with the Eastern Mediterranean Yacht Rally when night cruising would be required. We bought a low-power unit on the Internet at home and took it with us on the plane – the large radar dome was just small enough to be checked as luggage. It actually worked fine on the one night we were at sea, but it seemed to pick up only the biggest targets. We were nervous that a small fishing boat or potentially dangerous ocean debris might not be detected. After one night at sea, we swore off further night travel and used radar only once again, when we ran into thick fog between Greece and Italy. Bruce referred to it as his toy radar and played with it in good weather where he could compare nearby ships with the radar signals they give off. Even a large working radar unit (which costs several thousand dollars) is not foolproof and is no substitute for keeping a close watch in the fog or while cruising at night.

Depth Finder. Our boat had a depth finder that worked fine. It gave us no problems until we reached Greece, when it started to work only intermittently. It was old and we could find no replacement parts. We lived with it in a non-working condition for a month, taking care to stay in deep water and to watch carefully near shore. But that was not a good long-term solution. When we arrived at a large, well-stocked marina in Turkey, we replaced the system for about $400, including installation. Our new depth finder was so sensitive that installing it didn't require drilling a hole through the hull of the boat; it was just epoxied onto the inside of the hull. Putting extra holes in the bottom of a boat is not a good thing, so we were happy to have a new depth finder without having to add a new hole. Our new depth finder was good to about 200 meters of water depth, and at shallow depths read to the nearest tenth of a meter.

Autopilot. Our boat was fitted with a functioning autopilot, although it did do crazy things from time to time, and once caused the boat to spin in circles. But we found that the main consequence of a faulty autopilot was that we had to steer by hand now and then. Steering by hand gets tiring since it requires constant adjustments so a good working autopilot is definitely worthwhile.

Knotmeter. We had two independent knotmeters for measuring the boat speed, one built into our GPS/chart plotter system and the second protruding from the bottom of the hull in the form of a little paddlewheel that spun as it moved through the water. The GPS gave us our true speed over the earth's surface and the little paddlewheel recorded the speed we were actually making relative to the water. It is useful to have redundant systems, especially because the paddlewheel on the bottom of the hull seems to attract barnacles, which can change the speed readings in strange ways. Our hand-held GPS unit gave us yet another redundant reading of speed.

Navtex. The Navtex receiver gets a 24-hour weather forecast in English every few hours. These forecasts are sent by radio from each Mediterranean country. While Navtex is not adequate for long term weather forecasting, it was still a useful piece of equipment for us. However, new weather communications systems are even better, so check out the other options in the areas you plan to travel.

Binoculars. The importance of a good set of binoculars can't be overstated – and not just to see the pirates before they see us. All sorts of potential hazards show up in the water and need to be avoided, from fishing nets to stray channel markers. It's worth spending the money required to get good binoculars. Your reward will be the day that dolphins are swimming and leaping right in front of the boat and you have a ringside seat, thanks to your high-quality binoculars.

The binoculars we used daily cost around $300. We bought the waterproof version of the Nikon 7X50 binoculars with a built-in compass. The number 7 in the formula means that they magnify the images to be 7 times as big as seen with the naked eye. It's hard to use a larger magnification, such as eight or ten, because it's hard to hold the binoculars sufficiently still for clear viewing at that magnification in even the mildest of seas. The 50 in the formula relates to the width of the field of view through the eyepieces. The most common width of field is probably 35, but a wider field lets in more light, and lets you see more lurking hazards. The wider field of view also causes the binoculars to be bigger and heavier than the 7X35 versions. But that's not all bad. Bruce claims that heavier binoculars are actually easier to hold still on a boat than lighter ones. We have not used the built-in compass much (visible through the eyepiece), but if you need to fix your position on a paper chart based on two distant landmarks, the built-in compass makes the job easier. Good binoculars will last for many years, and will be used every day.

Books. All cruisers we met carried the "bibles" of Mediterranean cruisers, the (Rod) Heikell Pilot books on cruising each of the many coasts of the Mediterranean. There are two for Spain, one covering the eastern area where we would visit. There is one for France and Corsica, one for Western Italy, Sicily and Sardinia, a similar one (by Thompson) in the same series of books for the Adriatic (eastern Italy, Slovenia, and Croatia), one for Greece and one for Turkey and Cyprus. They are published in England by Imray Press, and they contain such a wealth of information that it would be foolish to leave port without the right Pilot book at the helm with you. We believe it is almost impossible to cruise without them. They have charts of each harbor and bay and list the amenities in each marina, including number of berths in total and the number available for visitors, availability of water, electricity and fuel, and existing repair facilities and marina shops. They describe how to contact the marina when entering and any marina dangers that may exist, as well as providing a brief but helpful tourist guide for each small port and marina, a guide that is a big help since most of these towns are not covered in traditional travel guides. The books also include coast guard phone numbers and VHF channels, as well as weather and safety information. All the boaters we met had a Heikell along with them. The Pilot books are available on Amazon but are rarely found in bookstores in the U.S. They are often available in boating stores in the larger European harbors, but the safest course is to buy one on Amazon before you leave. We have spent many evenings reading the Heikells while plotting our next adventure.

Some countries have a second guide that should not be missed if you want more local knowledge, but none should be considered a substitute for Heikell. Croatia has an excellent "blue" guide that shows every bay and harbor in detail, including the location and name of each hotel and restaurant in an anchorage, and often the exact location of mooring cans. Our Croatian guide was complicated since it was written in Italian, the only version available in the boat shop in Bari, Italy where we first saw it. Fortunately, we had just finished a beginning Italian language course, so the guide was fun for us. It is also printed in English, but that version was hard to find.

In Greece, there are a set of detailed guides consisting of dozens of local charts, each of which covers a region in Greece, with useful details about local ports and anchorages in both Greek and English. Much like the Croatian guide, they contain such detailed charts that they can replace paper charts. We found them less useful than the Croatian guide and extremely expensive, so after purchasing two, we stop buying them and relied on other charts. They do contain lots of detailed information, so you might want to take a look at them. They are available in virtually every Greek chandlery.

Instruction and Training

Before taking your boat out for the first time, you should consider hiring a professional boat captain to give you some basic instructions on the operation of your boat. Although boats have a lot of systems in common, each one operates a little differently.

We were advised that in Europe boaters are required to be licensed, even though no national licenses are issued by any Mediterranean country. We decided that the most impressive license we could have was one from the British Royal Yacht Squadron. In Mallorca, there are a couple of boating schools where one can obtain a license in a few days. One advantage of a British license is that the training is given in English. We signed up with an instructor that our British boat broker recommended. Instruction entailed taking the instructor (our broker's friend) and his wife out to sea with us for two days. During that time, we learned to plot our course by hand, anchor, berth, work the VHF communications system and carry out all the necessary boat checks each time we left and returned to port. Most of the information was a review for Bruce, who had taken several boating classes in California, but we learned much useful information about our boat in particular and about boating in the Mediterranean generally. And it was fun. Bruce received an Offshore Captain's license for non-tidal waters, and my license was the lesser Navigator's license for non-tidal waters, allowing me to pilot the boat on my own under virtually any Mediterranean condition. Nobody ever asked us to produce our licenses. But it gives us a subtle one-upmanship advantage at any Yacht Club bar if we pull out our official Royal Yacht Squadron licenses.

Daily Pre-Cruise Procedure

To be safe on the water, we figured we had to get organized. Since we tend to forget things at the most inopportune times, we wrote out an official pre-cruise procedure to be checked off each time we left port. It was posted on the wall in the main saloon.

Bruce's list included these captain's chores:

- Check the oil level and cooling water level in each engine and record it in the ship's log.
- Determine the course for the day on the paper charts and estimate the required time for the cruise.
- Check the fuel level and record it in the ship's log, making sure that there is sufficient fuel to reach the next destination and that more fuel is actually available there.
- Be sure the charts are on the upper helm, where the captain will be stationed.
- Stow the dinghy and its motor so it is secure under any kind of sea.
- Disconnect the AC power cord from the dock and stow the cord; disconnect any other cords (water hose, TV cable) that are connected to shore.
- Pull in the gang plank (passarelle) that connects the stern of the boat to the dock.
- Bring all portable electronics, instruments, and necessities to the upper helm, including detachable VHF radio microphones, hand-held GPS and binoculars.
- Start the engines, checking to see that the oil pressure and battery charger gauges are reading properly and that cooling water is flowing out the exhaust system along with the exhaust gases.
- Go over the appropriate sequence for releasing bowlines, stern lines, and anchor lines to keep the boat from damaging adjacent boats. In some marinas, the management provides staff or "marinaros" (who often run around in little inflatable boats), to help you leave the harbor. Take advantage of their help.

My list included the following:

- Close windows and hatches.
- Lash down movable furniture with bungee cords.
- Safely store phones and cameras.
- Put the U. S. flag out on the stern deck.
- Cover and tie down the bikes on the back deck.
- Tie the dog on the upper helm so she won't wander when we are underway.
- Secure the latch on the refrigerator door – a potential mess if forgotten.
- Confirm that kitchen cabinets are closed, flower pots stored, and no plates or other loose items are lying on any counter in kitchen or main saloon.
- Make sure needed books (especially a good novel), reading glasses, suntan lotion and a digital camera are on the upper helm.
- Prepare the lines for a smooth departure.

To be safe, all cruisers need a similar list. If it's not written down, you are sure to forget something important, only to be reminded when the resulting disaster occurs.

Boat Comfort

There are many little things to consider in getting a boat ready to be your "home."

We found that having enough plates, flatware and glasses for just six people was perfectly adequate since there were rarely more than four people at any meal. The rubber mesh shelf liners sold by boat stores are a must to keep plates and glasses, as well as small decorative items, from sliding around and toppling off the shelves. We enjoyed gradually replacing the existing boring serving dishes with interesting ceramic platters and dishes from local artisan shops. We replaced the ugly flatware avidly hated by Bruce with a new set of flatware, also ugly.

The mattress on our roomy queen sized bed was hard and uncomfortable. My back hurt after one night. We had a new foam mattress bed custom made and installed. It was still hard and uncomfortable. We ended up cutting grooves approximately three inches deep into the foam two or three inches apart, all the way across the mattress. That made a huge difference. We also bought a one inch latex pad to put on the mattress, which made the bed perfect. We bought a light weight double sleeping bag, called a "double-sided comforter" from West Marine and brought it with us. The bag zips open completely and has internal sheets that are fastened in by embedded Velcro strips. One side of the bag is heavier than the other, so it can be reversed to put the heavy side on top during cool weather and the light side on top during hot weather. The sheets can be pulled out easily for washing and the comforter itself rarely needs to be washed. The comforter is so large that I washed it on the deck with a bucket of soapy water and a hose. We loved it and bought one for our guest stateroom as well.

The multi-year task of decorating our boat with fresh flowers, posters and other art and pillows was a labor of love and made *Avanti* feel much more like home.

Time to Start Serious Cruising

When we left *Avanti* in April, the weather was cold and the sea rough. When we returned in May, the sea was calm and the sun was warm. All the interior refurbishing was complete, the drapes cleaned (but still stained), the boat underside splendid with its new anti-fouling paint, and the engine oil changed. We were ready to go.

We brought our dog Roka along with us this time, traveling on United Airlines where dogs are welcome in a small bag in the cabin.

The first few days back in Palma consisted of one intense shopping spree. We bought dishes, food, towels, shampoo, and bikes. We rigged up a box on Bruce's bike where Roka could sit to be chauffeured around town. We studied guidebooks and sea charts.

As the end of May arrived, we knew it was time to leave Mallorca. But we were happy and comfortable and the world outside Palma was frightening. We kicked ourselves – we had places to go, people to see. We waited and watched for a good patch of weather. Then one morning it happened: the sun was out and the breeze was light. We sighed, both excited and fearful. We slowly headed away from the marina. Our journey was underway.

CHAPTER 5
WHAT TO KNOW ABOUT MEDITERRANEAN BOATING

Haul out: it's a good idea to haul a boat out each winter; here we're in Rome

Wharf: this taverna sits right on the wharf in Kea, Greece, steps from *Avanti*

Wharf: An easy side-tie is appreciated at this bustling town wharf in Trogir, Croatia

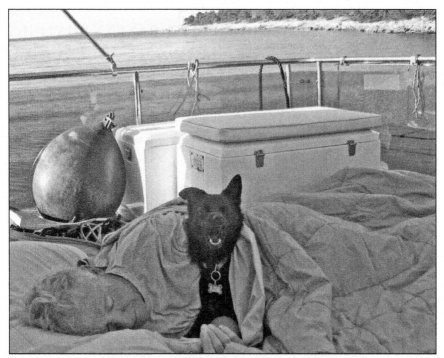

Anchoring: There's lots of privacy at anchor when sleeping on deck
on a hot night in peaceful Rab, Croatia

Maintenance: Bruce changes filters every 100
engine hours

There is a lot to learn before setting sail in the Mediterranean. Boating there can be surprisingly different and often confusing, especially the rules of the road and how to berth your boat. Education can also be vital on topics such as weather and sea conditions, boat maintenance and repairs, the various types of places to settle in for a night, a week or a few months, and the confusing rules for traveling from country to country.

Differences between Mediterranean and U.S. Cruising

Mediterranean Mooring

One major difference between boating in the U.S. and the Mediterranean is what is known as "Med-Mooring." In almost all marinas and ports, you must back your boat onto the dock or wharf to tie your stern to the dock. Your bow is held in place either by a heavy rope line permanently fastened to giant block of concrete on the bottom on the harbor, known as a "laid line," or by your own anchor dropped on the harbor floor as you back into your berth. If there is a laid line, a dockhand will typically wait on the dock to hand you a thin rope that is connected both to the heavy laid line tied to the sea floor and to the dock. This thin rope must be walked (or, more likely, raced) up to the bow, and while the dockhands are tying your stern to the dock, you frantically pull on the thin rope until the heavy laid line to which it is attached rises from the sea. You loop the heavy laid line onto a cleat on the bow of your boat and pull it in as tight as you can. The boat must keep running during this procedure to maintain control. Once the laid line is tight, the bow will be tightly fastened by the laid line to the concrete block at the bottom of the harbor and the stern will be tied to the dock.

A dockhand might hop aboard to assist. Don't allow him to take control of your boat – the boat captain remains responsible even if the dockhand causes an accident. In one of the fancier marinas in Turkey, a dockhand jumped on our boat and started to take control. Bruce mistakenly backed off, then watched as our boat plowed into the boat next to us. This would not have happened had the dockhand not tried to take over. A dockhand's appearance of knowledgeable helpfulness and his open assumption of control can cause you to believe, often erroneously, that he is competent. Beware!

Carrying out the Med-Mooring can be tricky, especially in cross winds; it takes practice. On-shore help is vital when winds are heavy.

Med-Mooring using a laid line is typical in marinas and city wharves in most of Western Europe, from Spain through Croatia, and in Turkey. In Greece, the laid lines tend to disappear. In place of a laid line, you must drop your own anchor off your bow and back up toward the dock or wharf until you can feel that the anchor has caught, then continue to back up, letting the anchor line pull out, until your stern is close enough to the dock or wharf to tie on. This is considerably more difficult than using a laid line. Sometimes your anchor doesn't catch. Sometimes it catches, then works itself loose. Sometimes there is no one on the dock or wharf to catch your stern lines to help you tie up. It is difficult, but not impossible, to tie up with no help. Sometimes you drop your anchor over someone else's anchor line, or late arrivals drop their anchors over your anchor line. Fortunately for us, we didn't hit the "self-anchor" harbors until our third year, when we were already reasonably competent in Med-Mooring techniques. If we had been forced to use our anchor while still learning the basic back-in procedures, we might have had some grim accidents.

Red Right Returning – Wrong!

Forget it! As it turns out, the U.S. is one of the few countries in the world in which the red running light is on the starboard side. In Europe, the lights are opposite. Green channel markers are on your starboard side, and red markers on your port side when entering a harbor in Europe, just as the harbor entrance is marked by red blinking lights or buoys on your port side and green blinking lights or buoys on your starboard. Finally, your running lights on your boat will be red to port and green to starboard, so a boat moving in front of you at night showing a red running light will be moving from your right to left, and a green running light will indicate movement from left to right. It can be confusing, but the motto "Red Right Returning – Wrong!" might be able to help you keep it straight. Cruisers in Europe have a different saying: "Port (as in the wine) is always red."

Weather and Sea Conditions

Have you read Homer's *Odyssey*? If you have, you likely thought that the sudden storms arising almost instantaneously and lasting for days, blowing Odysseus and his crew far from home, were obvious exaggerations. Not so. The wind and sea conditions vary dramatically from day to day, even from hour to hour. Sometimes there is no wind at all and then, suddenly, the wind comes up and blows so hard that no sane person leaves port. Often the wild chop made us cringe in fear at the thought of heading to sea. It is vital to understand local wind and sea conditions and predictions before venturing out.

Our solution was to stay in port when the conditions were bad. Normally, winds and seas calm down in a day or two. Sometimes this is not the case and boaters can be trapped for more than a week because of high winds, particularly in Greece. Encounters with high winds and rough seas are never pleasant.

Wind disasters are part of the scene in the Mediterranean. Our first serious wind encounter, in the Spanish port of Cadaquez near Barcelona, left us trapped at anchor for two days in high winds. Fortunately, we were in a protected bay. Almost a month later, in the Iles d'Hyeres near Toulon, we were again at anchor when a high wind came up. This time our anchorage was not well-protected and we were hit with four to six foot seas. We left our anchorage so quickly that we failed to batten down the interior of the boat, resulting in soaked papers, broken glass and a destroyed mobile phone. We learned from this disaster: in addition to being too careless about monitoring weather reports, we had failed to understand the importance of keeping the boat battened down so that unexpected winds and the resulting choppy seas wouldn't destroy our belongings.

Later we were trapped in Mykonos in a dangerous, persistent gale. We had planned conservatively and left ourselves what seemed to be plenty of time to travel from Mykonos to our plane in Athens to take us home, a trip normally made in two days, even in one long day in a pinch. But the winds howled, refusing to die. After more than a week of waiting, we became desperate and decided we had only one option: make a run for it. We survived the trip, but it was a memorable couple of hours, filled with terror and angst. Unlike our prior difficulties, this particular weather disaster was not caused by our carelessness or failure to prepare. There was not much we could have done differently. Our final and most traumatic wind disaster occurred crossing from Alanya, Turkey to Girne, Northern Cyprus, a distance of almost 100 miles. The trip started in calm waters, but as the day wore on, the wind kept rising. The wind and sea became so rough that we had to run the boat from the lower helm. We again were unprepared: our lower helm window cover, used to block the sun from baking the cabin, remained in place, blocking Bruce's visibility other than from the side windows. The roughness of the seas had a silver lining – no other boat was reckless enough to be out in those conditions, so there was nothing on the sea for us to hit. The passage took about ten hours but seemed like an eternity.

There are various tricks to staying on top of weather and sea predictions.

Our Navtex receiver provided regularly updated 24-hour weather predictions in English tailored for our present location. Many areas have a regular weather report, often in English, on the VHF radio. Nearly every marina and most ports and harbors also post a sheet of government-provided current and predicted weather and sea conditions. But often these postings provide only current conditions and predictions for the next 24 hours. Internet sites such as passageweather.com and windfinder.com are far more informative for longer-range predictions.

There are also internet sites for each country's specific marine weather predictions, usually run by the government. Some include cool color maps that can scare you to death with the huge splash of red (meaning highest winds) covering the map. The locations of these sites change on a regular basis; it's easy to find them with a search on Google. Being prepared won't keep the winds away, but at least you'll be ready.

Boat Maintenance and Repair

Regular maintenance and unexpected repairs are inevitable. There are certain problems you're bound to face, almost on a daily basis. Being in a different port every few days in a country where you must converse in a foreign language makes keeping your boat in top shape difficult.

Regular maintenance includes oil and filter changes, periodic battery replacements, annual antifouling paint, new zincs and through-hull checks. These can be planned in advanced and carried out in one of the modern marinas where you're likely to find good mechanics.

Repairs are another matter. Some are true emergencies and need immediate attention, even in backwater marinas where you're not comfortable with the available mechanics. Some, like toilet problems, can usually be deferred for at least a few days until you reach a reasonably-sized marina.

Our biggest repair occurred in Rome, where the black smoke emitting from one of our two Cummins diesels had worsened and the engine started to cough and sputter. We hired an engine mechanic recommended by the Cummins office in Rome. He concluded that we needed a new cylinder head and new injectors. Ouch! The cost exceeded $12,000 and took over a week to complete. We looked for a silver lining and shifted to Plan B, leaving *Avanti* with our adorable but expensive mechanic, Pumpellyo, and climbing aboard a ferry for a visit to Sardinia.

Our second worst problem was a leak in the shaft seal, the place where the propeller shaft exits from the inside of the boat into the water. Leaks in a shaft seal allow sea water to flow right into the boat, clearly a potential disaster. A bilge pump can handle a small leak, but an uncontrolled shaft-seal leak could sink *Avanti*. Our first trouble occurred in Turkey where we replaced one of the shaft seals. The same seal started to leak again in France a couple of years later and the shaft seal had to be replaced again, this time by an extremely self-confident mechanic who explained that his clients valued him so highly that they flew him around the world to repair their boats. His repair failed only one day later, as we crossed the Gulf of Lion. Not only did the shaft seal again start to leak, but the broken parts slashed a fuel line, causing us to limp into the marina at Cap d'Agde spewing fuel. We had to be lifted out of the water immediately to prevent *Avanti* from sinking. The formerly proud mechanic, that magician who fashioned our near disaster repair job, sheepishly drove four hours to Cap d'Agde to help with the new repair, seeming to realize that he'd screwed up. Each one of these repairs was expensive and time-consuming and often left us for days in an undesirable town (like Cap d'Agde).

We also had a series of troubles with our toilets. The motorized head in our master suite was fine until the day the motor stopped working. This turned out to be a much bigger job than simply replacing the motor. The exit pipes from the master head to the holding tank had clogged over time and waste had caked onto the inside of the plastic pipes like cholesterol plaque in an artery. Yuck! We had the pipes cleaned out in Croatia by an extremely brave mechanic who carried out this unpleasant task by removing the hoses and hammering them on the dock until the solid waste lining the hoses (we hope it was mostly toilet paper) broke up and fell out. After that, we tried to keep the waste hoses extra clean by flushing vinegar through the system every month or so to dissolve away any solid waste "plaque" buildup. Eventually we banned toilet paper from the heads entirely, thereafter using Greek and Turkish style trash bins for used toilet paper. We also had to replace our manual-pump guest toilet. It was old and the pumping mechanism started to leak (clean water, fortunately). We replaced the old head with a Jabsco, since it is a common brand in Europe. Our old head was an off-brand and no parts were available for it. Interestingly, Jabsco heads are manufactured about three miles from our home in California. Finally, we lost the macerator (grinding) pump from our holding tank that is necessary for emptying the tank at sea. Fortunately, a replacement was easy to find and install.

There seem to be an infinite number of boat parts that can fail. The only certainty is that something will break down from time to time. Just hope to find a silver lining, perhaps an extra day in an interesting port, and enough money in the bank account.

Marinas, Wharves and Bays: Where to Stay, Amenities

Marinas

Marinas are the easiest places to spend the night, the lazy boater's choice. Most marinas provide helpful goodies like workers to fix the latest boat problem, daily weather bulletins, water and electricity, food, shops and those always-critical on-shore toilets and showers. Some luxury marinas are impressive – air conditioned toilets and showers, gourmet restaurants, large grocery stores, huge chandleries, swimming pools, tennis courts and fashionable boutiques and gift shops.

Each boat in a marina has its own berth, a parking space that must be backed into, Med-mooring style, with boats on either side, separated only by inflatable boat fenders. Finger docks, those fixed docks that separate berthed boats in most U.S. marinas, are non-existent. Often you end up beside unoccupied boats so there can be lots of privacy, but having neighbors is half the fun. Each boat hangs a "passarelle" or gangplank off the back of the boat onto the dock for passage to and from the dock.

Between 2003 and 2010, the average cost for a berth in a marina for a 12 meter boat like ours was about $40-$80 per night, with a low of around $30 and a high of almost $200 (Ibiza was the all-time rip-off). Marinas charge based on a boat's length, and sometimes its beam, so smaller boats will cost less, larger boats more. We don't know how the rates have changed since 2010, but given the state of the European economy, it's hard to imagine that rates have increased much.

Some marinas have over 1000 berths, most for boats in permanent residence. Often the number of berths reserved for visitors (known as "transients") is small and these berths can fill quickly during the summer. In most cases, you cannot reserve ahead. Powerboats have an advantage in getting available berths because their speed allows them to reach the next marina earlier in the day than sailboats. A boat arriving after 5 p.m. may have trouble in many marinas.

When arriving at a marina, the typical approach is to idle around the entrance until the on-water marina dockhands (usually referred to as "marinaros") show up in their small inflatable boats asking about your needs and the size of your boat. In some cases, the marina asks that you call the office on the VHF radio upon arrival, and the office tells you the location of your assigned berth and sends dockhands to meet you on the dock.

Often isolated marinas provide bus service to town. The best marinas can arrange tours, airport transportation, taxi service, rental cars or motor scooters and most of the other services that a hotel concierge supplies.

Turkey and Croatia have consistently good marinas. Spain, France and Italy have some classy marinas, but most are of varying quality. The worst marinas are in Greece. Greek marinas in the Ionian Islands in the Adriatic Sea are fairly good, although there is only one full-service marina. Things go downhill as you move east. In most of Greece, marinas are non-existent, or of extremely poor quality.

We learned that construction of many Greek marinas is started with inadequate funds. The boxes for water and electricity are installed and the docks built, then the funds run out and the project is abandoned. We learned to assume, usually correctly, that the Heikell books were overly optimistic about both the availability of water and electricity in Greek marinas and the timing of the predicted opening of a new marina. Almost none of the new marina predictions were correct, even many years following the "opening soon" assertion. Fuel is also a problem in Greek marinas. Fixed fuel docks are rarely available and fuel is available only from visiting mini-tankers. Greece was where we were sold water-logged fuel by a mini-tanker that caused extensive damage to *Avanti*.

City Wharves

City wharves are our favorites. They are almost always in the historic center of town – those ancient ports from Greek or Roman days that are now too small for modern commercial and cruise vessels and thus given over to fishing boats and small pleasure craft.

Wharves often have some of the amenities of marinas, with dockhands, water and electricity in the best, and sometimes even bathrooms and showers. The amenities are generally provided by the town, or by private operators licensed by the town. Since they offer fewer services, the cost is usually less than at a full-service marina, normally $20 to $30, and often free. Wharves fill up fast and are often already filled before 5 o'clock when the sailboats start to arrive. The spaces are first-come, first-served. Sometimes a dockmaster wanders by, but often not. It is difficult to Med-moor on a wharf with no help, and if no dockhand is around, there will almost certainly be another boater, or even a passer-by, who will more than happy to help.

Since city wharves are in the heart of town, they are lively and fun. You can sit on board and watch the world go by, enjoying the hustling crowds and ancient churches and forts. Locals and tourists saunter by to gawk at the visiting boats and merchants set up shop in front of the boats to sell their wares. The ancient sites of the town are typically lit up at night, making for romantic on-board dining. Bakeries and fruit and vegetable markets are often a few steps away.

Bays: Mooring or Anchoring

The third type of overnight accommodation is anchoring or tying up to a mooring buoy. This is almost always free, although using a mooring buoy usually creates a moral obligation to eat at the restaurant that owns the mooring, usually the single building visible on the shore.

There are psychic benefits to anchoring. You'll normally have no close neighbors who make noise. Most bays are quiet and clean, conducive to swimming off the boat and even nude sunbathing. The swing of the boat with the changes in wind direction and tide creates a sense of exhilarating freedom.

But, alas, there are dark sides to anchoring. You're never totally secure on anchor and always subject to drifting into another boat or on to the shore, or having a neighbor's boat drift into you. And it turns out that anchoring takes skill. What appears to be a reasonable distance between your boat and another anchored boat may prove inadequate if the wind shifts 90 or 180 degrees during the night; figuring out the proper distance takes experience. You have to trust your neighbors to be competent at anchoring. If your neighbor takes a line from his boat to tie to shore in addition to dropping his anchor, his boat will not swing around with the wind. If you're swinging at anchor and your neighbor's boat is not moving because it is tied to the shore, there's likely to be trouble. If you find that your neighbor's boat is tied to the shore, you'll have to take a line to shore as well to avoid a nighttime collision. Real problems are created if you leave your boat swinging at anchor in the early evening and another boat arrives and is rude enough to anchor and also tie to shore. You may not notice the danger your neighbor has created, and even if you do, it may be too dark to take your own line to shore safely. You may even have to leave and try to re-anchor elsewhere, in the dark. Some boaters exhibit arrogant and dangerous behavior; others just aren't very bright.

There is less protection from the elements at anchor; quiet nights with calm seas can turn windy and create seas that are choppy and even unsafe. A wind shift can cause a quiet bay on the leeward side of the island to become a rough bay on the windward side. Sleep is never quite so sound at anchor because staying alert and aware is critical, as is listening for wind changes, sounds of an anchor dragging, or warning shouts from other boaters.

Anchoring also makes reaching shore less convenient. Going to shore to browse, get a paper, or have a meal means putting out the dinghy and trying to find a place on shore to tie up. And it can be a real pain for boaters with dogs to have to take the dinghy to shore for doggy duty after a lazy dinner, or first thing in the morning.

Regardless of the problems, anchoring in a secluded bay is an amazing experience – rocking gently on the quiet water all night, listening to the lapping of wavelets along the boat's hull and the chorus of crickets and frogs serenading from shore.

The primo places to anchor are in Croatia and Turkey. The quiet bays in Turkey, particularly Fethiye and Kekova, are the best anchorages in Europe, vying with the Kornati Islands off the coast of Croatia as winners of the "most beautiful bay" award. Greece has some gorgeous bays as well, but the winds in Greece are often blowing hard which makes anchoring risky. In France, the Iles de Lerin off the coast of Cannes and the Iles d'Hyeres off the coast of Toulon offer calm but often crowded anchoring. In Spain, several small inlets along the Costa Brava are comfortable for anchoring and the Balearic Islands are full of small bays. The anchorages around the Tremiti Islands off the east coast of Italy feature views of white cliffs and an enormous old fortress.

If you find a mooring can or buoy tied to the sea floor in a bay where you'd like to anchor, many anchoring problems go away. Anchor dragging, our biggest concern, is not a problem when mooring, but you still need to be aware of boats around you at anchor that could drift into you if the wind comes up. Mooring lines can rip from the sea bottom and set your boat loose, but we never experienced this scary event or even heard of it happening. Mooring cans are rare in the Mediterranean and most are owned by restaurants where you'll be expected to eat.

Sometimes a quiet, deserted bay can turn ugly. We stopped at a number of small bays that seemed great until the local disco in the pines on shore erupted at eleven p.m. and belched out techno music until six a.m. Beware the innocent looking taverna on the beach - it may turn into a raucous disco after you're happily asleep.

Water and Electricity Ashore

Genuine marinas and some wharves offer water and electricity beside your boat's berth. Whenever we neared a dock or wharf, we would scan the wharf for an electrical box and water faucet. Some of these boxes and faucets are located on only one section of the wharf, so it pays to look for the telltale box and faucet when selecting a spot.

An initial task in any marina or wharf is to plug in your electric cord extension and hope for power. For some unexplained reason, each marina uses a different style electric socket. It makes no sense, but we ended up with five or six different plugs, some with two prongs, some with as many as six, each purchased at the marina when the required plug was not already in our collection. If the electricity doesn't start to flow, a dockhand must be hailed, and the problem, usually a blown circuit breaker, remedied.

Much boat equipment runs on 12-volt electricity from the boat's batteries, so it is not absolutely necessary to plug into shore power. The stove and oven on *Avanti* did not work on 12-volt power. We rarely used the oven, but we did use the stove most mornings to heat water for coffee and to fry eggs. We solved the problem by buying a fancy portable camping stove that ran on butane. It worked just fine when we had no shore power.

We also used shore power for our floor fans. *Avanti* is not air-conditioned and the heat of the Mediterranean summer could get unbearable. We eventually figured out that an "inverter" that converts 12-volt electricity from our boat batteries into 220-volt electricity would help. It failed to produce enough 220-volt electricity to run the stove, but it did a great job on one or two fans. Two fans could get us through most but not all of the hottest weather.

Shore power is also required to recharge phones and batteries, but the inverter handles those electrical loads quite easily. Inverters do run the boat batteries down, though, so they should be used with care.

The boat's battery-based electrical system eventually runs down if not recharged by running the boat engines for several hours or by plugging into shore power. Our staying in a marina or bay with no power for more than a day or two resulted in *Avanti's* batteries running down. The solution is an independent generator that puts out 220 volts and not only recharges the boat's big batteries, but also permits the running of all equipment that needs 220 volts. The generator recharges the boat batteries, but recharges considerably more slowly than either shore power or power generated by running the engines. A generator can also be noisy and irritating, both to you and to your neighbors, especially in a quiet anchorage. Turn it off at night.

For us, having shore power made our life easier. We eagerly scanned each new port for the electrical boxes along the dock.

A source of fresh water is important as well and is commonly available even in sketchy marinas and ports. There is usually a water faucet by each boat berth. For us, lack of water was not a problem since our water tank was large, holding 100 gallons – enough water for almost a week. We used water from our tank for everything except drinking, including washing dishes and showers. The water from our tanks would have been fine for drinking, but it often picked up a slight taste from the tank so we preferred bottled water. When there was no water faucet by our boat, we could usually buy water from a water tank truck for a few euros. One important function of a water faucet by the boat is to allow for washing down the boat after a day on the salty sea. A few days at sea with no wash-down makes a boat sticky from the salt; most water tanks aren't big enough to hold the amount of water needed for a good boat wash.

Toilets and Showers

On-shore toilets and showers are a nice amenity. Our boat had a comfortable shower and two toilets, so we could be self-sufficient; however, *Avanti's* holding tank was extremely small so we used the toilet facilities on land when possible. Both shower and dish water (so-called gray water) flows directly from a boat into the sea, not into a holding tank. Use of holding tanks is spotty at best in the Mediterranean. As far as we could tell, the prior owner of *Avanti* never did use the holding tank, but instead set the valve so any toilet waste would go directly into the sea. Since *Avanti* was tied up about 20 meters away from the marina bathrooms in Palma, we hope that he used the on-shore toilets and not those on *Avanti*. If he did use the toilets on *Avanti*, the waste would have flowed directly into the marina. In most of Western Europe, boats are not required to use holding tanks, and there are no pump-out facilities in most marinas. Not a pretty thought.

Fuel

Ports and marinas are the only source of necessary fuel. *Avanti* used diesel fuel which was easy to obtain. If your boat has a gasoline engine, you could have problems since many ports sell only diesel fuel. We met a couple from Wales who had to spend several extra days in an unattractive marina in Southern Italy before they were able to locate a vendor who would haul tanks of gasoline to the marina for them.

Most marinas and ports have a fuel station that operates at a dock within the marina or on the wharf. When there is no fuel station, vendors bring fuel right to the stern of your boat via mini-tankers. The risk of taking on bad fuel is higher from a mini-tanker than land-based tanks. We were sold a tank of diesel in Greece that consisted of half diesel, half water, causing both our engines to die and resulting in time-consuming and costly repairs. We believe that the water seeped into the fuel as a result of a thunderstorm the night before; the mini-tanker likely had one of its upper tank lids partially open. After that disaster, we inspected every load of fuel before it went into the boat. Water is heavier than fuel, so it drops to the bottom of the fuel tank. Since fuel is sucked from the bottom of the mini-tanker, the heavier water will flow into the boat's fuel tank first during refueling. To confirm the lack of water, only the initial flow of fuel must be inspected. Bruce would pump a small amount into a clear bucket so he could inspect it closely for cloudiness, a sign that the fuel contains water. There are boat filters for filtering out water; however, they are small and not feasible for a boat that takes on hundreds of liters of fuel at once. For sailboats, however, they might be a wise investment. The best protection is to have the mini-tanker fill somebody else's boat before fueling yours. If there is any water in the mini-tanker's fuel, it will go into the boat that gets filled first.

The cost of fuel is wildly higher in Europe than in the U.S. For us, the cost of diesel fuel ran between $6 and $10 per gallon. Simply refilling our half-full 300-gallon tank cost over $1000.

Arriving in a New Country

Some countries require that you check in with a customs office when you first arrive. No EU country, with the exception of Greece, has such a requirement. No one in these countries ever even asked us for our passports.

In Croatia, Slovenia, Turkey and Northern Cypress, all non-EU countries at the time of our visit, we were required to enter the country flying a yellow "Q" flag – a flag that means we are not yet legally in the country – and immediately check in with customs at an official port of entry. We were required to check out when leaving as well. A list of official ports of entry for each country is posted in various places, most likely including the marina in the country you are leaving. Most medium or large port towns turn out to be official ports of entry. Checking in and out can be a bore and a pain, especially in Croatia and Slovenia, since this registration is supposed to occur exactly when you're arriving or leaving, meaning you can't go to customs a day early to check out, or wait a day after arrival to check in. In Croatia and Slovenia, the problems this created were worsened because the customs offices were not in the actual marina, so we had to figure out how to get to the right place. In Turkey, where the timing of checking in and out is more flexible, there was usually someone in the marina office who would help with the paperwork for a small fee.

Boaters must update the crew list in non-EU countries when anyone new arrives to stay on the boat and again when they leave, except in Turkey where this requirement either doesn't exist or is ignored.

The disaster is Greece – no other country comes close. The rule in Greece is that you must purchase a transit log from the port police when entering Greece. The log must be signed by the port police in each and every port at the time you arrive and again when you depart. These are the rules. Maybe. Two port police officers told us we needed to have our log signed only once a month. Who knows? That is a problem with Greece: the rules are never clear, but if you violate one, the penalty can be draconian. We had to pay over $1000 for one violation of a rule that even our marina didn't know existed. There has been a pushback by the EU against Greece enforcing these requirements against EU citizens since they violate EU rules, but no one questions Greece's right to enforce its rules against boaters from non-EU countries. Most boaters ignore these rules, but that's risky. We checked in or out with the port police now and then to build up the stamped entries and exits in our transit log, but certainly not at every stop. We were never asked to explain missing dates, even when the police could clearly see a one or two week stamp hiatus. If we had been asked, we were prepared to claim that we'd been anchoring. No sign-in is required if you're not docked in an actual port. There's also the ever-popular excuse that "the port police office was closed." It may be a little harder to convince the authorities of that one, but in fact many port police offices do appear to be closed almost all the time.

CHAPTER 6
LIFE ON BOARD

Lunch: Typical sunny lunch on *Avanti* with visitors

Breakfast: Bruce and Roka enjoy meal on upper deck

Getting Around: I enjoy playing tourist in Naples on a double-decker tour bus

Getting Around: Rental cars are a must. This car in Corfu is not typical – most are boring

Getting Around: Motorscooters for two plus dog are perfect for seeing the countryside

Local Area: We all three ran this race in Rome after learning of it in a local English-language newspaper

Life on board in the Mediterranean falls into a gentle rhythm, with many comfortably similar days, punctuated by unexpected adventures. My typical day started early when I hiked to the upper deck to watch the sunrise and write in my journal. Later Bruce emerged – he's not such an early riser. When we were both awake, we jogged with Roka to town to find a treat – a croissant perhaps, or maybe an apple tart or simply fresh bread. Returning to *Avanti*, Bruce made breakfast – perhaps an egg, prosciutto, our fresh-from-the-bakery treat, and plenty of hot coffee from either our Italian Bialetti or our French-press coffee maker, all of which we ate in the sun on the back deck on our wobbly plastic table – later replaced with a sturdier one – covered with a bright Spanish table cloth and a potted kalenchoe plant. This is the best time of the day.

If we planned to leave port on a new adventure, we checked the items on our departure checklist, turned on *Avanti's* engines and slowly pulled out of port. Four to five hours later, when we reached the next port, we scanned the marina or wharf eagerly for a good berth and if lucky we backed in, Med-Mooring style, with help from the marina dockhands or a passer-by, or found a quiet bay for anchoring, washing down the boat if water was available. Late lunch on board came next, usually a salad, perhaps with a beer or glass of wine if our sea passage had been less than calm. After lunch, we explored our new surroundings for an hour or two before returning to *Avanti* for a cold glass of white wine or a gin and tonic.

For dinner, we walked into the new town, or hopped on the dinghy and motored to town, along with Roka, to find a sea-side restaurant where we sat for an hour or two over dinner. In Europe, there is never any pressure to eat quickly and leave: tables are expected to accommodate only one sitting each evening. When you make a reservation, you may be asked when you'll come, but it doesn't much matter because the table is yours for the night. Making reservations early can snag you the best table though. Even without a specific request, many restaurants will place the earliest reservation at the best table. Restaurants hold your table for the whole evening. After dinner we returned to *Avanti* to drink a glass of port or ouzo on the deck, talk with any visitors who might be with us, or just soak in the view of the glowing castles, forts and cathedrals surrounding the port. Then we were off to bed, with *Avanti* swaying gently in the harbor or quiet bay.

If, on the other hand, we weren't leaving port in the morning, the day started the same, but then we ventured out to visit local museums, cathedrals or mosques, castles and forts. We bought fruit, vegetables and cheese in the outdoor market and other groceries at the local supermarket. Or we might ride our bikes to places too far to walk, or swim in the sea, or perhaps rent a car for the day to visit special ruins, castles or hill towns too far away for our bikes. We usually still returned for lunch on board, but sometimes ate lunch in town.

This is a perfect life. It's hard to overstate how satisfying life was on *Avanti*. Those ordinary days on the Mediterranean will always be some of our most precious memories.

But perfection takes work. There are things to learn and problems to solve every day, things that need to be mastered to reach the ideal. What follows is a list of several of them.

Learning About the Local Area and Getting Around

We carried piles of guidebooks brought from home – English versions are hard to find in Europe and expensive. We collected a half dozen for each country. Most guidebooks provide useful information, and each provides different insights, but the problem with most mass publication guidebooks is that they generally include only big cities, ignoring the quiet port towns visited by boaters.

Some guidebooks, such as the Blue Guides and the Cadogen guides (both British and both recommended) cover many small towns as well as the big cities and are therefore more helpful for boaters than the guidebooks published in the U.S. The Heikell books are the most valuable. They provide brief descriptions of each port, marina and bay, often the only information available about some of the smaller villages. An Internet connection allows you to find information for some of the towns, but many seaside villages are too small to have websites.

Marinas often provide brochures and pamphlets describing places of interest in the surrounding area. English language newspapers can be found in some countries at news kiosks. These papers fill in the details about local cultural and civic events. The most helpful of these was the English version of the Greek newspaper Kathimerini – it was included in the daily International Herald Tribune and contained information about local Greek plays and other cultural events, as well as articles that gave us a better understanding of the politics and culture of Greece and how Greeks view the U.S. In Italy we learned about the Susan G. Komen Race for the Cure in Rome from an English-language paper. We signed up and ran an historic course around the Baths of Caracala, the Forum and the Coliseum.

Once you know about the area, you have to figure out how to get to what you want to see. For us, our bikes were a basic necessity, taking us to most points of interest, markets and restaurants. We rode them almost daily. Bikes are ruined quickly from exposure to salt in the sea and air, so buying expensive bikes doesn't make sense. They'll last three to four years, then start to have major repair problems due to rust; it's time to replace them. We used public transportation from time to time, but rarely. We took a multi-hour bus ride from our marina in southern Italy to Rome one year, and sometimes we'd take a train from a port town to another near-by town to visit a museum or other interesting site. The local train was a quick and efficient way to reach to Rome from our coastal marina, Porto di Roma. More often, we rented a car. Car rentals are easy, but sometimes expensive, even for total wrecks. Roka loves cars, so having a rental car gave us lots of flexibility when visiting neighboring towns or attractions – if she wasn't allowed in, she was happy to stay in the car. Rental cars also freed us from the hassles of bus or train schedules. We rented motorscooters frequently, mostly Vespas designed for two people; I would sit behind Bruce with Roka between us. This worked only in rural areas where traffic wasn't insane.

Shopping for Necessities

Shopping around the Mediterranean can be a treat. The local vegetable and meat markets are especially busy and entertaining. When we purchased *Avanti* in Palma, we needed lots of new stuff: serving dishes, wine glasses, a coffee maker, picture frames, towels and washcloths, shampoo and soap, dog food, a table and four chairs for our deck, new pads for our outside chairs, beach towels, bicycles and boat equipment. The list was long.

We filled up an entire SUV-style taxi with necessities we bought at the French-based Carrefours big-box store in Palma. On another Carrefours trip we overloaded my bike so dramatically that we were sure the bike tires would pop. Bruce thought the two eight-pound barbells and the DVD player might be the guilty culprits.

We found the well-stocked Ikea store in Palma and bought a big rug. We hauled it back to the boat by taxi along with all those other Ikea items we couldn't resist. We couldn't resist the Ikeas in Barcelona and Naples either.

The large Target-like stores in the bigger European cities – Carrefours and Migros are examples – were, like Target, of varying quality, but we could buy almost anything there, including groceries. We bought decorative pillows, dishtowels, dishes, sunbathing pads, and bed sheets, together with milk, meat, cheese, olive oil, yogurt and interesting canned goods. El Corte Ingles department store in Barcelona was our favorite – an old-fashioned department store with an enormous grocery store in the basement full of gourmet foods. El Cortes Ingles also delivered groceries for free, even to boats. We took advantage.

Large food stores are similar to the big grocery stores in the U.S. Their products are somewhat different and some foods not readily available. Peanut butter fanatics are advised to bring your own supply. In Turkey, good coffee is hard to find except for those who happen to enjoy Turkish coffee. We don't. We brought our own coffee from California in bulk, sticking a few pounds into our suitcases. We purchased bread daily at the local bakery. Bread must be bought daily since it contains no preservatives and dries out quickly. The breads in France are the best, but bread in every country is good when warm from the oven. And it's cheap – usually less than 50 cents a loaf.

Most fruit and vegetable markets and grocery stores carry only fruits and vegetables that are in season, unlike grocery stores in the U.S. There are rarely raspberries from Chile, for example. When apricots are ripe, they are everywhere and delicious, then suddenly they are gone. It's the same with peaches, cherries, plums and tomatoes. There might be a grocery store here and there with the same sad out-of-season fruits and vegetables common in the U.S., but they are rare. Fruits and vegetables are best from the outdoor markets found in every city and town. Meats from the butcher shops were difficult for us to buy. Butchers rarely speak English, so it's hard to figure out the identity of the meats since the cuts look quite different from those in the U.S. We rarely cooked dinner on board and had little need for fresh meat. Even the smallest of towns has at least one "supermarket," often smaller than our 7-Elevens, but adequate for basics like eggs, milk, bread and olive oil. Prices for food are similar to those in the U.S., although fish can be wildly expensive.

We found the grocery shopping carts confusing because they are locked together. We soon learned that we had to put a euro coin into the slot that locks the short chain on one cart to the next cart in order to free a cart for use. This is true in all countries we visited. When you return the cart, you just relock it to another cart and your euro pops back out. It's an efficient system that keeps carts from being left in the middle of the parking lot. Why don't we have such a smart system in this country?

Clothing stores abound, usually in the form of small boutiques, but the selection is just fine in the large department stores, such as El Corte Ingles in Barcelona.

We had to buy bicycles – a basic necessity. In Palma, we located a used shocking-pink bike at a local bike store for just under $100. It was too big for me, so Bruce was stuck with it. It was a bad buy. A few days later, I bought a brand-new red bike for around $120 at Carrefours. We also bought two plastic milk boxes and Bruce attached them to the racks on the backs of our bikes. They could hold what we bought and also provided a seat for Roka to ride along with us.

When my bike was stolen in Barcelona, I found a new bright orange one at the local Decathlon, a cool store similar to REI. Meanwhile, Bruce had learned to hate his pink monster bike. He was disappointed that it hadn't been stolen in Barcelona. The thieves had cut both bike locks, but had taken only my bike – even crooks have taste. Bruce finally "accidentally" knocked his pink monster into the bay in the marina in Monaco. Fortunately, Roka wasn't tied into her box; otherwise she would have gone down with the bike. The thought of Roka sinking into the marina with the bike gave us nightmares. Bruce swore that the loss of his hated bike was an accident, a claim met with great suspicion, especially since I knew he had just seen a Decathlon store only a block away from our marina. He soon had a nice new Decathlon bike, just like mine except blue.

You may decide that a TV and DVD player are necessities. When we bought *Avanti*, she was equipped with a TV. But there isn't much to watch on the available satellite stations unless you understand the local language well, or German. We could get BBC and MSNBC part of the time. But when we were forced to watch them for more than a half hour, we found that they get repetitive quickly. We found we rarely watched TV. There are knock-off DVD's available for sale on many street corners and we did watch one or two, but found there were more interesting things to do. Don't considering bringing a TV or DVD player from home. U.S. televisions and DVD players don't work in Europe. TVs in Europe use a different broadcast frequency, and DVD players have a different electronic format than in the U.S. You can find DVD players to buy that accept both U.S. and European style DVD's, but they are expensive.

Shopping for Local Artisan Goods

Shopping for local artisan goods is the most fun of all shopping. We bought interesting ceramics in many countries – particularly France, Italy and Turkey – and we bought glass vases and candlesticks in Mallorca. The rugs in Turkey are hard to resist, especially the ones from the far eastern Kurdish provinces, and especially when you're waited on by an entire Turkish family and being plied with hot tea. We bought colorful straw baskets in Sardinia. Greece, Sardinia and Rome had interesting museum reproductions for sale, including replicas of pre-historic jewelry made by the people living in Sardinia 4000 years ago, reproductions of cycladic statues in Greece, and replicas of Etruscan ceramic animals in Italy. We bought Murano glass and carnival masks in Venice and silver jewelry in Greece.

In Turkey you must bargain; the Turks will not respect you otherwise. Our rule of thumb was to start at 40 to 50% of the initial price asked (assuming the initial price wasn't ridiculously high) and compromise at perhaps 60%. In other countries you can try to bargain, but in Turkey it's essential.

We carried everything we bought in Europe home in our suitcases. After an unfortunate shipping experience in Turkey in 1997 (when it cost us hundred of dollars to get a Turkish rug through US customs – more than the value of the rug), we no longer ship anything home. Most people ship their purchases home and haven't had an experience like ours, but we don't want to be burned a second time.

We found that our bags hold a lot. Because most of the clothing and equipment we brought from home in our luggage was intended to stay with the boat, we had extra luggage room when returning home, perfect for filling with the cool things we had bought. We filled all our carry-on luggage space with the delicate local crafts and breakables we purchased. When we returned to Europe each spring, we filled any extra space in our check-on bags with bubble wrap to use to protect our delicate treasures when we brought them home in the fall. Shops that cater to tourists sometimes wrap items with bubble wrap, but just as often they use newspaper or nothing. Extra bubble wrap comes in handy. Turkish rugs are usually placed in special bags by the rug sellers that can be checked as luggage on an airplane. In Istanbul, we put all the rugs we bought (perhaps 4) in a $5 soft suitcase we bought in the bazaar and checked it as luggage. The bag had nearly fallen apart by the time we arrived home, but it served its purpose. We filled our check-in luggage with the unbreakable items we had bought, often wrapped in our clothing for extra protection.

Prescription Drugs and Medical Help

Unfortunately, even healthy boaters get sick, and most of us are on at least one prescription medication, so it's important to know how to handle medical problems and drugs. Pharmacies are abundant in Europe and many drugs that are sold by prescription only in the U.S. can be purchased over the counter in Europe. Since the names of the drugs are usually different from the names in the U.S., it can be almost impossible to figure out the identity of the drug you need, although it helps to know the generic names. To avoid confusion, we always took along all of the medications we needed for the entire summer. This meant ordering 90-day supplies and reordering as soon as permitted by the insurance companies, usually a week or more before the end of the current supply, in order to aggregate a few extra pills. With our hoarded pills, we usually had more than enough medication to get us through four months.

In a pinch, we asked guests to bring along a refill of a couple of our prescriptions when they came to visit. It's easy to refill an existing prescription from a pharmacy with offices throughout the country (RiteAid, CVS) if you have the name and number of the prescription. They can be refilled anywhere by anyone.

Anyone planning to be gone for substantially longer than 4 months could have issues. While there are pharmacies everywhere in Europe, we never tried getting a U.S. prescription filled there and we have no idea whether it's possible.

If you need medication or have a health problem, there are many excellent doctors in Europe and most speak English well. The European medical systems are generally outstanding and the cost is dramatically less than in the U.S. Some countries even provide free medical care to tourists. As in the U.S., most of the best doctors and medical facilities are in the large cities.

Bruce ended up with bronchitis in Spain – bad cough, high fever – and had to go to two different doctors, one in a small port town, and a second in Barcelona, the second being necessary because the first doctor hadn't prescribed a sufficient dose of antibiotics. In Barcelona we waited in a packed hospital waiting room for endless hours with rising frustration to see a doctor. Newly arrived patients seemed able to see a doctor immediately while we sat and waited. We finally found an English speaking doctor who told us we were in the wrong place – this waiting room was for emergencies only, so seriously ill arrivals were put in line in front of us. He sent us down the street to a different clinic where Bruce was seen immediately by an efficient doctor who took blood tests, shot a chest x-ray, and gave Bruce a prescription for more antibiotics and a tongue-clucking over the inappropriate prescription given to him by the first doctor. Total cost for the visit, blood tests and x-ray: $100.

We had one false alarm in Greece when we thought we might need medical help for a visitor. We did some research on medical care in

Greece and learned that the main hospital in Athens has a sterling reputation, but those in small towns may be dicey. Another of our guests actually did need a doctor on Hydra in Greece. A kindly woman in one of the port shops told us where to find the only doctor on the island and even called his office to let him know we were on our way. He seemed competent, but he smoked during the entire visit, dropping ashes on the floor as he examined our guest, so it wasn't an ideal experience. The visit cost $40 and the prescribed medication cost all of one euro. The medical problem was solved so the visit was deemed a success.

Guests

We loved hosting visitors. We bought *Avanti* in part because she was guest-friendly. Her guestroom was located at the opposite end of the boat from our master stateroom and had its own bathroom.

In our eight years of travel we had almost four dozen visitors. Some years we had many, some years only one or two. We had fewer visitors as we traveled farther east – not surprising since travel to the boat takes longer and costs more the farther east one goes. We regretted that. We thought that Turkey was by far the best country to visit on *Avanti* and only three couples visited us there.

We told our visitors to pick a date or a place, but that we could not guarantee both. We could never promise that we would actually be at a particular place on a particular date. While we were usually close to where we had predicted, sometimes it took some effort to reach us – our visitors traveled by train, taxi and ferry to find us after they arrived in the local airport. Sometimes we rented a car to pick visitors up at the airport when we thought we would be too difficult for them to find.

Our most challenging visitor connection occurred when our son Adam visited us in Italy. We were on the east side of the country near the Gargano Peninsula when he arrived in Rome. The trains and buses from Rome to the Gargano Peninsula are sketchy at best and our son knew no Italian. Being overprotective parents – even though he was 30 years old – we drove to Rome to pick him up, a four-hour drive each way. Then we drove him back to Rome at the end of his visit. The things we do for our children!

Friends who visited us in the Greek Islands landed in Athens and usually took a ferry to reach us. Ferries to some islands have only sporadic service or require changing ferries and most of the ferries are slow. There are a few high-speed ferries but only to the most popular islands. It's possible to fly from Athens to some larger islands such as Santorini and Crete, but flights are often delayed by weather. Ferries are more dependable.

At times a guest's planned arrival limited our travel options. Being a couple of days early to a planned meeting site meant extra days in port, often resulting in an unplanned adventure. Hurrying to reach the meeting site on time could mean missing a desired extra day in an interesting town. In Turkey, we planned to participate with dozens of other boats in a yacht rally to Cyprus, Syria and Lebanon, then quickly return to Antalya, Turkey to meet visiting friends. We ended up dropping out of the rally early, which left us with two extra weeks near Antalya to wait for our friends to arrive. We thought about renting a car to visit the Turkish interior, but we had been there before. We needed a different plan and quickly hit on visiting Egypt. Our problem was that we had only two weeks to both plan and complete the trip. I contacted travel agencies on the Internet but they all laughed at the thought that they could arrange a trip in only one or two days. We had to put the trip together ourselves using a local travel company for our plane tickets and the Internet for places to stay. We decided to add a side trip to Jordan since we had heard about the wonders of Petra. We were gone for ten days. Everything went smoothly and we loved the trip. We would not have had the chance to visit Egypt and Jordan if not for that unexpected two weeks with nowhere to go.

At the same time, we are firm believers in limiting the length of time that guests feel welcome to stay. We told visitors that a stay of fewer than four days wouldn't be worthwhile. It takes a day to settle in, and the departure day usually isn't all that useful, leaving only two good days in a four-day visit, hardly enough time to go anywhere. But we also told them that we would get cranky if they stayed more than a week. At the end of seven days, a boat with visitors starts to seem small and crowded. Most of our visitors stayed between five and seven days. They all still claim that they had a great time and we have no reason to disbelieve them. We certainly enjoyed their visits.

We forced all guests to endure a safety talk when they first arrived. We showed them the location of fire extinguishers, life jackets and the life raft (the raft that inflates automatically when thrown on the sea and contains drinking water and other survival equipment). We went over the rules to follow if anyone happened to go overboard. The rules were simple but important.

Working on Board

I was still fully employed as an attorney during our first year of cruising. My Blackberry was essential for work emails, but I also needed to review long documents. This meant spending a few hours in every port at the local Internet café. I was on countless phone calls with clients and opposing counsel, but I made sure they initiated the calls since there is no charge on European mobile phones for incoming calls. We tried to create an effective connection between our on-board computer and the Internet, spending a fortune in Spain on a worthless connecting device. Nothing really worked until wi-fi finally became popular in the later years of our travel.

Many Internet cafes did not have the printers I needed to print out documents for review, and often the printers that did exist were slow and expensive. This became a problem. Eventually we bought an inexpensive printer, downloaded documents at the Internet cafe on a primitive USB flash drive or a CD and printed them out on board.

That was a big help. After I retired, we stopped using the printer and tossed it a couple of years later when it stopped working.

During our first summer, my largest client completed a major multi-property partnership so I found myself on many long conference calls. Fortunately I was working with other lawyers in my law firm who could handle most of the document drafting, so my job was limited to reviewing the documents and helping to negotiate.

I tried to schedule calls for 10 a.m. California time. That was 7 p.m. in Europe, just the right time to participate in a call from our upper helm with gin and tonic in hand. Fortunately, some of my clients were in Europe or the Middle East, so my desired conference call time often worked well for several participants.

The connections were never easy but they were not impossible, and it would be much easier now because of advances in technology. Mostly it was a big pain. When I received an unexpected call in the middle of a day of sightseeing, it meant stopping to take the call for an hour or so while Bruce and Roka cooled their heels. Often a scheduled conference call meant returning from town early or cutting short an interesting activity to be on the phone at the right time, documents in hand. Bruce was always understanding and helpful. He kept Roka quiet and refilled my gin and tonic glass whenever necessary. He also entertained our visitors during any particularly stressful work periods.

After our first year, I retired, continuing minimal work for one client. It was less stressful. I completely stopped working on the boat after our second year.

Periodically we ran into boaters who had elaborate communications facilities in their boats, easily enabling them to work effectively. Each year's advances in communications were startling. Now it is not much more difficult to work on a boat in the Mediterranean than at home, except of course for all those distractions.

Food and Wine

People have written entire books on this topic. We are not wine or food connoisseurs. We are more gourmands than gourmets. But we did form strong, though maybe subjective, opinions about the food and wine in the Mediterranean, which I am more than happy to share. Our normal routine on the boat when not at anchor was to make breakfast and lunch on board, then head into town each evening for dinner. This routine allowed us to control our intake and our budget for most meals, while opening up many opportunities to sample local goodies at our 'big' meal of the day.

We converted to a cosmopolitan European breakfast of prosciutto and cheese, with perhaps an egg with toast and coffee. Our lunch consisted of either the salad of the country we were in – Niçoise in France, Caprese in Italy, Greek in Greece and Turkey, or a sandwich with local salami and cheese or a bit of our hoarded peanut butter.

We loved dinners out. That's where we found the most interesting foods, from local meat or seafood dishes to bottles of local wine. Few of our meals were memorable, but eating out is a good way to learn about regional foods and to get to know the locals. Best of all, somebody else does the cooking and the dishes. The only times we ate dinners on board were when we could find no restaurant – a problem that occurred from time to time in remote areas – or when we anchored out, or the weather was rainy and we didn't want to walk to town. We always kept emergency dinner rations on board – pasta and tomato sauce, some Italian farro to cook with onions and mushrooms, or pre-cooked sausage that doesn't spoil for months if properly refrigerated.

The one major problem with eating out in Europe is the lack of variety. There are so many ethnic foods in the U.S., from Italian to Thai to Ethiopian to Mexican, often as close as the nearest shopping mall. That isn't so in Europe. Large cities have ethnic restaurants, but not the small port towns we normally visited. Generally we found only Italian food in Italy, only French food in France, only Greek food in Greece, and each restaurant in any country had a menu essentially identical to the restaurant next door. Eating in the Mediterranean is much like going to the old-style Midwestern diners, where one can get meat loaf, burgers, mashed potatoes, grilled cheese, cole slaw and pie, and each diner offers essentially the same menu as every other diner up and down the highway.

We eventually tired of the food in each country. We greeted each new country with joy because we finally got to eat new and different dishes. But, alas, we soon tired of the food of that country, too.

In Italy, the menus are mostly pasta, risotto and pizza, some uninspired beef steaks, interesting veal and sometimes chicken; we almost never found lamb, duck or pork on any Italian menu. Inland Northern Italian cuisine is a whole different story – always exquisite and delicious. But around port cities the food is pretty uninspiring standard fare, especially south of Naples. These are not the glorious meals found in Tuscany and Umbria.

In Greece and Turkey, lamb is the dish of choice. Its preparation and taste are completely different from lamb in the U.S. We love roast lamb, but not the bony, fatty lamb chops served in both Greece and Turkey. In these countries, the "mezes" are the most fun – lots of interesting small dishes usually selected by visiting the kitchen, many made with eggplant, yogurt, cucumber and various types of fish.

While France is the clear winner of the "best Mediterranean food" prize, even in France we tired of the same menu every night. In France we could choose duck, lamb, beef, stuffed zucchini flowers and of course the ever-present French fries. Notwithstanding the French reputation for great food, the food can often be mediocre in portside restaurants.

Croatia is proud of its variety of meats. One popular dish consists of a giant pile of various chops and sausages. It's delicious the first few times, but like other meals, eventually becomes tedious.

In Spain, the answer is always tapas – the best the country has to offer.

The salads in each country are also the same from one port to the next. Many of the countries offer a "national" salad plus perhaps a small green salad or a tuna salad. The national salad of Italy is the tomato, mozzarella and basil Caprese salad. In Greece, it's the tomato, feta, cucumber and olive Greek salad, also served in Turkey. Salad Niçoise with tuna, green beans, hard boiled eggs and potatoes is the salad in France. In France it was hard to find a Caprese or a Greek salad. No country other than France offered a salad Niçoise. Fortunately, we rarely grow tired of salads and each country had a specialty worth eating nearly every day.

We never warmed up to some popular native dishes. We had paella in its original home of Valencia in Spain and had trouble finishing it. We splurged in Marseille on bouillabaisse at one of the city's most renowned and expensive bouillabaisse restaurants and hated it. We initially found the pizzas in Naples to be mediocre, although we warmed up to them on our second visit. We ended up eating far too much pizza in Italy.

We learned that we're not fans of most Mediterranean fish. That turned out to be a problem since fish are a big part of the local diet. We've never been calamari or other small fish eaters. Neither of us cares for anchovies (other than in a Caesar salad). We don't much like the shrimp in the Mediterranean, where they are expensive and are served "whole-body" style in the shell, making them difficult to dig out and often soggy or mealy when, after great effort, the shell, which includes the eyes, is finally peeled away. The little Mediterranean lobsters are excellent, but they don't hold a candle to a Maine lobster, plus they are extremely expensive. The sea bass is our favorite – known as lubina in Spain, bronzini in Italy, and lavraki in Greece – tender and moist but often served in a bland fashion, and extremely expensive. The best is a whole sea bass baked in a thick coating of salt. Same with the dorado, which is a bit more bony, but still tasty and slightly less pricey.

What we loved were the cheeses, the salamis, and the fresh fruits and vegetables. The cheeses are best in the Western Mediterranean and in France they are memorable. By the time we got to Turkey, we found cheeses weren't worth eating and since there is no pork available, there was no good salami, so we started bringing our own cheese and salami from home or asking our visitors to bring some, or, as in one case, flying to Romania for good salami.

We weren't enthusiastic about desserts in the Mediterranean, other than gelato in Italy, flan in Spain, and just about anything in France. We didn't warm up to the sweet honey baklava-style desserts common in Greece and Turkey. When we visited Switzerland at the end of one trip, after spending an entire summer in Turkey, we were like kids in a toy store with all those cakes and tortes.

We always tried to drink local wines and especially enjoyed visiting local wineries and vineyards, even when the wine wasn't all that tasty. We found that some places, sadly, just produce bad wines. Turkey is probably the most difficult. Although it has some good vineyards and wineries, the fact that it is an Islamic country means that the wine industry is of interest to only a limited portion of the population. The wine in Greece is good as long as you stick to wines from the northern Macedonian regions and Santorini. Croatian wines were mediocre but drinkable. Many small Croatian towns reek of fermenting grapes being aged by the citizens in their garages. They sell their wine by pouring it into empty used water bottles brought by neighbors who want to buy. In Turkey, Greece and Croatia, restaurant house wines were often not drinkable so we ended up buying a full bottle of wine, often a liter size which is larger than wine bottles in the U.S. That probably wasn't all that great for our health. Sometimes we cheated on our "local wines only" rule and bought French or Italian wine when they were available. We always kept a stash of reasonably good wines on board if we got desperate.

In Italy, France and Spain, it's hard to go wrong no matter what you drink and we always ordered the less expensive house wines at dinner. We especially enjoyed the wines from Northern Spain and the Cote du Rhone wines in France. In Italy, each region has fabulous wines, even in the far south, though the wine quality seems to go downhill the farther south you go. We were disappointed with Sicilian wines, now touted as "fine wines." Sicily has been the largest producer of cheap table wines in Europe for more than a thousand years. Several decades ago, some of the local vintners decided to try making some fine wines, the result being wines like Nero d'Avola that now are exported around the world. We found them overpriced for the quality.

Inevitable Disasters?

Common questions we get: "What happens if your engines fail? What if you hit something? What if someone goes overboard? Aren't you afraid of pirates?"

Although things often go wrong and create huge levels of stress, we never experienced an event that put our lives or boat in serious danger, although the leaky shaft seal came close. Our fears were usually far greater than any actual danger. Our natural caution likely left us prepared for most problems.

We read what we could find about handling major problems. The Heikell books have information about rescue groups to call on your VHF or cell phone. The Coast Guard in each country will respond quickly to emergencies if you call on Channel 16 with a "Mayday" (meaning life threatening emergency) or a "Pan Pan" (meaning a non-life threatening emergency). Some countries, such as France, have an independent boat rescue service available 24 hours a day to help boats in distress.

We made sure we had all necessary safety equipment on our boat – life jackets, lifeboat, radio, flares, life ring, fire extinguishers. The U.S. Coast Guard publishes a virtual safety check that helps you determine what safety equipment you should carry. It is consistent with information provided by the Coast Guards in other countries, making it a good place to start. The virtual safety check can be found on the Coast Guard Auxiliary website.

We practiced the man-overboard drill. We made sure someone watched whenever anyone on board went down from the upper helm or came back up while the boat was moving. If a boat lurches suddenly or even if someone simply slips, the result can be a man-overboard. If no one is watching, it could be hours before the person who has fallen overboard is actually missed.

We did rescue one elderly gentleman from the sea several miles from the French shoreline. We felt quite professional pulling him up on deck using our crack safety training. He had fallen off his windsurfer and lost sight of it in the large swells. We spotted his windsurfer easily because of the height of our boat. We offered to rescue it and take both him and his windsurfer to shore. Notwithstanding his advanced age, he insisted that we simply reunite him with his windsurfer. We acquiesced, he jumped off the boat back into the water, hopped on the windsurfer and off he went.

We learned to study the weather reports and stay in port when high winds were predicted, other than the one unavoidable and terrible trip from Mykonos to Tinos. Bruce checked the oil and fuel levels every time we prepared to leave port. Our engine troubles were a huge pain and cost us time and money, but we were never in any danger. We put a dent in *Avanti*'s side on the Rhone which cost us plenty to fix, but it wasn't dangerous.

We got accustomed to little disasters – the irritating ones that can just plain ruin your day – but never lost sleep worrying about the big disasters.

Another reason that our adventures were generally disaster-free is that Mediterranean waters are extremely safe, other than in winter storms. Real disasters are hard to find. Ports are close to each other and the Mediterranean Sea, while sometimes unruly, is not as wild as the open Atlantic or Pacific Ocean. We were almost always close to a port we could call if we were in trouble. In our many years on the Mediterranean, we heard only one "Mayday" call on our radio. Within minutes, it was clear that other boats were on their way to help.

And, by the way, there are no pirates in the Mediterranean.

CHAPTER 7
TRAVELING WITH YOUR PET

Roka meets a water buffalo, source of the best Italian mozzarella

Roka lounges in the Roman amphitheater in Pula, Croatia

Roka's favorite relaxing spot on *Avanti*

A new friend on the trail in Croatia

Roka is an expert motor scooter rider

These women admire Roka on the streets of Trogir, Croatia

Roka's favorite perch, at the bow of the dinghy

Our Dog Roka

We have had a dog underfoot since we were first married, usually a small rescue dog from the local pound. We can't imagine a dog-less life.

When we started thinking about life at sea, we worried about what to do with our dog. We heard that Europe is dog-friendly, so we took heart and started researching.

First we learned that a dog must be small to ride in the plane's cabin. We didn't believe we could bear to check her as luggage in the plane's belly. We also learned that most airlines refuse to even allow dogs to be checked as luggage during the summer months due to the potentially deadly heat. So we needed a dog small enough to comply with the airlines' in-cabin regulations, meaning a maximum of 14 or 15 pounds.

After mourning the loss of our beloved Pepper in early 2000, we started thinking about a new doggy pal. We searched shelters for a small, mellow dog. We learned that small dogs are in great demand so they don't stay long at a shelter. We looked for a couple of months and finally found Roka, a stray, at a far-away shelter in a sketchy LA neighborhood.

Adopting her required a long, hot drive to the shelter three days in a row. She weighed only 12 pounds – a perfect weight to meet the 15 pound maximum we had set. However, when she arrived home, she quickly grew to 18 pounds. She must have been almost starved when she arrived at the shelter. We named her Roka, the word for "fox" in Hungarian since she has a distinctively fox-like face.

To us, she was a black mutt of no apparent breed. Then people we met on the street started asking us about our "schipperke." We checked out the breed on the Internet and there she was! Her face and curly tail are totally schipperke, a Belgian barge dog. She has just enough anomalies, like a longer and slimmer body than purebreds, to make it clear that one of her parents was definitely not a schipperke.

Roka turned out to be the perfect travel dog. Her only imperfections are that she is slightly too large under some airline rules, she possesses an independent streak that can show up as a desire to wander off, and she often barks when left alone. But we were lucky. After her adoption, we worked hard at training, knowing how important her good manners would be when traveling. She's smart and learned quickly. While she knows what she's supposed to do, her independent streak results in her often opting to ignore us. She travels quietly, sitting or sleeping for hours in her soft-sided airplane bag on the plane without the slightest movement or noise. We could never have guessed she'd be so quiet. But we need to credit our good choice mostly to luck, not brilliant training skills.

Joys of Taking Your Pet with You

There are obvious joys in traveling with your pet. If you love having a dog or cat at home, you'll love having your friend on your boat. Pets on board open up a new world of local friendships. Roka is a friend-maker – everyone wants to meet her and pet her. We had many conversations with people in the street that would never have happened if not for Roka.

Roka went with us everywhere. She learned to sit between us on a motorscooter seat. She sat quietly under the table during dinner. She is an expert at taking escalators and elevators and riding buses. She learned to ride in a basket on Bruce's bike attached behind his seat and trotted on her leash alongside my bike, even in heavy traffic. She seemed to relish her time with us on the boat and the many adventures she experienced, especially the aromatic garbage bins.

Problems with Taking Your Pet

A dog or cat on your boat can also create major problems. The frequent need to go to shore for doggy business can get tiresome, and there are places where she's just not welcome. There are problems when leaving the boat for a few days, and with Roka, we had a constant fear that she'd wander away.

Our travel style was different when Roka was along. We knew we could leave her on the boat in complete safety from morning until evening. But we had to take her along if we planned to be away longer. This meant we were limited in what we could do, and we had to arrange our trips carefully. During one year in Europe without Roka along, we flew to Egypt and Jordan for ten days, and then to Romania for a week. This would have been impossible if Roka had been with us.

Pets Usually Welcome, but Sometimes Not

Western Europeans generally welcome pets in their shops, in outdoor markets, and always in the outside patios of restaurants. Since it's warm in the summer, the question of whether we could bring Roka inside a restaurant rarely arose. The few times that we needed to eat inside due to cold or rain, or because there was no outside area, the results were mixed. Some restaurants said no, period. Others looked at our quiet, well-behaved dog and allowed us all to eat inside. Roka always sat quietly under our table, so once we were allowed in, she was never an issue. Sometimes, we carried her into a restaurant in her soft-sided airplane bag and no one had any idea that we had a dog with us.

Options When Pets Not Permitted

Most museums and historical sites do not allow pets; neither do most hotels. There are various ways to deal with this problem.

- <u>Leave your pet on board</u>. We left Roka on the boat when we had to eat inside, or went to a museum or other area where dogs were not permitted. She was never happy about that. At first we left her to roam the boat while we were gone. After she peed right in the middle of our bed one evening and didn't even look guilty when we came home, we assumed it was revenge for our having left her. We started to tie her up when we left her on the boat so she couldn't get to any vulnerable places.

- <u>Try renting a car</u>. When we were planning to be away from the boat for a night or even an extremely long day, we rented a car. We could leave Roka in the car if we were eating inside or if she was not welcome at a hotel where we spent the night. Fortunately, she loves all cars and never objects to staying in one. During the day, the heat and sun in a car can be a problem, particularly when visiting a tourist site or museum, so we always looked for a well-shaded parking spot and left the windows cracked. On excruciatingly hot days, we would take her to the entrance of the site and ask the ticket sellers to watch her, which they were generally happy to do. Many hotels do not allow dogs. You can find dog-friendly hotels on the Internet, but sometimes they aren't where you want to stay. With a car, we could take Roka along and sneak her unseen into the hotel in her airplane bag, then put her back in the car when we went to dinner or other places she wasn't allowed. If your dog hates being in a car, this probably wouldn't work as well as it did for us.

- <u>Take your pet anyway</u>. In addition to sneaking her into hotels and restaurants, we often took Roka to other places where she was not allowed. It became a bit of a game. We would zip her into her airplane bag and tote her into museums and tourist sites. Of course, that doesn't work in museums where visitors are not allowed to bring in bags or where the bags must go through an x-ray machine.

Before St. Peter's in Rome started to x-ray all tourists' bags, we put Roka in Bruce's backpack and took her into the basilica with us. She is perhaps one of the few living dogs to have had a close-up view of Michelangelo's *Pieta.*

- Find a kennel. If you go somewhere for a day or two where pets cannot go, your options are limited. There are some kennels in Europe, but far fewer than in the U.S. Our only experience with finding a kennel was a near disaster. When we were scheduled to return home from Nice, France for two weeks one August, we decided to leave Roka at a kennel, never thinking that finding one might be a problem. We visited the tourist bureau near Nice for help. The two women working there were gracious, but struggled to understand what we wanted. Their English wasn't great; our French was worse. It was clear that our question was not expected; we imagine that no tourist had ever asked them about a dog kennel. When they finally understood, they looked in the yellow pages and found only three kennels in the area. We were dumbfounded. In our small town at home, there are dozens of places to leave a dog. Nice is a big city. Even worse, only one of the kennels was in the city proper. The second was almost an hour's drive north of Nice, and the third several hours north. We panicked.

We drove to the first kennel, in Nice proper. The young, sophisticated woman in the office spoke some English, but her response to my query was to laugh. She explained that all spots for boarding for the busy month of August had been filled months ago. She found it amusing that I thought there might be a spot for my dog. She had no suggestions as where else to try.

The next day we drove an hour north past La Colles sur Loup to the second kennel, located in an obscure corner of the countryside. We finally saw the sign, "Le Grand Chenil du Midi." We were in the middle of nowhere. Our hearts sank when we saw a chained gate at the entrance. I fiddled with the chain and managed to get it unlocked and we drove in, following a dirt road for about a half mile. I was resigned to failure; if I could barely communicate with the sophisticated woman at the kennel in Nice, how could I ever communicate with a local in the countryside?

At the end of the road, we stopped at some low buildings. A woman walked toward us. I called out, hoping for a miracle, "Do you speak English?"

"Why of course," she laughed. The miracle had happened. Barbara was born and raised in Virginia. She met and married a Frenchman many years ago and has lived in France ever since. She and her husband run this low-key kennel, set in the woods, and, as miracles piled up, they had space available for one more dog during the time we planned to be gone. She explained that many of the dogs and cats she boarded belonged to Parisians vacationing on the Riviera who refuse to leave their pets at home, but their resorts do not allow pets. So they bring their beloved pets anyway and board them close enough for a visit or two during their vacations.

Two weeks later, we were back, having never worried about leaving sweet Roka with such a friendly woman. It was probably too much to hope that Roka would pick up a few words of French while she was at her "summer camp." We suspect that her failure to learn French was because the American owner spoke to Roka in English the whole time.

Moral of the story: don't count on finding a kennel. I expect it's easier in some places than others, but you won't find many. And don't expect help from the local tourist office.

Not all Airlines Take Dogs in the Cabin and Rules Differ

Some airlines will not take dogs in the passenger cabin over the Atlantic: American, Continental, British Airways, and Air France were among those we could not patronize because of their no-dog rules. A few do, or at least did when we needed pet travel – United, Lufthansa, Delta, and Swiss. The rules as to pet size vary and are both confusing and difficult to find. Some of the soft dog carriers sold for airplanes are actually larger than the airlines' published rules allow, although in practice no one seemed to check or measure. Some airline rules for pets are based on the pet's weight, not carrier size. We concluded that the maximum dog weight is around 14-15 pounds, though Roka is usually closer to 16 or 17 pounds. When asked, we'd say 15 pounds. The maximum weight given by airlines is often 18 pounds, but that weight limit includes the carrying bag as well as the dog. Keep that in mind and try to find a relatively light-weight bag. The pet should be able to fit fairly comfortably into the bag and is supposed to be able to stand, but Roka is far too big to have any hope of standing in hers.

Special Issues in Greece and Turkey

After spending part of one summer with Roka in Greece, we decided Greece was simply too unfriendly to dogs and we assumed the same would be true in Turkey. Roka didn't visit Turkey so we don't actually know how she would have been treated there, but we saw few pets on Turkish streets. The joys of having Roka with us in Greece and Turkey would be outweighed by the problems. We decided that she would have to stay at home. Fortunately, our daughter had recently bought a house so there was a place for Roka to stay while we were gone.

It's not that there aren't plenty of dogs in Greece. But they are treated differently there than in other parts of Europe. In France, Italy and Spain, and even Croatia, dogs are family pets, pampered and loved.

Many people stopped in the streets to admire and pet Roka. Children wanted to play with her. Faces glowed when she appeared.

In Greece, dogs are generally ignored and sometimes reviled. Each dog in Greece has its own personal neighborhood where other dogs aren't welcome. Generally, dogs don't belong to a particular family; they hang out in the neighborhood and local residents provide them with food. It takes a village to raise a dog in Greece. When Roka suddenly appeared in another dog's territory, fur rose and the local dog charged, bristling with hostility, teeth bared. We soon learned that none of these dogs had any issues with Roka once their noses let them know that she was a spayed female. But the hostile approach got tiresome. In Athens, female dogs often wear wide red collars and male dogs wear blue. The collars mean that the city has picked them up, neutered them, and then returned them to the streets. Thus in some sense, the country is dog-friendly. It's just that the role of dogs is vastly different than what we are used to.

It turns out that vicious cats are another problem. Our first problem with cat aggression was actually in Croatia. In the picturesque walled town of Korčula, a local cat spied Roka from the other side of the town square. The cat raced toward Roka at full speed and threw itself on top of our astonished dog, hurling its body and claws into her. Roka screamed. Visitors to the square stopped to watch, stunned at the ferocity of the attack, clearly sympathetic to Roka's plight. Fur flew – mostly Roka's. I had to pick Roka up and pull the cat off of her. In the process, I was scratched. Poor Roka cried for a long time.

Like dogs, cats in Greece tend to live in the streets and some become wild and often aggressive. Roka suffered another cat attack in Paxos, Greece, leading to more loud doggy screaming. Every person in earshot simply stared at Roka, this time clucking disapprovingly, since they believed she must be at fault. No dog sympathy here. The cat did have nearby kittens, but Roka's only crime was that she was in the area. Roka was attacked again in Mykonos for no reason. We didn't even see the cat until it was on Roka's back. Typical of the

Greeks, they again blamed Roka, claiming she was disturbing the cat's kittens. However, this time there was not a kitten in sight. Roka remains fearful of cats to this day, and even of small dogs that look like cats.

These experiences, when added to the visible fear and disgust on the faces of many older Greek women at the sight of Roka walking down the street, led us to decide that it would be best for Roka and us to leave her home when we returned to Greece and visited Turkey.

Requirements for Bringing Your Pet to Europe

The requirements for bringing a cat or dog to Europe can be found on-line, but they aren't simple and can be confusing. Calling embassies results in inconsistent answers, but this is not surprising. Few Americans take their dogs with them when they fly to Europe so officials aren't prepared with answers.

The belief that dogs must be quarantined applies only to the British Isles, not other parts of Europe. The European Union now requires a "European pet passport." It can be accessed on-line, but is difficult to understand. To obtain the passport, we were required to get an "official" U.S. government stamp on a certification that Roka had been properly immunized. It turned out that this stamp could not be provided by our vet. We had to drive to Los Angeles to obtain the stamp from the Federal Veterinary Office, taking along the proper documents from our vet. This was an inconvenience that served no real purpose since the man with the government stamp based his approval solely on our vet's signature.

Authorities in Europe paid no attention to our dog when we entered a country anyway. One reason is that most of the time no one even knew she was there. We brought her into each country either on our boat where we could put her below decks or in her airplane bag if we flew in. When we entered a country by plane, customs officials never actually looked at our bags or asked us any questions. There are no questionnaires as we have in the U.S. about what we are bringing into the country. When we boarded planes, both in the U.S. and in Europe, we were asked at times to produce her documents – generally a health certificate signed by the vet and a rabies vaccine have been adequate, although a pet passport is now technically required in Europe. No one ever wanted to actually look at Roka.

Our biggest problem turned out to be the airline officials at the ticket counters who were stumped when we arrived to check in. We always had the required reservation for Roka, but most airline personnel have apparently never checked in a dog. They often can't figure out how much to charge (usually about $120) or how to ticket it. Those in line behind us tended to get hostile since we usually caused a commotion and delayed check-in for the whole line.

Once past the confusion at check-in, the security check must be navigated. Pets must be carried through security since they cannot go through the x-ray machine. All collars and leashes must be removed since they will set off the metal alarm. A pet that is able to wiggle out of your arms can be a problem, especially since you're juggling with luggage and putting shoes on and off as well as controlling a pet. Roka, fortunately, is happy to just sit quietly on the conveyor belt while we get organized. Then she goes back into her airline carrier. She actually loves her carrier. When she sees it on the floor, she'll often try to get into it. To her, the airplane bag means that she gets to go with us – a happy event for her.

She is supposed to stay inside her bag on the plane, under the seat, during the whole flight. Since she is so quiet, and her black coat makes her hard to see in a black bag in a dark plane, we always open her bag so she can get some air. After a brief look around, she will always settle back for many hours without a sound.

Only once did we have a scare about her size. A little martinet flight attendant saw her on the plane before takeoff, sitting happily in her bag, which I had prematurely unzipped. He looked askance at her and proclaimed, "That dog is too big – I'm getting my supervisor!" We panicked, visualizing being thrown off the plane. We quickly zipped her back into the bag, waiting for the axe to fall. A large, frowning female flight attendant marched down the aisle to our seats, followed by the little squealer. He pointed a guilty finger at us, huffing that we were the culprits. She looked stern. She informed her assistant that he could leave and she would handle this problem herself. He reluctantly left, clearly wanting to stay to watch our punishment. As soon as he was out of hearing range, the large woman's visage changed from that of brooding enforcer to friendly flight attendant. She smiled at us, asked to see Roka, and then started cooing and petting, gushing about what a sweet dog Roka was. As we breathed a sigh of relief, she explained that some flight attendants were a bit anal and it was best to just humor them.

Pet Requirements Within Europe

We could discern no special laws or rules concerning pets in Europe. No one ever asked to see Roka's papers, not even in bureaucracy-crazed Greece. We were never questioned about her.

The only rule we learned is that in most parts of Europe dogs are required to be muzzled on trains and buses. Our first clue about this rule occurred on a train in Spain. The conductor vigorously waved his arms, talked wildly and pointed at Roka. We didn't understand. We smiled blankly until the conductor gave up. After we learned the rule about muzzles, I wrapped her leash around her nose when boarding buses or trains to make it look as though she were muzzled. The popular Halter leashes might do the same since they look a bit like muzzles, although they don't prevent a dog from biting somebody. It may be wise to take a muzzle. We finally bought one, but Roka never let us put it on her and we gave it away.

Returning to the U.S.

Dog fun also occurred each time we returned to the U.S. The U.S.

customs form asks each passenger if he or she is carrying any "plants, food or animals," and we of course checked "yes," causing us to be diverted into the agricultural line. The agricultural inspector always asked the same question, "What food do you have?" We would respond with a laugh and answer, "We have a dog." This response always elicited a surprised look, and the question, "Where?" When we pointed to the dog carrier, the inspector would always chuckle heartily – this was not what he expected. We never had to show any documents even though a rabies certificate is legally required to bring a dog back to the U.S. Instead, we were always waived right through.

CHAPTER 8
HOW MUCH WILL IT COST?

How much will it cost? Can I afford it? This is perhaps the scariest question, the one that makes even the bravest soul quiver. Everyone knows that boating is for rich people, not for those lacking an extra few million dollars.

The answer surprised us. We learned that our cruising life was far less expensive than we anticipated. It's not for the poverty-stricken, but you don't need to be wealthy either.

I've tried to provide a rough cost breakdown. So much depends on the boat, where you go and your style of living that this can be no more than a starting guideline for understanding the financial issues you may face. There are lots of caveats and assumptions to consider that will likely require adjustments.

The first and extremely important caveat is the value of the euro versus the dollar. This makes a huge difference. If the euro is worth $1.50, everything will cost 50% more than if the euro and the dollar have the same value. When we bought *Avanti*, the euro had a value of $1.05. In 2008, its value rose to $1.60, making everything far more expensive for us. Costs in this section are provided in dollars and assume a euro worth $1.30. As the euro increases or decreases in value relative to the dollar, the costs increase or decrease accordingly.

Initial Cost of the Boat

As described more thoroughly in the chapter entitled "Buying That Boat," the cost of a boat in Europe can vary from under $75,000 for an older sailboat of 36 to 50 feet, to $500,000 or more for a newer powerboat of 35-45 feet.

We initially anticipated paying at least $350,000 for a boat, possibly more. We actually paid about $180,000 for a boat that was perfect for us. After nine years we sold *Avanti* and netted approximately $95,000 after paying the commission. We would have suffered a greater loss if not for the increase in value of the euro. But we put *Avanti* on the market in 2010, one of the worst years in history for selling a boat. If we had sold her in 2007, she likely would have fetched a far higher price. As it was, it took over a year to find a buyer and we felt lucky when we did. We've heard of many boats that sit unsold for years. For us, the cost of the boat itself ended up averaging about $10,000 for each year we owned her, a big number, but still a bargain compared to chartering.

Boat Repairs and Maintenance

The "rule of thumb," we were told, is to assume a cost of ten percent per year of the initial cost of the boat for repairs and maintenance. For us, that would be $18,000 per year, but we never came close to spending that much, even though our boat was over ten years old when we bought her. Our average was closer to five percent. We concluded that several major repairs would be required to reach the ten percent figure.

Although some boat repairs and maintenance costs, such as oil changes, are similar to auto expenses, a better comparison is to costs of home ownership. Expenses such as fixing or replacing appliances, repainting, and plumbing or electrical problems make up the bulk of the costs.

One thing to remember and simply accept is that you'll likely be paying at least ten percent more for everything than you'd be charged if you weren't a foreigner. It's the price you pay for not being fluent in the language. Just don't let it get to you. You have no choice.

Our largest repair cost was the rebuilding of one of our engines due to a cracked cylinder head, a cost of over $12,000. It was painful, irritating and time-consuming. The problem showed up as excessive black smoke from the engine. We had no choice but to gulp hard and pay. The only silver lining was meeting Pumpellyo, our adorable Italian mechanic, recommended by our engine manufacturer, Chicago-based Cummins. He spoke no English so had to bring an interpreter, but he was a picture-perfect older Italian, short, cheery and always wearing tattered overalls. Our second priciest repairs were caused by the repair of our three shaft seal leaks and averaged about $1300 each. Our crash into a pylon on the Rhone damaged Avanti to the tune of $10,000, but insurance paid $8000 of that bill. The 100 liters of water dumped into our fuel tank by a negligent mini-tanker operator in Greece cost us a couple thousand dollars to clean out and fix. We also had two sets of replacements of our two giant 8D boat batteries, each time costing close to $1000. These batteries start the big engines and run the electrical system when there is no shore power. After the second replacement, we paid our winter marinas to keep our batteries charged all winter so they didn't sit untended for eight to nine months. After that, our batteries lasted far longer. We figured they should last for at least four years of cruising and maybe more if we treated them well.

All other repair costs were smaller, although several things broke each year and had to be replaced, including coolant hoses, an engine alternator, a salt-water heat exchanger, an engine fan belt tensioner, an engine diesel fuel return line, a manual toilet, a fresh-water shower faucet, a fresh-water pressure pump and various electronic instrument parts. These repairs weren't cheap, but usually cost a few hundred dollars, not a few thousand.

For reasons I fail to understand, Bruce relishes fixing things that go wrong on a boat, but sadly some of it is beyond his skill level or patience. *Avanti* was no stranger to technicians and mechanics who could both diagnose and fix problems. But when he was able to do the repairs himself, Bruce saved us hundreds of dollars.

There are also periodic maintenance requirements, as with autos, but the marine version is always far more expensive. The engine oil must be changed about every hundred hours of engine use. For us, that meant changing oil twice a year at a cost of a several hundred dollars each time. When we changed oil, we also changed fuel filters – two for each engine – and had the mechanic check a half dozen other parts that tended to go bad, such as the impellers in the engine cooling system. The regular maintenance bill was seldom over $1000, but often came close. Every other year, we had the bottom of the boat repainted with anti-fouling paint. Some people roll on the anti-fouling paint themselves to save money. We often touched up the paint ourselves in the years we didn't have it professionally repainted. A gallon of anti-fouling paint costs over $200 and multiple hours of labor are required to apply it, even for touch-ups. We paid around $800 dollars for a professional anti-fouling paint job. Bruce figured it was cheaper to pay someone to do the anti-fouling than to pay the hospital bills for the lung damage from the highly toxic paint vapors.

Non-Boat Travel Expenses

In our early years of travel, we flew across the Atlantic two times each year and spent up to five months in Europe. Later, we shortened our stay to three months and flew to Europe and back only once each year. We were able to obtain good air fares since we bought our tickets early. The cost of each flight increases as you fly farther east.

We also used frequent flyer miles, particularly since one or two trips across the Atlantic garner enough miles to come close to paying for a free trip. We traveled one time on business class using frequent flyer miles. Deciding well in advance when and where to go and when to return allows you to bag those frequent flyer seats. But I tend to be obsessively thrifty, so we typically flew economy.

Once on our boat, we had minimal land-based travel costs – a rental car now and then for an inland excursion at $40 to $100 per day, depending on location, and perhaps a motorscooter for local use, usually costing $20 to $50 per day. We rarely spent nights ashore in hotels unless we were taking a few days to visit a destination too distant for a single-day trip. We took one or two of those trips each summer and budgeted for six or seven nights in a hotel each year.

Cost of Boat Fuel

Boat fuel is the big hit. The cost of fuel was our largest expense. Let's face it: motorboats use lots of fuel. Sailboat use substantially less, even when under power, since their engines are much smaller, but they also travel more slowly. A general rule of thumb is that a sailboat can travel under power efficiently at about five knots (5.5mph), a full-displacement motorboat at seven to eight knots, and the semi-displacement boats like ours at ten to twelve knots. Under those conditions, sailboats can get four to five miles on a gallon of fuel. Motorboats, on the other hand, can range from one to two miles per gallon for a full-displacement boat and one mile per gallon for a semi-displacement boat such as ours, and that's on a good day. At $7 to $10 per gallon, fuel costs add up. We tried not to think about the size of our carbon footprint on *Avanti*. Fortunately, newer boat engines are more efficient.

We traveled between 1500 and 2000 miles per year. At that rate, it took eight years to complete our cruising path. We started and ended in the Balearics in Spain and got as far east as Northern Cyprus. Our total voyage was approximately 15,000 miles.

Based on 1800 miles per year, assuming a cost of $8 per gallon for fuel and mileage of one mile per gallon, we spent approximately $15,000 for fuel per season. Painful. A sailboat covering the same mileage would likely pay closer to $2000 per year for fuel, partly because it would be under sail for at least part of the trip.

We tried to put the best light on these fuel costs by mentally offsetting them against other costs we would otherwise have incurred – costs such as gas and upkeep of our cars at home and other types of transportation we would use if not on the boat. The cost of fuel for our boat also permitted us to take our "home" along with us and to live in marinas, ports and bays at a far lower cost than the nightly rates at a typical hotel, and usually in a far nicer place. But it's hard to successfully rationalize such extravagant use of fossil fuels.

Marina Fees

Rather than hotel costs, or costs to rent or own a home in Europe, we paid a charge to spend the night at almost every marina. There was also a charge on many city wharves. Anchoring is almost always free.

The highest marina charge we paid was on the island of Ibiza in Spain, the shocking cost of almost $200 per night. The average cost to stay in a marina in the Western Mediterranean for our 39-foot boat was $40 to $80. This usually included a free hook-up to both water and electricity and access to marina showers and toilets.

In parts of southern Italy and most of Greece, there are few marinas, but many city wharves. The nice marinas are rare and cost about the same as marinas in other countries. More common in Greece is the unfinished marina. There is no charge to stay in these unfinished marinas, but also no electricity, water or other services. There is often a minimal charge at a city wharf in southern Italy and Greece, perhaps $20, and that may or may not include water and electricity.

In marinas and wharves without water, water tanker trucks normally ply the wharf – usually $5 of water would fill our 100-gallon tank and last us for up to a week.

To save money, or simply to enjoy some peace and quiet, boats regularly anchor in harbors or nearby coves. Travel to and from shore is by inflatable dinghy. There is usually a place on a convenient dock or even a rock to tie up the dinghy for a few hours for shopping or a dinner ashore. Since there is no charge for this, anchoring for a few days is a good money-saver. Going ashore by dinghy is more of a hassle than just walking off the passarelle, but for many boaters, the isolation and sense of freedom provided by anchoring is well worth the hassle, and of course the cost saving is substantial.

Food

We ate breakfast every day on the boat on our aft deck or occasionally on the upper helm. This was always a cheery occasion with our bright Spanish tablecloth and red flowering kalenchoe. We had an interesting view of the world each morning.

Lunch varied – if we were on the boat, we would eat lunch there, normally a salad or sandwich; if touring a local town, we would often eat lunch out.

We almost always ate dinner out. Many boaters eat every meal on board. We have concluded that they must enjoy cooking more than we do or they need to live more frugally. By evening, we were worn out from working on the boat, walking through town or simply sunning ourselves. We had no desire to cook dinner.

Just as at home, the total amount you pay for meals is directly proportional to how frequently you eat at restaurants. The cost of basic food in Europe is similar to the cost of food in the U.S. – some things are less expensive, some more. The cost of eating out varies from country to country, but it is no longer the "steal" that restaurant eating in Europe used to be. With a bottle of house wine (usually quite delicious and inexpensive), our dinners for two were often $20 to $50. It's certainly easy to pay less, but we never sweated paying for our dinners. They were too much fun.

In some countries the house wine is not so delicious. House wine is generally inexpensive – less than five to seven dollars for a liter (somewhat larger than a normal bottle of wine) vs. up to $20 for a bottle of a vintage wine – still less than the normal wine bottle at a U.S. restaurant. In some countries the house reds were fine, but not the house whites; in others, vice versa. Generally, the quality of the wines is consistent over a region, or even a whole country, so in places such as Croatia, we tended to drink more red wine, and tried to avoid whites. But in Greece, the house whites were fine and we drank those more than reds. In Italy, France and Spain, most house wines, of either color, are excellent. Saving costs by ordering the house wine usually makes sense.

You can control the cost of food and meals, just as you can at home. In general, food and dining should not be much more, or much less, expensive than you are used to paying at home.

Off-season Storage

Boats can be left either in the water or on the land over the winter. The costs are similar, although land storage is usually less expensive. We have seen marinas that charge as much as double to leave a boat in the water. Most boaters who do not plan to use their boats for the winter have them hauled out. Hauling out adds a few hundred dollars to your wintering bill. However, boats left in the water may need to be hauled out for a new coat of anti-fouling paint anyway, so the hauling costs often even out.

Because the Mediterranean is relatively warm, boat hulls are prone to osmosis, the process of forming tiny blisters when water seeps into the outer layers of the fiberglass on the hull. The cure for this is outrageously expensive and takes months. Drying out the hull now and then helps prevent this condition, another reason for hauling out for the winter. It also helped our mental health to haul out since it meant that we didn't have to worry about the fate of *Avanti* during huge European winter storms. If you live on your boat all winter, that's different – of course it has to be in the water. Rates vary from one marina to the next, so it pays to shop around. Some small marinas may offer excellent rates, but likely have limited amenities.

The cost for boat storage for the winter for our 39-foot boat ranged from about $2500 in Croatia to $4000 in France and Spain. The cost is more for a larger boat, less for a smaller one. The cost to keep our batteries charged added $300 to $400 to our winter costs, far less than the cost of continually buying new batteries.

Insurance

Our boat insurance cost ran about $2000 per year, or one to two percent of the boat's value. The price increases slightly the farther east one travels, which we never understood. Perhaps the insurance company figures that eastern Mediterranean countries are not so safe, but we did not find that to be true. Our only claim resulted from an accident in France.

Bottom Line Costs

I have tried to estimate the total annual costs for two people based on the following assumptions, and excluding the initial cost of the boat:

- a cruising season of 4 months in the Mediterranean
- a winter haul-out and storage
- travel of 1800 miles
- fuel costing $8 per gallon

One additional set of assumptions applies to the low cost, frugal cruiser and a second to a more moderate life style with more luxuries, but nothing outrageous.

For the frugal traveler, I make the following assumptions:

- 36' sailboat costing around $80,000
- many repairs and most maintenance performed by the owner
- anchoring at least half the time
- four miles per gallon of fuel

- motoring approximately half the time

Here are the total costs:

> Fuel: $ 2,000
> Repairs/Maintenance: $ 3,000
> Marinas: $ 2,400
> Winter Storage: $ 2,800
> Insurance: $ 2,000
>
> Total: $ 12,200

With care, the costs could be lower by doing more self-repair and maintenance, anchoring more, and keeping travel to a minimum when the winds are not sufficient for sailing

For cruisers desiring a more moderate level of comfort, with more marina nights and a powerboat (that's us), I made these assumptions:

- a $200,000 40' semi-displacement motorboat
- some basic repair and maintenance performed by the owner
- staying at marinas when available
- One mile per gallon of fuel

Here are the total costs:

> Fuel: $ 15,000
> Repairs/Maintenance: $ 7,000
> Marinas: $ 4,500
> Winter Storage: $ 3,000
> Insurance: $ 2,500
>
> Total: $ 32,000

There are lots of variables that can put you between "frugal" and "moderate" cost. For example, the medium cost assumes a powerboat – a sailboat would be substantially less. Traveling 2000 rather than 1800 miles would increase costs. Anchoring more often also changes the costs considerably.

There's no point in even calculating the cost for a "high end" expenditure cruise. The sky is the limit if the boat is large. Winter storage costs increase, as do insurance and especially fuel, as well as repairs and maintenance. At some point, perhaps when a boat reaches over 55-60 feet, owners may need to hire a crew member or two to help run the boat and keep it in good condition. Now we're talking about a rich person's life, not ours, and I don't know much about that.

To help rationalize paying these amounts, we considered some possible savings offsets: (1) mortgage and home ownership costs saved if you sell your house, or rental payments saved if you're a renter; (2) income received if you rent out your home; (3) other travel you might take if not cruising (many one or two week tours cost well over $5000 per person); and (4) gas and maintenance on your automobiles that you are not using when away on the water.

Not included in my cost analysis are travel expenses to get to and from your boat, clothes and gifts you may buy, rental cars and motorscooters, and other miscellaneous purchases. Travel expenses can vary wildly, depending on the style and level of luxury you prefer when you travel. For these other costs, you are best able to estimate your own budget based on the types of expenses you normally incur on other trips.

My analysis of our expenses in the Mediterranean led me to the conclusion that our cruising actually resulted in costs not dramatically different from those we would have incurred if we had stayed home. This is mostly because we have high expenses when we're home – a large monthly mortgage payment and high property taxes. We didn't have these expenses when on *Avanti* because the rental payments we received on our house covered these costs. If we hadn't rented out our house, our travel would have imposed a greater financial burden. On the other hand, if we hadn't been on *Avanti*, we would likely have taken two or three traditional vacation trips to Europe or Asia each year, each trip lasting three weeks or so; I expect that, with the costs of transportation, hotels and restaurants, each trip would likely cost at least $15,000 for a couple ($30,000 for two trips), plus airfare, and often considerably more. We concluded that our three to five months on Avanti cost more than we would have spent for a couple of fancy three week trips, but not outrageously more. And we thought our months on Avanti were far more satisfying and, actually, a terrific bargain. Everyone has a different financial situation. But you may be surprised at how little extra you'll need to spend.

And, by the way, every penny we spent was worth it.

OUR WONDERFUL GUESTS, WITH HOME LOCATION AND YEAR(S) OF VISIT

Maleah & Scott Ashford
Corvallis, Oregon 2010

Wendy & Bill Birnbaum
Sisters, Oregon 2003

Gaudenz Bon
Aarau, Switzerland 2008

Jim & Sally Chesebro
Corona del Mar 2003

Adam Clark
Seattle 2004

Adam Clark & Meagan
Yoshimoto, Seattle 2008

Andrea Clark
Corona del Mar 2003

Jason, Andrea & Sienna
Clark Bone
Davis 2005, 2010

Jan Clausen & John Lohr
Encinitas 2004, 2009

Jean Enersen & Bruce Carter
Seattle 2005, 2009

Fred & Marg Elliston Harris
Corrales, New Mexico 2007

Jan & Malcolm Johnston
Menlo Park 2004, 2006

Lindell & Sheila Ivary Marsh
Newport Beach 2005

Sue Michaelson & Lois Jacobs
Newport Beach 2005

Candy & Monte Midkiff
Lopez Island, Washington
2005, 2008, 2009

Tricia Nichols
Denver 2005

Alicia, Rodolfo & Rodolfo
Katuneric Prieto
Punta Arenas, Chile 2003, 2005

Bill & Barbara Roberts
Newport Beach 2005

Loretta Sanchez & Jack
Einwechter
DC/Santa Ana 2008, 2009

Polly & Eric Stanbridge
Corona del Mar 2008

Megan Upham
(with Andrea Clark)
Bay Area 2003

Cathy Voreyer & Kim Coates
Corona del Mar & Bay Area 2008

Rob, Sarah, Cameron, Luca
& Lexi Weibel
Zurich, Switzerland 2010

Winston Vickers & Susan Winston
Long Beach 2003, 2005, 2010

CPSIA information can be obtained at www.ICGtesting.com
Printed in the USA
BVOW06s1230091015

421356BV00010B/137/P